# BLIND PERSISTENCE

## THE STORY OF THE BEFORE COLUMBUS FOUNDATION

Edited by
Ishmael Reed and Justin Desmangles
with Carla Blank and Tennessee Reed

Baraka Books
Montréal

For reprint permissions see page 285

ISBN 978-1-77186-398-8 pbk
ISBN 978-1-77186-415-2 epub
ISBN 978-1-77186-416-9 pdf

Cover photo: Andrew (Andy) Hope III and Ishmael Reed at the Southeast Alaska Native Cultural Festival, Sitka, March 1979.
Cover by Leila Marshy
Additional editors: Carla Blank and Tennessee Reed
Book Design by Folio infographie
Editing: Robin Philpot
Proofreading: Anne Marie Marko

Legal Deposit, 4th quarter 2025
Bibliothèque et Archives nationales du Québec
Library and Archives Canada

Published by Baraka Books of Montreal

TRADE DISTRIBUTION & RETURNS

Canada
UTPdistribution.com

United States
Independent Publishers Group: IPGbook.com

We acknowledge the support from the Société de développement des entreprises culturelles (SODEC) and the Government of Quebec tax credit for book publishing administered by SODEC.

PUBLISHED & PRINTED IN CANADA

**Ishmael Reed** has authored fifty works of fiction, poetry, non-fiction, plays and librettos, and edited numerous anthologies. He has received prizes in every category. The fourth novel in his "Terribles" series, *The Terrible Fives*, is forthcoming from Baraka Books in 2026. Other recent works include *Why the Black Hole Sings the Blues* (2022), and *The Shine Challenge 2025*, premiered at NYC's Theater for the New City on January 30, 2025. Reed is also a cartoonist, songwriter, musician and composer, public media commentator and publisher. Books published by Baraka *Books include Bigotry on Broadway* (with Carla Blank), *The Complete Muhammad Ali*, *The Terrible Fours*, and *Why No Confederate Statues in Mexico*. He lives in Oakland.

**Justin Desmangles** is chairman of the Before Columbus Foundation, administrator of the American Book Awards, and creator of the radio broadcast New Day Jazz. A member of the board of directors of the Oakland Book Festival, Mr. Desmangles is also a program producer at the African-American Center of the San Francisco Public Library. His poetry and journalism have appeared in *Amerarcana*, *Black Renaissance Noire*, *Drumvoices Revue*, *Konch*, and *Musiqology*.

# BLIND PERSISTENCE

Dedicated to Will Hearst III
and to our deceased pioneer directors,
Andrew Hope III
Alta
Robert Callahan
David Meltzer
Joyce Carol Thomas
Rudolfo Anaya
Willie Hearst III

Also to the late president of PEN Oakland, Floyd Salas,
and a PEN Oakland founder, Reginald Lockett.
Special thanks to Henry Louis Gates, Jr.

"Eight American writers were honored in Manhattan last weekend at an awards ceremony by the Before Columbus Foundation. The foundation was established four years ago by the novelist and poet **Ishmael Reed** to recognize Afro-American, Asian-American, Mexican-American, and other writers whose works he believes are usually excluded by the established literary tributes such as the National Book Awards.

"We think the other book awards are corrupt,' said Mr. Reed, whose satirical novels have included *Mumbo Jumbo* and *The Last Days of Louisiana Red*, 'because they do not represent the entire spectrum of American writing.' Among those honored were **Rudolfo Anaya,** a novelist, and **Jayne Cortez** and **Quincy Troupe,** who are poets.

"Mr. Reed himself has 'been treated very well' he said by the organizations his foundation was formed to counter. As the winner of a 1975 award from the National Institute of Arts and Letters and the Academy of Arts and Letters, he was 'glad to get it.' But that 'doesn't mean I can't see my job as to reform the establishment' if it ignored others, he said."

—Judith Cummings, Robin Herman, *The New York Times*, March 6, 1980

# Contents

## INTRODUCTIONS



## FICTION

## NON-FICTION



## POETRY

## TRIBUTES



## AFTERWORDS



## APPENDIX

# INTRODUCTIONS

# The Origins of the Before Columbus Foundation

by Ishmael Reed

*On March 14, 2024,* The Atlantic *magazine announced a list of "*The Great American Novels.*" Four directors of the Before Columbus Foundation made the cut.*

Two of the best decisions I've made were to leave for New York City from Buffalo in 1962 and to leave New York for California in 1967.

In New York, during the 1960s, I came under the influence of black cultural nationalists like Askia Touré. Through the Umbra Workshop, I became acquainted with black history and culture. I also had contact with black painters like Joe Overstreet, Algernon Miller, Gerald Jackson, Al Loving, Jack Whitten, Ellsworth Ausby, and others. Musicians Cecil Taylor, Sun Ra, Archie Shepp, and Albert Ayler were acquaintances. White artists like Art Bevacqua and Walter Bowart were also influences upon my work.

Walter and I founded *The East Village Other*, an underground newspaper which I named. Both Carla and I had connections to the downtown art world.

Andy Warhol, Carla Blank, and I discussed film when we would run into the artist at Max's Kansas City. I appear on a recording with Warhol called *The East Village Other.* As an example of how the middle class sometimes absorbs the underground, this "experimental" record is on sale at Target. I'm one of a handful of people who know how Max's Kansas City, a gathering place for writers, filmmakers, and painters, got its name.

My world was black and white, straddled between the white counterculture and black cultural nationalism. I was one of three writers cited as the counterculture's favorites in the Woodstock program, but my work also appeared in black publications like *The Liberator* and *Cricket*.

The Beats influenced us. They brought American poetry from the parlor rooms of the elites to the streets. We were not aware of the proletariat writers of the 1930s who preceded and influenced them. But like the parlor poets of the elite, the Beats were a white male movement, which Anne Waldman pointed out effectively in *Women of The Beat Generation*, an anthology edited by Brenda Knight. That straddling between black and white ended when I met Carla Blank.

N.H. Pritchard, the poet, introduced me to Carla Blank. The three of us performed in "Black," a multimedia work directed by the late sculptor/visual artist Aldo Tambellini. I began writing my first novel, *The Free-Lance Pallbearers*, in a Chelsea apartment where Carla and I shared the rent. She grew up in a Pittsburgh home where her parents, Ethel and Marcus Blank, hosted dance, music and theater groups composed of different nationalities.

When I met her, she had links to the Indian and Japanese avant-garde. Carla and dancer Suzushi Hanayagi's collaboration would lead to one of the first artistic responses to the war in Vietnam. Called "Wall Street Journal," it included one section of choreography based on their score of photos about the war, clipped from *The New York Times* and other print media. Soon, Carla and I were members of a circle that included Chinese, Japanese, and Iranian artists. Among the circle were the late futurist F.M. Esfandiary and an Iranian cartoonist whose cartoons I got Walter Bowart to publish.

My organizing gene fired up; I assembled a group that included Carla, the feminist lawyer Flo Kennedy, folk singer Len Chandler, and Leah Bernstein, a writer. I called it International Mind Mining. This group was the predecessor to the Before Columbus Foundation. Although Carla is mistakenly identified as one of its founders, her example guided my thinking into conceiving a multicultural organization.

The first sign of my implementing a new multicultural awareness was the anthology *19 Necromancers from Now.* This anthology was supposed to prove that there was no uniform way for black writers to tell a story. I added a Hispanic writer, Victor Hernández Cruz, and Frank Chin, who is Chinese American. Victor was a teenager when I met him. He'd published one chapbook: *Papo's Got His Gun.* We've maintained a relationship with Victor since 1966. He now lives in Morrocco, and Carla and I published his most recent book of poetry, *Guayacán.* I'd read an excerpt from Frank Chin's unpublished novel, *A Chinese Lady Dies*, in a newspaper called *The Great Speckled Bird.*

*19 Necromancers* became more than its original purpose, which was to highlight the different styles of black writing. Because Frank was included, Asian American writers met at the book party for the anthology, held at the Oakland home of Luther Nichols, the West Coast representative of Doubleday. Following that meeting, Frank Chin, Lawson Inada, Jeffrey Chan, and Shawn Wong began a collaboration. They became known as "The Four Horsemen of Asian American Literature." They published a manifesto for the Asian American Renaissance, which Charles Harris published at my suggestion. At that time, Harris was the publisher of Howard University Press. The anthology, *Aiiieeeee! An Anthology of Asian American Writers*, edited by Frank Chin, Jeffery Paul Chan, Lawson Fusao Inada, and Shawn Wong, has gone into a third printing and is celebrating its 50th anniversary this year.

After that party for *19 Necromancers*, a god of Variegation seemed to steer us in the direction of the founding of the Before Columbus Foundation, a literary multicultural organization, but at that time, multiculturalism meant "third world."

In 1972, Al Young and I began a magazine called *Yardbird Reader.* We handled the editorial, and Glenn Myles and Doyle Foreman handled the graphics and production. *Yardbird 3* was the Asian American issue. Al Young and I also co-published *Y'Bird* and *Quilt,* which, like *Yardbird*, published writers who were unknown at the time. They are now part of the canon.

In 1974, a historic conference occurred in Ellensburg, Washington, where Al Young and I met Native American writers Leslie Marmon

Silko, Phil George, and Neil Tall-Eagle Parsons. Lawson Inada, who attended the *Necromancers* party, was also present.

My position as editorial director of *Yardbird* made me eligible to join the Coordinating Council of Literary Magazines (CCLM). As a member and later chairman of the organization, with the help of Rudolfo Anaya, I expanded the board of directors to include Hispanics, Asian Americans, Native Americans, and black writers. A former chairperson, William Phillips, editor of *The Partisan Review*, accused me of nominating writers who were not qualified. I had nominated Leslie Marmon Silko, who was recently elected to the American Academy of Arts and Letters, and the great writer Toni Cade Bambara, whose work merited a whole page in *Newsweek*, a week after Phillips announced that the author of a book he hadn't read was unqualified. Phillips had sponsored a hatchet job on Richard Wright executed by James Baldwin because in his memoir, *A Partisan View*, he found the Richard Wright he encountered in Paris to be unpatriotic. His magazine, *The Partisan Review*, received money from the CIA.

CCLM provided seed money for black, Latino, Asian American, and Native American magazines. Under this program, seed money was also available for distribution. I received a grant totaling $5,000 to start the organization, which I called Before Columbus Foundation, inspired by a series of books that posited a black presence in the Americas before the arrival of Columbus, principal among them Ivan Van Sertima's *They Came Before Columbus* and Lerone Bennett Jr.'s *Before the Mayflower: A History of the Negro in America: 1619-1962*.

For his book. *Forced Into Glory: Abraham Lincoln's White Dream*, Lerone Bennett, Jr. was severely criticized by the moribund good old boy historical scholars' establishment, for daring to suggest that Lincoln was less than a saint. Historian Gerald Horne compared Bennett Jr.'s drilling by pro-Lincoln historians with Galileo's appearance before Father Vincenzo Maculani da Firenzuola. Bennett Jr. received our American Book Award in 2002 during a ceremony held at the Southgate Tower Hotel in New York. Horne received an American Book Award in 2021.

> The Before Columbus Foundation operates on the premise that storytelling traditions existed thousands of years before the arrival of Europeans, which counters the myth that storytelling begins with the Puritan settlement. Puritans weren't even the first Europeans to arrive in North America.

The Spanish were followed by the French. Edition after edition of the *Norton Anthology of American Literature* fails to recognize the Spanish tradition in North American literature. Records show that the Spanish West's literary traditions began in the 1600s.

Leslie Silko supported our claim with her theory that Native American orature and literature have existed for thousands of years. Civilizations existed in this hemisphere before Greece and Rome. The Mayans used pictographs, which show up in our alphabet. The letter A, for example, represents the face of an ox. The Aztecs used codices to document the invasion from Spain and its consequences.

To be eligible to receive the $5,000 from the Ford Foundation for the distribution project, I was required to name a partner. I chose Victor Hernández Cruz, whose work I had included in *19 Necromancers from Now.* We began distributing magazines like *Maize*, *Puerto del Sol*, and other publications.

A turning point in the organization came when Bob Callahan accused us of discriminating against white ethnics; Callahan's letter changed the direction of the organization. By embracing brown, yellow, and Native Americans we had expanded from a position of Cultural Nationalism with a nod to the white Counter Culture toward multiculturalism. We hadn't thought of whites as ethnics. Callahan, like me, was an ethnic gatecrasher with ties to Hispanic and Native American communities. It was through Callahan that I met Andrew Hope III, (pictured on the cover of this book) the Tlingit poet who became the president of Before Columbus.

This meeting led to several trips to Alaska. Carla and I published a book of poetry by his spouse, the late Sister Goodwin, an Inupiat, whose book *There Is a Lagoon in My Backyard* was the first book published by an Inupiat woman.

Andrew Hope and Bob Callahan became members of the Before Columbus Foundation's Board of Directors, as did Rudy Anaya.

Bob Callahan, Ishmael Reed, Carla Blank, and Shawn Wong.

Al Young, Ishmael Reed, Lawson Inada,
and Leslie Marmon Silko.

Lerone Bennett, Jr. and Tananarive Due receive
American Book Awards from Ishmael Reed

Sister Goodwin is standing second from right holding her baby Ishmael Hope, who was being baptized that day. Second from left is Carla Blank beside Sister's daughter. Andy Hope is sitting with Andy and Sister's first son, and Tennessee Reed, dressed in a traditional dress made by Sister, is front left. Taken on the front steps of St. Michael's Russian Orthodox Cathedral, Sitka, Alaska. (Photo by Ishmael Reed)

Joyce Carol Thomas

From left to right, Marie Anderson, the late Alta, the late Bob Callahan, Kathryn Trueblood, Ishmael Reed, and Shawn Wong standing in front of the Raymond House in Preservation Park, Oakland.

Mary Burgess

The late Bob Callahan, Victor Hernández Cruz, the late David Meltzer, Simon Ortiz, and Shawn Wong.

Callahan introduced us to Italian American writer Lawrence Di Stasi and Jewish American poet David Meltzer, who along with Alta, a poet and publisher of Shameless Hussy Press, also joined the Foundation's board. At my invitation, author Joyce Carol Thomas signed on.

In 1980, at my suggestion, we began the American Book Awards due to my experience with the National Book Award, which, given my expanded view of American literature, came up short in terms of diversity. The National Book Foundation has changed since then.

In 1973, the National Book Award (NBA) nominated me for two titles: *Conjure*, a book of poetry, and *Mumbo Jumbo*, a novel. Eric Pace of *The New York Times* ignored the press release issued by the National Book Foundation, which featured my nomination for the two awards, even though this honor was highlighted. *The Saturday Review of Literature* announced that I was "a shoo-in" to win for my novel, *Mumbo Jumbo*. I lost. My friend, the late novelist William Gass, was on the panel. He said that the Southerners had nixed my winning the award. Something like this happened to John A. Williams. He received the Prix de Rome from the American Academy, only to have it rescinded, something about which he protested until his death.

I noticed during this experience that few black authors had received literary awards. Ralph Ellison received a National Book Award for his innovative novel *Invisible Man*, but he was lucky to have friends among the judges. I noticed that at that time, no Native American, Latino, or Asian American had received an award for their writing.

It wasn't until 1999 that a Native American, Ned Blackhawk, won a National Book Award; Ha Jin was the first Asian American to win the award, for his novel *Waiting*, published in 1999. A Hispanic writer, Isabel Allende, received an honorary award in 2018. Noting these omissions, in the early 1980s, we started presenting the American Book Awards.

The first awards were held at the West Side Community Center in New York. In preparation for the ceremony, Gundars Strads packed the winning books and award plaques, and I carried them to New York to present them to the awardees. Quincy Troupe arranged this event. Winner Jayne Cortez and her husband, the visual artist Mel Edwards, were in a hurry to catch a plane, so we were rushed.

The following year, our awards were also presented in New York City, at Joe Papp's Public Theater. Toni Morrison, Donald Barthelme, Stanley Crouch, the famous hoofer Howard Sandman Sims, and South African trumpeter Hugh Masekela were on the program. Ntozake Shange and Amiri Baraka were in the audience.

When it was announced that the late Doubleday editor, Ken McCormick, was among those who began an award with the same name months later, I called him. I informed him that our American Book Award's name had originated a few months before, because we were using that name when *The New York Times* announced the creation of the Before Columbus Foundation awards. Because three ABA ceremonies occurred in New York, *The New York Times* covered that award and two others. But we didn't want to confine our ceremonies to Manhattan. We held awards ceremonies in other cities, including Washington, D.C., Philadelphia, Chicago, New Orleans, Miami, Seattle, and various cities in California—Anaheim, Los Angeles, San Francisco, and Oakland. We wanted the American Book Awards to cover the nation. Because *The New York Times* covered the beginnings of the American Book Awards, I was surprised to see the following *Times* article in 2011:

**The Short, Unsuccessful Life of the American Book Awards**
By Craig Fehrman

> In the summer of 1979, the Association of American Publishers made a stunning announcement: The National Book Awards were no more. In their place would rise the American Book Awards, offering some 30 prizes.
>
> "It will be run almost exactly the way the Academy Awards are run," a spokesman told reporters. Indeed, the industry tripled the awards' budget, hiring an, "official accounting agency, "securing a Broadway producer to design the set, even pushing the idea of office betting pools. (*The New York Times Sunday Book Review*, Oct. 28, 2011)

I wrote to the author of the article:

> Mr. Fehrman : Someone directed me to your article about the 'short life' of the American Book Awards. The American Book Awards are alive and well.

When Ken McCormick, my editor at Doubleday, announced the other ABA, I called him to tell him that we already had one. The discussions went back and forth. Eliot Fremont-Smith, then book reviewer at *The Village Voice*, wrote that the other ABA, 'the short lived one,' should yield the name to us.

In 1981, *The New York Times* covered our second ABA. Since then, we have held awards ceremonies in a number of cities, including Chicago, New Orleans, Philadelphia, Seattle, Los Angeles, San Francisco, and Washington, D.C.

Among the distinguished writers who have attended our awards at their own expense have been Don DeLillo, Edwidge Danticat, Gloria Naylor, and others. Maybe that's because we are writers and accept not a single corporate dime!

Among our directors are a recipient of a presidential medal for literature, the current poet laureate of California, a chancellor of the American Academy of Poets. I am a recipient of a John D. MacArthur Fellowship. On Nov. 23, our awards ceremony will be held at the Miami International Book Fair as they celebrate their 40th year.

You might find some ABA ceremonies at the C-SPAN archives.

Thank you

Ishmael Reed, A Director, The American Book Awards sponsored by the Before Columbus Foundation.

On Sat, Oct 26, 2013, at 8:37 AM, Craig Fehrman wrote this email to me:

Dear Mr. Reed,

Thanks for taking the time to write. And, as an aside, thanks for your wonderful novels—I've taught "Flight to Canada" at Yale a couple of times, and my students always love it.

Anyway, I remember coming across that Fremont-Smith column in my research for my NYT article. My editor and I decided there wasn't enough space to talk about the two versions of the ABA, but I'm genuinely happy to hear the one you're affiliated with is doing so well. I hope this year's ceremony in Miami is a big hit!

Best,

Craig

We may be invisible to *The New York Times*, who sided with their hometown institution, the National Book Award, against us, but their denial of our existence is not shared by writers, some of whom *The Times' Book Review* has honored. Ours was the first major literary award received by Toni Morrison.

There are memorable moments from the American Book Awards and our other programs. A community forum about drug trafficking which included authors Norman Solomon and Professor Peter Dale Scott. Students at Berkeley High School were offended by a PBS documentary about their school. It aired on October 18, 1994. The Before Columbus Foundation sponsored a forum in which the producer, who flew in from the East, engaged in an exchange with the students. Our present Chair, Justin Desmangles, has organized a number of author forums under the sponsorship of Before Columbus in cooperation with programs at San Francisco Public Library's Koret Auditorium.

Jos Knipscheer, the late publisher of *In de Knipscheer*, said that the One World Festival held in The Netherlands was inspired by Before Columbus. As a result, I visited the festival. Kathy Acker and Gregory Corso were also guests. Our most controversial award went to James O. Freedman, who had come under fire from the far-right *Dartmouth Review*. Fox Butterfield, a *Times*' writer, reported the story on Jan. 10, 1991:

> "The Anti-Defamation League of B'nai B'rith said today that it was a *Dartmouth Review* staff member who placed a quotation from Hitler in the conservative weekly last fall.
>
> Supporters of *The Review* in conservative circles in New York and Washington had repeatedly insisted that the insertion was sabotage and done by someone outside the paper. But the paper's editor has said from the beginning, and repeated today, that someone inside was clearly responsible.
>
> The Dartmouth campus erupted in fury after *The Review* carried the passage from Hitler's *Mein Kampf*, his political autobiography, on its masthead last October on the first day of Yom Kippur, the most solemn Jewish holy day. The passage read in part, 'By warding off the Jews, I am fighting for the Lord's work.'

> Supporters of *The Review* later suggested that Dartmouth officials, including President James O. Freedman, seized on the incident to try to destroy the paper. For example, at a news conference in Hanover shortly after the incident, Dinesh D'Souza, a trustee of *The Review* who is a scholar at the American Enterprise Institute in Washington, called the insertion 'a criminal act of sabotage.'"

When the father of one of *The Dartmouth Review*'s writers attempted to block Dr. Freedman's candidacy for Harvard president, members of the Dartmouth faculty cited his receiving the American Book Award at the Miami Book Fair International as evidence of his leadership.

In a letter to *The Harvard Crimson* printed on December 17, 1990, they wrote: "His selection as the 1990 recipient of the American Book Award's Educator of the Year is evidence that we are not alone in our opinion."

Great musicians performed at the American Book Awards. Besides those mentioned above, who performed at the first ceremony, Allen Toussaint played piano at the New Orleans ceremony. Blues legend Charles Brown ("Merry Christmas, Baby") who performed when we held the ceremony at the Great American Music Hall in San Francisco, credited this appearance as the beginning of his comeback.

While the "short-lived" American Book Awards had money, beautiful people, and enormous publicity, for years, BCF operated out of a two-story building on Sixth Street in Berkeley, where we distributed magazines. Visitors occupied the upstairs apartment on occasion. Novelist Chester Himes, playwright Adrienne Kennedy, whose play, *The Ohio State Murders*, reached Broadway in 2021, and poet Ted Joans lived there rent-free.

Gundars Strads and, before him, Mary Burgess, managed Reed, Cannon & Johnson, our small press operation.

In 1981, while teaching at Dartmouth, I received a call from the owner of the Sixth Street building. She offered to sell it to us for $91,000. I passed on the offer. In November 1987, I was named writer-in-residence for *The San Francisco Examiner* by Will Hearst III, and this residency came with use of a nice apartment in Pacific Heights. I'd returned from Harvard and found my inner-city neighborhood occupied by a crack operation. I wrote a series of articles about how this crack house affected my neighborhood. These articles caught the eye of the developer who headed Bramalea, Incorporated, which had developed Oakland's nearby Civic Center. He told me that the city was developing Preservation Park, which would include sixteen historic Victorian era buildings, five of which stand in their original location north of 13th Street, and eleven of which were moved from elsewhere in Oakland to avoid demolition. The sixteen houses are arranged to resemble a late 19th-century Oakland neighborhood. He was responsible for our gaining a residence in Preservation Park. First, we were located in the Ginn House, an 1890's mansion. Later, we moved to the Colonial Revival style home of William J. Raymond, who was a professor of physics at U.C. Berkeley, where we have resided ever since.

On November 18, 1991, my article about the Before Columbus Foundation appeared in *Time* magazine. Accompanying the article were pictures of Preservation Park in color. We had arrived. We'd graduated from 1446 6th Street where the furniture mainly consisted of chairs from a destructed movie house that had been thrown away. We were poor and struggling. At one point, the situation became so dire I asked Gundars how we were going to make it. He said, through "blind persistence." Gundars was unlike most of my students at Cal. They were privileged, from beautiful homes. Gundars' family escaped the Soviet occupation of Latvia. As refugees, they settled in Berkeley. Mary Burgess writes about her role in laying the administrative groundwork for Before Columbus.

> Hi, Ish. Good news that you're doing a history of Before Columbus—it deserves the acknowledgment for all the writers you've brought to our attention and celebrated, and for its long-ass run (and still running!). I wonder what in my experience you're interested in hearing about? My involvement was as admin, finding Fred's place on 6th St and setting up a system to run the office, which was necessary but uninteresting. What was fascinating was watching you collect writers and works to represent, distribute, and honor at the Book Awards, but you're the voice for that. What I witnessed was your force, your energy driving us along, starting at zero and still going. The essential ingredient. Most organizations fizzle for lack of consistent energy. BC had you and others constantly blowing life into it, bringing in talented people, keeping on. And putting BC's mission ahead of the inevitable squabbles.

I got a huge part of my literary education at BC. I owe you for that.

Let me know if you want something more specific, and I'll see what my memory holds.

The administrative history of Before Columbus, and after Mary Burgess built its structure, can be divided into the Strads years and the Desmangles years. Before Columbus began with $5,000. We'll be fifty years old in 2026. How was it done? **Blind Persistence.**

## The Early Days

### Executive Director Gundars Strads remembers the origins of the Before Columbus Foundation

by Gundars Strads

We began by distributing books and magazines by multicultural authors and small presses back when it was still called minority literature.

**Ishmael Reed:**
I remember. Magazines with titles like *Tin Tan*, *Puerto del Sol*, and *Maize*. What else were we doing?

**Gundars Strads:**
We became an official nonprofit organization in 1978. There's only so much you can do, and you can only write grants and fundraise if you've got your nonprofit status. So 1978 was when we all got it together, and the founders signed the official declaration and the bylaws—everything you need to do to become a legal California charitable corporation and a 501(C)3 for the Feds. And then, in 1980, we held the first American Book Awards.

**Ishmael Reed:**
Did we do readings or sponsor readings during that period?

**Gundars Strads:**
We sponsored and produced readings, panel sessions, and discussion forums. We engaged with other similar-minded literary groups and educational organizations.

Originally, we were operating out of one-fourth of a fourplex, which was also our warehouse. We had to install a bed and some pots and pans to make it a "live-in workspace" to get zoning approval. That's what's interesting. At the University of California, I met you, Ishmael, and eventually got involved with your publishing company and with BCF. I remember the only speeding ticket I've ever gotten was trying to get to the post office in time to mail off Before Columbus material. When I started working there, the office manager was Mary Burgess, who helped put the business together and managed all aspects of administrative operations and bookkeeping. She was also a fantastic typist and editor because back then, computers hadn't automated everything like today. She taught me a lot. I even learned to become adept at ten-key touch on an accounting machine. After several years we published two volumes of our celebrated catalog/anthology that included a statement of our broader vision of American literature. Distribution was becoming more and more of a big players' game requiring bigger capital investment than grants could sustain. We were more of a multicultural collective geared at promotion and education than a strict business venture.

The business end was to distribute Native American, Hispanic, Black, Asian American, and Euro-American books and magazines. We had a rep traveling around the country on a commission basis. We'd suddenly get a bunch of orders from Denver, and then from Salt Lake City, then St. Louis, Chicago, and so on—a string of map pins. The middle of the country turned out to be more hip to what we were promoting than anyone expected. Not huge numbers, but numbers nevertheless. It wasn't just the usual bi-coastal sophisticates attuned to multiculturalism, but still calling it minority literature. And it was a sign of how all this stuff spread because people suddenly became more aware of what was then still called minority literature. So, we got through those early years, and when Mary left to start her own business, I took over all those duties. I took a job at the University as an editor to help pay my bills. I ended up working with the same typesetters we used at Before Columbus and our small press. They were also a West Berkeley radical crew. They were very supportive of our cause and treated us like family. They even got a visit from the FBI (classic black suits, black ties, and shiny black shoes), who showed up at their offices and wanted to inquire about one of their customers whose book they typeset, *The Weatherman Handbook*. They had nothing to hide. They never met them and only dealt with them by mail. The Weather Underground was a violent offshoot of Students for a Democratic Society (SDS), an activist organization in the 1960s. The name came from a Bob Dylan song (there is currently a website called the Weather Underground, which actually tells you "which way the wind blows"). We were all suspect. Over the years, BCF got anonymous mail from racist hate groups seeking to educate us about the error of our ways.

One of the many things I learned from Ishmael Reed's influence and mentorship was to have pride in your identity and your culture, however complicated it might be. There were a lot of Americans who would have trouble with my name and would ask me, "Don't you have an American nickname we can use? Why do you have to be different?" And that's one thing I came to resist, while many second-generation immigrants tried hard to fit in, accept acculturation, and translate themselves into American names.

I started working at Ishmael's publishing companies in the late 70s, my post-college apprenticeship. At one point, Berkeley had a hundred small presses in the city limits. While 90 percent of publishing in this country (the big money) was in New York City, I was interested in the other 10 percent. Independent publishing has always been diverse regardless of where the big money lies. It was about publishing what you care about rather than pure profit. (It's also been estimated that 5 percent of book authors make 95 percent of the money). A lot of people tried to get Before Columbus to go for the big money and sell our concept to someone else (like a good idea in a venture capital market). We resisted that because we weren't willing to relinquish control, choice, and discretion. Before Columbus started out with just a few people representing African American, Asian American, Hispanic American, Native American, and European American writers. But we eventually gave awards to a widening diversity of people through the American Book Awards. And then we would often ask them to come on the board and serve. That's actually how we kept expanding and getting more board members, with broader representation. We recruited more women onto the board as well. One of our earliest board members who was also an award winner was Alta, who founded the only American press owned by a woman at the time, Shameless Hussy Press, which had published a lot of stuff that was way ahead of its time. She even bucked trends in feminist literature by calling out hypocrisy and self-stereotyping.

We were broke. We didn't have any money. You know, nothing. We'd give an award and then some, uh, major organization would give the same person an award. They always copy us. They copy us. That was one of the interesting things, besides the fact that there was another American Book Awards for a while. And they offered to give us money to go away and then they said we tried to bribe them. They told me that theirs was run so badly that they finally went back to the name of National Book Awards because they developed themselves such a bad rep.

Gundars Strads and Justin Desmangles at the 2023 American Book Awards. (Photo by Tennessee Reed)

## Justin Desmangles introduces the 2024 American Book Award Ceremony

The Before Columbus Foundation didn't need a war to honor the poet Mosab Abu Toha. We didn't need anybody to die in order for us to return to the front lines for the advocacy of diversity or equity or inclusion because we've been fighting that fight from the very beginning.

We weren't taking any cues from the so-called mainstream, what we used to call the press and what today we call the media. Because, collectively, we've understood, from the very beginning that one of the distinguishing characteristics of the history of the United States is that, for centuries preceding the Declaration of Independence and for more than a century afterwards, literacy was punishable by death for almost 20 to 25 percent of the entire population. I believe in many respects, this attitude about education, about literacy and what it is for, is still maintained in the status quo.

As the chairman of the Before Columbus board, I read far more books than the law allows, the law of averages, and, increasingly, the laws of this country. This is very dangerous. But I want to point out something that the founders of Before Columbus understood intuitively and practically, which is that the insight and the understanding of language as a resource, both intellectually and sensually, to gain and maintain power, comes from that specific legacy of having once been put to death for being able to read and write. And everyone here today who is receiving an award is part of that tradition and is part of that resistance. And make no mistake, the war is with us today.

And to bring a little bit of focus onto that particular point, I had shared this with Ishmael, I think, last year. It's quite striking. It's the so-called father of the country, George Washington, in 1795, and he's writing to a friend of his, Edmund Pendleton. And he's saying this about those Washington describes as "the ignorant savages from whose hostile conduct we experience much distress." "But it is not to be overlooked," Washington continues, "and they in turn are not without serious causes of complaint from the encroachments which are made on their lands by our people who are not to be restrained by any law now in being or likely to be enacted. They, poor wretches, have no press through which their grievances are related." Pick up on that. "And it is well known," he continues, "that when one side only of a story is heard and often repeated, the human mind becomes impressed with it insensibly."

Well, there it is. So we're not just fighting for ourselves and each other. We're also opening a horizon of possible freedoms for those who will continue this legacy, which began with the Before Columbus Foundation almost fifty years ago.

When Before Columbus first started, it actually began as an outfit that was distributing literature, as a book distributor. And this was the first effort of its kind to consolidate and bring together multicultural literature from throughout the Americas under one roof, for the possibility of mutual understanding and promoting each other's work. Now if anyone wants to take a look at this [*Before Columbus distribution catalog, held up by Justin*], I'd be more than happy to pass it around. But I will just tell you very briefly that the contents of this catalog and the books that were made available through Before Columbus in 1978, at this late date, twenty-five years into the 21st century, really read like a Who's Who of the imminent and preeminent writers who have changed the entire landscape of American literature to the state of inclusivity or sometimes not that it is today.

Before we begin the award series formally, I'd also like to share with you something I believe is also quite important about the early history of Before Columbus. [*Justin shows the audience a poster.*] This was one of the earliest events that was organized by Before Columbus. It is a down-home reading in 1978 by Harryette Mullen and Amos Zu Bolton. You can see that. But here's the point I want to make here. Poetry disco dance party. Okay? Okay? If the poem doesn't boogie your body, that's part of your ailment. Okay? So here's the thing— that the sensual world and the role of the imagination and the possibility of real freedom, that is to say how we move, how we groove, and what we do and the choices that we make comes, from that poem. The origin of those lines is not on paper. They're from the mind song of the poet who brings the being to your imaginative horizon. Now you decide which way you're gonna move. You're gonna sit there with that subvocal. Right? Get your groove on. Let that freedom move you where you need to be. And that's where the poem is coming from, and that's where we acknowledge what that tradition really comes to . . .. That's still where it's at, and that's where we are today.

# Imagining America

by Wajahat Ali

You need to learn two lessons quickly if you want to survive and endure in the country currently called America.

First, if you aren't telling your story, your story will be told to you by others.

Second, the streets in America aren't paved with gold, they're paved with blood.

It's the blood of tribes and communities that suffered so the rest of us could walk or in some cases drive overpriced testaments to capitalism's bad taste like the Cybertruck.

These invisible, forgotten, and ignored communities are often referred to as the salt of the Earth by those whose linen and dirty laundry are cleaned by workers who are individuals with names and not generic condiments.

These denizens of America show up throughout the country's history as characters without speaking parts. They're the background fillers, the extras, the hired help, or the token henchmen beaten up by the Hollywood hero who would otherwise get his clock cleaned if the screenplay wasn't rigged in his favor.

These essential workers who are treated as inconsequential annoyances include descendants of formerly enslaved people whose history and stories of overcoming oppression are deemed inappropriate and too sensitive for school children who are otherwise expected to survive and endure weekly school shootings. These alleged criminals and rapists can be Mexicans born in Texas or Venezuelan immigrants who are told to go back to their country by white men whose grandfathers were born in Scotland. These vermin attempting to replace us are both Jews and Muslims who have to prove their moderation and safety to a country that celebrates white vigilantes who keep shooting and choking unarmed Black people to death.

We live in interesting times. Some people would rather risk their kid getting shot at school than read a book written by Toni Morrison. In 2025, we have book bans but no bans on assault rifles. We have criminals as President promoting Nazi conspiracies about Haitian immigrants eating pets, and librarians and teachers losing their jobs for promoting books that acknowledge different religions, ethnicities, and sexualities.

We had a qualified Black Indian woman running for President who had to be near perfect as a rich, vulgarian white supremacist could talk about Arnold Palmer's penis and still barely win an election by a Hitler mustache hair.

But then again, this *is* America. This is how it has always been. Now, the hoods are off. The dog whistles have been replaced by tweets, podcasts, and bullhorns. There's no need to play Taboo. There's no "economic anxiety." It's pure. It's raw. Organic. Out in the open.

These are forces of white supremacy trying to replace the stories of a multiracial, multifaith, and multicultural America with the monoculture of White Christian Nationalism and corporate greed.

In 1976, the Before Columbus Foundation was founded by a group of writers "dedicated to the promotion and dissemination of contemporary American multicultural literature" and highlight the stories of all the communities that have been existing in this country, especially those who are still missing from our children's history books. Multicultural was a scary word then, and it has become even scarier now. You might recognize a few of its synonyms: diversity, wokeness, and CRT. If these words weren't so terrifying, they wouldn't be trying to ban books, would they?

Thankfully, we at the Before Columbus Foundation love scary stories and horror movies. So what terrifies the miserly forces of white supremacy and conformity, delights the rest of us, the majority. Unlike the enemies of progress, the Before Columbus Foundation welcomes and embraces stories that make us temporarily uncomfortable because we know the only way forward is to expand and stretch ourselves, our hearts, our communities, and our imaginations.

Writers are often the cultural workers with the talent and skill to do just that. If the forces of constriction and hate are Thanos, then consider us the Avengers. “No capes!” to quote Edna from *The Incredibles*. We contain multitudes and our numbers keep growing. To honor the immense talent that exists within American literature, the Before Columbus Foundation has presided over the American Book Awards for nearly half a century.

These are annual awards given to writers by writers.

These are awards given to those writers who don’t obey in advance, who don’t bend the knee to fascists, and who don’t abuse their pen and talents to sanewash the truth, who don’t twist themselves in Cirque Du Soleil pretzels to engage in performative “both sides” bullshit, who don’t sell their integrity to placate corporate donors, who don’t hold their figurative punches against bullies, tyrants, demagogues, and twice-impeached criminal vulgarians who quote Hitler.

These are awards given to writers by writers who never concede an inch or a word to a fascist. These writers resist, they provoke, they mock, they ridicule, and they punch back. These writers also use their pen and talents to speak uncomfortable truths, to uplift marginalized communities, to give comfort, shelter, and shade to those deemed illegal or who allegedly hail from “shit hole countries” or threaten to “poison our blood;” these writers fight for our collective freedoms and rights even if it means they lose cable news contracts, NYT columns or teaching positions; these writers will write and publish editorials warning against America electing an authoritarian even if it upsets their billionaire donors or bosses.

These are writers who excavate stories and revitalize ancestors who were erased and forgotten and who criticize this country’s numerous sins and injustices out of love and a bold hope that still imagines a better future. These are the writers who are the recipients of the annual American Book Awards. Every single recipient is chosen due to one trait and one trait only—the quality of their word. We don’t waste time with tokenism or cronyism. We are independent, which means we can say what we want without fear or favor. There are no corporate interests attached. There are no runners-up. Everyone is on an equal footing. This means you will have wealthy, accomplished writers sharing the stage with independent, first-time writers. Again, all we care about is the word and the quality of the word.

The recipients are nominated by members of the BCF board who come together to discuss, debate, and then unanimously pick the list of winners.

Speaking of our board—let us flex for a moment. We have MacArthur genius winners, Pulitzer Prize winners, poet laureates of the United States, Booker Prize winners, poets, academics, playwrights, novelists, journalists, historians, and I once wore makeup on TV as well.

Some founding members have since passed on or retired, but the Before Columbus Foundation and the American Book Awards keep living. A young generation picks up the pen and writes the next chapter. The story is still being written even if it feels like all hope is lost and we're headed toward a tragedy.

However, no one has typed, "The End," so that means there's still a chance and a blank page waiting to be filled by the next generation that can keep resisting, dreaming, and building a better future for this country in which all of its children will have the chance to be an equal co-protagonist.

# FICTION

## An excerpt from the short story

### "The Poorest Boy in Chicago"

### by Mitch Berman

I was allowed, until I was much too old, to punch my maternal grandfather as hard as I wanted, provided I didn't hit him in the stomach. I used to climb him like a mountain, pummeling as he laughed. His head was enormous, its leading feature the family nose, broad and bulbous and quite equal to the task of holding dominion over a wide, powerful face. His hair, though thin, never went completely gray; he Brylcreemed it straight back, the comb tracks visible, in the way of men of his generation. He bore a striking resemblance to Babe Ruth.

Grandpa drove a succession of new white Cadillacs with white leather upholstery. Parked in one of those Cadillacs in front of our tract home in the Los Angeles suburb of Buena Park, Grandpa opened his wallet to show me twelve hundred-dollar bills. He was my idea of a high roller.

When I was seven, Grandpa outfitted me with my first blazer—bright red with embossed brass buttons—and drove to Las Vegas so fast the wind from the window hurt my face.

A highway cop pulled us over near the Nevada border. Somehow Grandpa got him talking about the Dodgers, and was on the verge of charming his way out of a ticket, when I piped up shrilly from the back seat: "I told you you were driving too fast, Grandpa!"

Grandpa put the inevitable ticket next to the millions of dollars in his wallet and pulled back onto Interstate 15, grumbling, "I'll give you a slap."

At the Golden Nugget Casino, Grandpa and I had Shirley Temples while Grandma drank something that made her expansive enough to laugh at everything Jimmy Durante said and invite me on their upcoming trip to Hawaii. Grandpa raised the back of his hand to his mouth and told me confidentially, "Your Grandma's soused."

When Grandma said he had been elected president, I took for granted she meant of the United States. Actually, Grandpa had been elected president of the Sanitary Suppliers' Association of Southern California. He was a founding father of that organization, having started his factory, Captain Kleenzit, Inc., in 1936. Our home was full of Captain Kleenzit paraphernalia: not just the all-purpose household cleaner, pink and perfumy, but playing cards, pens and pads, and the calendar, all bearing the art-deco Kleenzit logo Grandpa had never changed. One of his company's two annual calendars depicted a different vintage car each month, the other the semi-nude frolickings of a plump and rather overaged nymph named Hilda. The family always got the version with the cars.

There were two Grandpas as well. Mine never swore and rebuked me for doing so ("You've got a filthy mouth, like your father"); the Other Grandpa, I learned after his death, when it fell to Grandma to run the factory, had been the source of innumerable off-color jokes that a Kleenzit trucker would repeat only after issuing warnings to the ladies. I was astonished to discover a massive collage of soft-core pornography splayed out across the wall above the urinals where my Grandpa had peed every weekday of his adult life.

In his last years Grandpa had developed a mysterious blood disease that doctors called a precursor to leukemia. Though he required increasingly frequent transfusions, his life went on more or less as usual, except that he was forced to relinquish his vice presidency of the liberal California Democratic Committee.

On a visit from college, I drove up to my grandparents' home in Laurel Canyon as Grandpa and Beau-beau, the miniature poodle he spoiled rotten, jogged across the road. I embraced Grandpa while he put up a mild struggle and his customary protest: "C'mon c'mon c'mon c'mon."

Physical contact made him uncomfortable now that I had grown up, a fact in which I took a perverse delight. I kissed his fat cheeks until he said, as always, "I'll give you a slap."

Only then did I release him. "You look like you're in good shape, Grandpa."

"What do you mean?"

I had pressed a nerve. "Well," I fumbled, "running across the street and everything."

"Big deal!" he snapped. "I'm only seventy-one-and-a-half."

And a half. He had begun again to count his years in fractions, as a child does.

Long, long before, when the notion of achieving such an age would have seemed preposterous, the *Chicago Examiner* had announced a weeks-long search for "The Poorest Boy in Chicago," upon whose waifish head would descend six dollars "in Silver." My grandfather, then six years of age—"'Most six'nt and a half!' he cried fiercely," according to the *Examiner*—was the fruit of that search. In a sepia-toned photograph in the August 10, 1915 *Examiner*, Grandpa sat on a kitchen chair with one bare foot folded under him, peeling a potato into his lap with a small knife and wearing clean pinstriped overalls and a paper-sellingly wide smile. As the *Examiner* quoted him,

> "Me poor!" he laughed. "Quit kiddin'. Ain't I got a shoe that 'most fits an' a roller skate with three wheels on it an' a job an' a family? Poor! Course I gotta work, but b'lieve me I get paid for it!"
>
> He gets "paid." One day last week he earned 17 cents, and all he has to do with it was to feed and clothe and shelter his family of five—mother, two little sisters, and a baby brother.
>
> **WON'T LET SISTER HUNGER.**
>
> Four-year-old Norma was gnawing a crust of bread. Goldie would have taken it away from her.
>
> "Joe oughta eat it," she said. "He's gotta keep strong so's he can work."
>
> "Aw, let 'er eat," said Joe grandly. "I'll get some more to-night."
>
> He jingled his coppers proudly.

Grandpa never spoke about his origins, perhaps because he did not like their memory, or perhaps because he scoffed at the notion that

TUESDAY, AUGUST 10, 1915. Chicago Examiner... The Best Newspaper for the Best Po

# ROCKEFELLER INQUIRERS IN CLASH; SPLIT IN 3 FACTIONS

**Controversy Over Report to Congress Nearly Disrupts United States Industrial Commission.**

**Contention Hinges on Whether Oil King Shall Be Condemned, Lauded or Ignored in Findings.**

John D. Rockefeller and the conditions prevailing in the mining districts of the Colorado Fuel & Iron Company, of which Rockefeller is the principal stockholder, as well as the scope of activities of the $100,000,000 Rockefeller Foundation in New York, constituted a bone of contention among members of the United States Commission on Industrial Relations in secret session yesterday. The differences all but disrupted that body and brought to a termination its efforts to prepare a report of its work to be submitted to Congress.

Even as matters stand now, there is every indication that three separate reports will be sent to Congress, representing the three divisions of opinion among the commissioners.

The controversy hanged on whether Rockefeller should be condemned, ignored or lauded in the report.

**THREE REPORTS SUBMITTED.**

Three tentative drafts of a report were submitted. The first was written by Basil M. Manly, director of research and investigation for the commission. The second was presented by Commissioner John R. Commons, a professor at the University of Wisconsin, and the third came from Commissioner Harris Weinstock, a merchant of Sacramento, Cal.

Manly's report was supported by Chairman Frank P. Walsh and Commissioners A. B. Garretson, James O'Connell and John B. Lennon. The latter two members are vice president and treasurer, respectively, of the American Federation of Labor. Garretson is secretary of the Railway Conductors' Association.

The Manly draft dealt with the testimony in connection with the Rockefeller interests, particularly with the allegations that the Colorado Fuel & Iron Company had furnished money to corrupt the Colorado electorate; that saloons were conducted by the company within short distances of public schools and that literature favorable to the mine owners was distributed by keepers of saloons.

**NO MENTION OF ROCKEFELLER.**

Professor Commons' report dealt with sociological conditions and is said to have made no mention of either Mr. Rockefeller or any of his interests. Mrs. J. Borden Harriman is said to have approved this draft.

The third report is said to coincide with the views of Commissioners R. H. Aishton of Chicago and S. Thruston Ballard of Louisville.

In the course of the discussions reference was made to the $10,000,000 Russell Sage foundation at New York, the Baron de Hirsch fund and the benevolences of Andrew Carnegie.

The Commons report recommends creation of various committees and bureaus to continue certain lines of inquiry on which the Industrial Commission has touched.

**THREE REPORTS PREDICTED.**

The commission will meet to-day. Predictions are made that the final result will be the submission of three separate reports to Congress.

The principal opposition to the Manly report is that it makes unsupported attacks upon corporations and voices the views expressed by labor leaders.

The document submitted by the group of employers on the commission is objected to on grounds that it enters into a defense of capital and arraigns labor organizations.

Commons' draft met opposition on the grounds it is neither clear nor constructive and contains no conclusions that will give Congress a comprehesive grasp of the commission's work. It is asserted the paper represents the personal convictions of the professor rather than concrete views drawn from the investigations.

## Indian Tells Healey Dog Is Tax Exempt

Is a full-blooded Indian exempt from city taxes? C. Strack, a Miami Indian, who lives at 1232 Fulton street, told Chief of Police Healey yesterday he was exempt from paying taxes. He asked that an order be issued saying that he did not have to pay a license fee for a dog. It was too much for the chief, who referred the matter to the law department for an opinion.

## Umpire Quigley Is Disabled by Blast

A few minutes before the ball game started on the West Side yesterday Umpire Quigley touched a match to the gas heater in the umpire's dressing room to see how the thing worked. An explosion knocked him unconscious and he was sent to a hospital close by. Dr. Davis, the

# "Poorest Boy" in City Found Supports Five on 17 Cents

JOE LUPOWICH AND HIS SMILE

## "Newsie" Declares He Really Isn't "Poor"; Gets $6 Intrusted to Examiner.

The poorest boy in Chicago didn't know he was poor at all.

"Me poor!" he laughed. "Quit kiddin'. Ain't I got a shoe that 'most fits an' a roller skate with three wheels on it an' a job an' a fam'ly? Poor! Course I gotta work, but b'lieve me I get paid for it!"

He gets "paid." One day last week he earned 17 cents, and all he has to do with it was to feed and clothe and shelter his family of five—mother, two little sisters, and a baby brother. He himself, the poorest boy, is six years old.

His name is Joe Lupowich, and to-day he will get the handful of silver coins that were entrusted to the Examiner to be given to the poorest boy in Chicago. That was the order the Examiner received. Give them to "the poorest"—not the most miserable, not the sickest, not the most terribly crippled boy in Chicago, but "the poorest." And the Examiner has decided that means Joe. The fact that he manages to be happy has nothing to do with the case. And his ignorance of his own poverty is immaterial, too. He gets the silver —$6 worth.

**WHOLE CITY LOOKED FOR JOE.**

At least a dozen persons telephoned or wrote to the Examiner about Joe. The whole city was looking for the poorest boy. Some of the searchers sent in lists of half a dozen boys, because they could not decide. But those who mentioned Joe did not mention anybody else. Easy enough to decide in his case.

So the Examiner found him yesterday, in a little room in the rear of 1248 Washburne avenue. The mother was sitting in a crippled rocking chair. She has been "weakly" of late —malnutrition, a doctor might call it. Goldie, seven years, and Norma, four, were playing under the table. Willie, eight months, lay on his mother's lap. Joe himself was studiously counting coppers near the one window.

"Earned 'em," he said proudly. "Sellin' papers. I'll earn a lot o' 'em, too, when I get bigger and have a stand where all the people go by. But I got all I need right now—'cause I know a place where you can go late at night an' buy a whole lot o' day before yesterday's bread for fi' cents. I know a boy that makes $3 a week an' spends it all. He don' know how to buy bread. Gee, 'f I had that kid's money!"

**WON'T LET SISTER HUNGER.**

Four-year-old Norma was gnawing a crust of bread. Goldie would have taken it away from her.

"Joe oughta eat it," she said. "He's gotta keep strong so's he can work."

"Aw, let 'er eat," said Joe grandly. "I'll get some more to-night."

He jingled his coppers proudly.

"You're six years old, are you Joe?" said the visitor.

"'Most six'n a half!" he cried fiercely.

It isn't always wretched to be poor. The only danger is that Joe, when he gets that $6, will become a giddy philanthropist.

## $125,000 Back Pay Is Given to Carmen

## Jury Disagrees in Brazelton Sanity Case

# GRAFT CASES GO TO JURY TO-DAY

**Prosecutor Johnston Will Close Argument for State in Trial of Egan and O'Brien.**

Denouncing the state's witnesses as thieves, convicts and swindlers, banded together in a "perjury club" to punish the honest policemen who had arrested them, and censuring the state's attorney's office for using their testimony, counsel for William Egan and Walter O'Brien, detectives charged with grafting, began their final pleas to the jury yesterday in Judge O'Connor's court. Attorney Charles E. Erbstein, for Egan, completed an impassioned plea, and Attorney John E. Northup, for O'Brien, was in the midst of his argument when court adjourned last evening. When Northup concludes this morning Prosecutor Frank Johnston will make a last demand for a conviction and the case will go to the jury.

Northup appealed to the reason of the jury. He argued that no credence should be given the testimony of men who are confessed criminals and who are now under sentence to the penitentiary — "Barney" Bertsche and James Ryan.

"If the story of Barney Bertsche is proved false," he said; "if it is found to be perjury, then you cannot find these defendants guilty. If you find his story false the whole case of the state fails—there is nothing you can do but return a verdict of not guilty.

**BRANDS BERTSCHE A "WRETCH."**

"Is there anything in this evidence to show that Barney Bertsche is not an abnormal wretch and that he would not hesitate to falsify for a purpose? Wasn't he convicted time and time again? Wasn't he sentenced for swindling Mrs. Hope McEldowney? Wasn't he sentenced—though he is not serving that sentence—to the Joliet penitentiary for that? And has he not good reason, in his own criminal mind, to falsify here to better his own chances for pardon?"

Attorney Erbstein's plea was frankly to the emotional side of the jury. He appealed first to their prejudices, picturing Bertsche and Ryan, convicts, living at a fine hotel at the expense of the county and enjoying luxuries which are forbidden jurors.

Then he pictured the private lives of the accused Egan and O'Brien, brought their wives and children into the foreground and set forth their grief and sorrow if the defendants should be sent to prison.

"Since you men were sworn in to hear this case have you had your cigars, magazines and drinks every day?" demanded Erbstein. "No! That's only for the state's witnesses. You men are only jurors and you can't have any luxuries. Among the witnesses for the state are James Ryan and Barney Bertsche. According to their own testimony they are now under sentence to the penitentiary. But, gentlemen, I'll wager they are downstairs in the State's Attorney's office. I'll say, gentlemen, that the whole perjury club is downstairs in the State's Attorney's office.

**JURORS WEEP AT PLEA.**

"Some of you gentlemen are married and some of you have children. When you leave here will you go home to your wives and children? With you, gentlemen, rests the question whether Egan, the man who has helped protect your homes from the night prowler, is going home to his wife and children. Are you men going home to your wives and say to them, 'Yes, I sent him down to a whitewashed two-by-four cell, where he will see no sky?'

"And are you men going to place the scarlet letter upon the breast of Ean's wife and children on such flimsy testimony as this? Are you men going to have his little children taunted by others when they go to school and play? Why? Because the other children will say: 'We don't want to associate with you. Your father is a criminal and a thief. He betrayed this city.'

"Are you going to hold up those little darlings to public scorn and contempt on such testimony as Bertsche and the Ryans gave? Here we have three thieves, not forty thieves; here we have not twenty pieces of silves, but $500. How do we know? Three members of the perjury club said so."

Two purors wept. One wiped the tears away with a handkerchief.

## Bank Clerk's Body Is Found in Lake

The body of Clarence V. Burnson, 22 West One Hundred and Twelfth street, was taken from the lake at Carr's beach, Miller, Ind., yesterday. Burnson and his three sisters went to Miller Sunday. He disappeared while the girls were in the locker room dressing for a swim. The sisters, believing that their brother had drowned, returned home. They asked the police to search for him. Burnson was a clerk for the Union Trust Company.

# TIFF IN WOMEN'S OIL CORPORATION

**Mrs. William Severin and Mrs. Dora Earle Will Quit If Men Are Given Hand.**

There is revolt in the camp of the Woman's Federal Oil Company. Two of the officers of the organization have resigned. One of the officials took with her a promise of the purchase of 1,000 shares of stock.

The resignations are final. The purchase of stock may be made, however. It all depends on whether arrangements can be made to suit the former officers. If this is done stock will be acquired by them. If not, Mrs. William Severin and Mrs. Dora Earle will no longer be connected with the first business concern of the suffragists of the country.

The difficulties are dual. The two Chicago women expected the organization would be entirely of women, and it developed that two men wanted a finger in it. Also, Mrs. Severin and Mrs. Earle had been led to believe that the central headquarters of the company would be in Chicago. Instead, the Woman's Federal Oil Company has been incorporated under the laws of Louisiana and that prevents the main work from being carried on in this state.

Furthermore, a quantity of stock was to have been sold before any of the proceeds could be diverted to the suffrage cause.

Mrs. H. H. Honore, president of the business, said yesterday that within the next two or three days a complete reorganization will be effected. The company will be much more exclusive, according to present plans.

Mrs. Severin, who also is president of the Illinois Women's Republican League, was to have been secretary of the oil company. She had made arrangements to invest $5,000 in the venture.

"There are no stockholders yet—at least, not a cent of money has been turned over to the corporation," said Mrs. Severin last night. "Everything is tentative. It is believed that stock can be sold at a lower price, according to the plans as I know them.

"If, however, the women have their company by themselves, then I shall be willing to put money into it. I want to see it a woman's company exclusively. If it is not, I think I shall keep my hands out of it."

But Mrs. Honore declared Mrs. Severin still is a stockholder, and Mrs. Earle as well.

"I am not a stockholder," said Mrs. Severin. "I am waiting to see what happens."

The masculine member of the company to whom the women objected is J. L. Tucker, fiscal agent, now in Shreveport, La. Mrs. Honore said yesterday that Tucker is still connected with the concern.

The company will refine the oil from 4,800 acres of Louisiana oil lands, leases to which are now being looked over. The Chicago office of the company is on the fifteenth floor of the Lytton Building. Mrs. Honore, who is a resident of the Congress Hotel, says she is in the concern to stay.

"We are going to organize a new company and we shall make money," she said. "It is one of the biggest things women have undertaken."

## Tardy Taxpayers Halt Property Sales

Taxpayers who rushed in at the last minute to pay their taxes in the County Building yesterday halted the sale of property for unpaid taxes. It was continued until to-day to permit the readjustment of the lists. County Treasurer Stuckart said the unpaid items totaled almost $100,000. The value of the property to be sold for taxes this year is $2,500,000, or $500,000 advance.

## Sunday Burglars Get $1,258 From Homes

"Sunday afternoon burglars" stole property worth $1,258 from five South Side homes, according to the victims' reports to the police. Those robbed were: Alexander Harris, 4736 Michigan avenue, $145; Thomas W. Bell, 4740 Michigan avenue, $395; Charles Smith, 6042 Michigan avenue, $112, and Mrs. D. Leslie, 839 East Forty-seventh street, $240.

## City Horse Foreman Under Charges

C. T. Griiner, foreman of horses for the police department, was suspended yesterday and charges filed against him by Chief Healey. It was charged that the foreman charged the city $35 a month for the maintenance of an automobile and that in six months his machine was in the repair shop seventy days.

anything could have held him back. He was fond, however, of telling the story of how he had quit his four-pack-a-day smoking habit. It was a remarkably short story. "One day I said, 'Who's the boss? Me or these cigarettes?' I never smoked another. Never missed it." He would give a quick sharp stare to each of his listeners, daring someone to deny it, to deny the lesson in it.

The lesson was that Grandpa had, through clean living and indomitable force of will, rendered himself invulnerable to the weaknesses of ordinary men. And so it dumbfounded us all when a minor piece of oral surgery went sour, Grandpa's red-blood-cell count plunged, and he was taken by ambulance to Cedars-Sinai Hospital.

I flew in from New York, and spent the next month with Grandma. Every morning she stuffed me full of eggs—scrambled with green peppers, with fried salami, easy over, in omelettes—and then we were off to Cedars-Sinai, where I listened to my grandparents debate about finances and the factory. "You shut up!" he'd tell her, when things had reached a certain point.

"No, *you* shut up!" she'd tell him.

Maggie, my youngest aunt, came daily to the hospital, and together we giggled as her parents carped. When we became too much for Grandpa, we found ourselves—politely but firmly, Grandma being his ambassador in matters requiring tact—expelled from his room. We would wander to Beverly Center, the six-floor shopping mall newly opened on the grounds where, as a child, my grandparents had taken me for pony rides in the middle of Los Angeles. Maggie and I would anesthetize ourselves for hours by popping chocolate-coated coffee beans and touching things we could not afford. Finally we would sink into the Star Trek lobby furniture and look at each other's haggard faces.

After visiting hours, Grandma would take me for a run on Fairfax Avenue, it being imperative that her only grandson be constantly supplied with his favorite foods—strawberries, T-bone steaks, Canter's Delicatessen's onion bagels and lox—all the foods she called my favorites turning out to be her own. I stalked her with my new Minolta in the open-air produce markets; "Oh no, I look awful," she would say, patting her hair like a forties film queen.

We returned to watch old movies on TV as she crocheted throw rugs to cover up the spots on the white wool carpet that were Beau-beau's legacy. "Beau-beau," she would murmur, "was a *pisher.*" Grandma loved Paul Muni and Charles Laughton, hated sex scenes and subtitles. One night we made Droste's cocoa with fresh whipped cream and watched *Pygmalion.* It was her opinion that Leslie Howard had beautiful eyes.

Specialists were swirling around Grandpa at Cedars-Sinai, but I considered myself the only doctor assigned to Grandma. I blanketed her with good intentions, insisting that she eat when she wasn't hungry, setting her alarm an hour forward while she slept. She puttered endlessly in the kitchen and bore my ministrations with a girlish resistance that she usually allowed me to beat down.

There were many reasons why Grandma's yellow-tiled kitchen had always been my favorite room in their home—the laughter of my aunts, the smells of chicken soup and kasha varnishkes—but perhaps the best was that it was not the living room, where Grandpa sat at his card table doing jigsaw puzzles under a goosenecked lamp and occasionally peering over his half-framed glasses and giving the TV's remote control a dour pump. Only Beau-beau could violate this sanctuary with impunity; Grandpa would buffet the dog with big blunt hands until he elicited his phony snarl, pluck out any ribbons his daughters had tied into Beau's black curls, and dispense Chips Ahoy cookies from a glass jar kept close by for that purpose.

I once calculated that the number of Chips Ahoys the tiny poodle devoured would be equivalent, for an adult human, to fifty-four chocolate-chip cookies per day. Grandma laughed at me: "Try telling that to Grandpa!"

I never did, and Beau-beau lived to be seventeen. When Maggie came home for family dinners, Beau-beau jumped all over her; Grandpa could say only, "The dog's happy to see you, Margaret."

My grandparents had put five years between each of their three daughters. Though Maggie was thirteen years older than me, she had always seemed of my own generation. She had introduced me, in my teens, to rock music and marijuana, taken me to Fellini films with her friends. Now, until such time as Grandpa got better, both our lives were on hold.

Grandpa would get better; that was our common coin. Maggie clung to a form of hope that I couldn't abide: not only would her father live, but the hospital was the best in the world, and the nurses were nice, and in fact everyone was very nice, and no one was ugly. I rubbed her raw with constant arguments that the only realistic thing to believe was that Grandpa would recover: though the doctors now said that Grandpa had crossed the border into leukemia, and the odds were ten to one against him, the odds did not take into account Grandpa's extraordinary constitution, his iron will; the odds, when viewed rightly, were all in his favor. In one picture snapped by a stranger in Beverly Center, Maggie and I were leaning against each other like adjacent buildings slowly collapsing together.

It was as if the entire family had smoked marijuana and the high was lasting a month: if something was good, it was very very good, if bad, it was unbearable; and in either event we immediately forgot it. Grandpa had reached the point where he had good days and bad days, and we had all become Grandpas.

Grandpa had taken his chemotherapy with no vomiting or hair loss, seeming to prove my childish theory that he was more than human. The initial blood and bone-marrow tests were clean, but soon a few cancer cells were discovered.

The second round of chemo was as hard as the first had been easy. Grandpa's hair fell out in bunches, and solid food became an impossibility. A second intravenous unit appeared beside his bed, dispensing clear foodstuff while the other dripped noxious chemicals into his bloodstream. The doctors told us he was vulnerable to infection and asked us to wear surgical masks in his room. Grandpa insisted on his daily shower more adamantly now that strangers were regularly inspecting his body, and the intravenous units had to be disconnected every morning, reconnected when he finished.

He had always been something of a dandy. My mother had recalled to me her amazement, long before Captain Kleenzit became successful, at seeing her father bring home silken boxer shorts. All his socks were Egyptian cotton, their colors fastidiously coordinated with the loud, expensive Italian slip-on shoes he favored. Now Grandpa lay naked in his bed at Cedars-Sinai, waiting to be exposed by anyone who cared to lift his sheet.

Judge Jimmy Eisenberg, an alert, narrow man in a tailored brown suit, came to reminisce with Grandpa about their lives in California politics. I listened, encouraged by Grandpa's energy. When he dozed off suddenly, the judge, waiting for him to awaken, talked with me for a while about New York, rents, and crime. He said he'd heard I was a writer.

Before I could answer, Grandpa awoke and roared, and not only awoke and roared but actually sat up to do it, "Ask him how much *money* he's made on his writing!"

He had always had a knack for the killing interpolation. When I called from college to talk to Grandma, chattering for half an hour about her daughters, my professors, her latest short story and the letter she'd had in Tuesday's *Times*, Grandpa would seize the phone and say, "Listen to me: Don't ever forget you're Jewish!"

Not forgetting we were Jewish did not, however, mean forgetting Christmas, but we displayed no holiday decoration that bore the likeness of any figure from the New Testament, and when my first grade sang "O Come All Ye Faithful" at the year-end assembly, I silently mouthed the words "Christ the Lord," feeling it inappropriate to give an enemy deity my personal endorsement. We had to neuter the holiday in order to claim it.

On Christmas Eve, my grandparents' living room—and the baby grand piano, with gifts piled high, spilling off, stacked on the floor—became the center of the family. And at the center of the center sat Grandpa, playing the piano both well and badly. More particularly, his right hand played well while his left played badly; he could read the treble clef but not the bass, and as he unerringly picked out the melody of "Tea for Two" or "Begin the Beguine," his left hand crashed and bumbled randomly among the deep notes. We saved Grandpa's gifts, always the most lavish, for last; his card always insisted, *Happy Hanukkah.*

As Grandpa grew more prosperous and more irascible, it became increasingly hard to find presents that pleased him. Finally we began giving him intentionally foolish objects, like a horribly large plastic leprechaun with a grinning head mounted on a spring. You hit the leprechaun's head, and, after a preliminary *werrrrrrrrr*, it began to laugh—"HahahahahaHEEHEHEEHEHEEHAHAHEEEEH-HAAAHAAA HAAA"—and just when it was winding down, could not possibly have another breath in it, would start all over again with renewed vigor. There was no way to stop it short of the great violence that it inspired.

We had little reason to believe Grandpa liked these things any better than the chromatic harmonica that was instantly recycled back into my own family, or the neckties that never made it to his electrical tie rack (two people had, in desperation, given him electrical tie racks); but Grandma swore he loved them, which only meant that she did.

The room at Cedars-Sinai contained nothing to hint at how difficult it had become to get anything, do anything for this man. Suspended between beige walls and beige linoleum, between the odors of human illness and the false denials of sweet antiseptic, between intervals of darkness and fluorescent light, between intervals of silence and soft trebly Muzak, between artificial night and artificial day, lay a fully insured elderly white male patient, waiting for blood tests and medications, waiting for puncture and palpation, waiting for change, simply waiting, waiting and wearing the plastic ID bracelet that hospitals affix impartially to old men, babies, teenagers, and corpses.

In an ongoing attempt to infect that no-man's-land with a few germs of personality, we were exporting Grandpa's household effects to the hospital. Like gift-giving, it was a hit-and-miss proposition, with the misses coming considerably more often than the hits. One morning we put the mechanical leprechaun in a brown Ralph's supermarket bag and smuggled it in.

The large elevator car was already crowded with nurses and interns when several patients' families got on with us in the lobby. Everybody in this elevator was headed toward a cancer case—lung and lymph on the third floor, leukemia on the fourth—and no one spoke above a whisper. In the quiet, the hospital's Muzak became foreground. It always seemed to be playing something from *Fiddler on the Roof.*

A platoon of nurses and orderlies boarded on the second floor. I moved toward the rear, slid sideways, hunched my shoulders, flattening myself to the wall, compressing myself, when somebody elbowed the package in my hands. There was an ominous *werrrrrrrrr.* Grandma and I exchanged a look of horror.

"*Hahahaha!*" began the paper bag. Conversation stopped as every eye stared at me. Like all hospital elevators, this one was torturously slow, and while we inched upward to the leukemia ward the paper bag howled and screamed in irrepressible hilarity.

"Get that goddamn thing out of here!" Grandpa barked as soon as he saw it. We took the leprechaun back that night in the trunk of the car, and when we bumped over the old trolley tracks on La Cienega we could hear the muffled hooting of its interminable laughter.

Unless I am forgetting a perfunctory goodbye that evening, "Get that goddamn thing out of here!" was the last thing Grandpa ever said to me. A little after midnight the hospital called to tell us that Grandpa had taken a turn for the worse. He'd been moved to the Intensive Care Unit.

Our family reunited from its diaspora that morning at Cedars-Sinai: Grandma and me, my mother and her sisters Maggie and Evelyn, Grandpa's younger brother Charlie and his wife; from Laurel Canyon and New York, from Seattle and Venice and Marina Del Rey and the San Fernando Valley, all of us embracing and reassembling the lobby furniture until, armchairs and sofas and love seats and end-tables, we were in a circle like an embattled wagon train.

Uncle Charlie was the first to go in. When my grandparents had been courting, Charlie had introduced himself to Grandma by riding a horse into her mother's Brooklyn candy shop to deliver a love letter from his big brother. Over the years Charlie had developed the embarrassing habit of falling asleep after dinner when company was present. Because I had always visited with my grandparents, I had never seen him do it; Charlie could listen to Grandpa for hours.

Charlie spent only a few minutes in Intensive Care. When he emerged, his arms rigid at his sides, his face utterly composed, we converged on him. Charlie gave a hoarse bark and collapsed into a chair. Looking around at us, as if our hopeful faces would contradict what he had seen in there, he cried, gasping and choking like a man who had not cried since childhood and thought he had forgotten how. With his bulk and his thick nervous fingers, now drumming on his knees, now barring his broad face, he seemed more than ever before a slightly smaller, slightly younger version of Grandpa.

"Joe!" Grandma was up and into hallway across the lobby, striding to Intensive Care and throwing the door open and demanding to see her husband. Maggie and my mother and I followed. Evelyn remained, paralyzed, in her chair, watching us and shaking her head slightly.

Grandpa writhed. He was naked to the waist, very white and still fat, although he'd lost thirty pounds. Under the respirator, strapped into restraints, completely unconscious, he tossed his great wild bald head from side to side as an electronic monitor implacably flashed readings of heartbeat and blood pressure. We asked questions, as if the readouts proved that this heaving figure was still Grandpa, using loud voices as if he was merely hard of hearing: "Are you warm enough? Can you hear us? Squeeze my hand once for 'yes.'" The nurses assured us he was very comfortable. His yellow nails protruded half an inch beyond his toes.

Grandma knelt beside the bed and buried her face in the huge white hand that lolled, upturned and passive, over the metal railing. "Don't leave me!" she sobbed. "Don't leave me, Joe!"

For fifty-two years Grandma had not only remained married to this man, but had remained happy with him. Now, at her signal, the rest of us lost control at once: me telling Grandma in a sober, masterly voice not to upset Grandpa; Maggie telling me to leave Grandma alone; and my mother imploring generally for peace: all of us bawling and shouting advice at one another as Grandpa began to die.

After a while we retreated to the lobby, where we stayed for hours, waiting for news and trying to sleep on furniture that seemed continually to change form, usually for the worse, beneath us. I kept seeing the whiteness of his body, under the respirator, the harsh lights, under restraint: I knew I'd never easily dislodge that image and hang any other picture of Grandpa in its place.

A week later, on the flight back to New York, I sat in the shaft of the overhead light, flipping through the photographs I'd taken in Los

Angeles, while a movie caused the other passengers, under their headphones, to laugh in response to stimuli I did not hear. The family had dispersed: my mother to Seattle, Uncle Charlie to the Valley, my aunts to Venice and Marina Del Rey. I always returned to one photograph, the way you will, if you turn over each card in a deck, keep coming back to the ace of spades. I had taken it two nights after Grandpa died, following Grandma out into her garden as she went to cut a rose for the kitchen table. I'd used a flash and it had illuminated Grandma while failing to penetrate the blackness of the night around her.

# Hare Diary

by Maxine Hong Kingston

September 22, 2011 —Thursday

Phoenix — > Tucson. Picked up by Sharon Zapata, small as me, efficient, cheerful, driving a big van. Always a relief to find the person who's to meet us actually show up. Sleepy, I fumblingly asked about the boycott of Arizona being called off because of the passing of a bill that gives citizenship to children born in the U.S. Said aloud, this trade-off didn't make sense. Children born in the U.S. (such as moi, and former slaves) *are* citizens. The Fourteenth Amendment. Redundant for AZ to pass such a bill. From the backseat, Earll read us the article in yesterday's *Chronicle*; La Raza announces the boycott over. Sharon said that she didn't know of any such discontinuance. She spoke evenly, that the boycott was doing good *and* doing harm. She's taken years off work to donate time to Derechos Humanos. I praised and thanked her. She called the Fence a "funnel"; it funnels the migrants to the worst of the desert.

Our hotel was Lodge on the Desert, designed like a pueblo, mazes of courtyards and adobe-covered buildings. Our room had a balcony with a view of parked cars and hills. I opened the balcony door, and turned on the automatic fireplace. We unpacked, and went straight to the Palm Room. We'd already missed a day and a morning of proceedings. Ken Chen gave us a shout-out, "Maxine Hong Kingston and Earll have arrived!" Everybody applauded and cheered. The room was full of tables / work stations, where people were finishing lunch, holding discussions, and working on projects. The walls were covered with lists of ideas for actions. People told us, we just missed the most amazing speakers, fortifying the group for the journey to the border.

I put on the book table *Neighbor: Christian Encounters with "Illegal" Immigration* by Ben Daniel. And one of each kind of Santo Toribio Romo holy cards. Rev. Ben Daniel himself had sent the cards from San José, bought at the Catholic church across the street from his house. (He called the prayer cards, medals, and novena booklets "tchotchkes" and "swag.") Earll and I got some food, and sat at a table with a comedy team* who were touring the country. One of them asked me about *Neighbor.* "Do you always put that many Post-its in your books?" Earll answered, "Yes, when she's teaching." I talk story: Making the crossing, hundreds of migrants have had appear to them a man who brings water and food, and sometimes money. Lately, he's been known to drive a pick-up truck, and give rides. He points out the direction the immigrant should continue traveling, and where to find shelter, and even a job. When you've made good in El Norte, he tells them, come back south, and give thanks at Santa Ana de Guadalupe in Jalisco. People who've completed that pilgrimage were surprised to find a picture of that very man they'd met in the desert; he's Father Toribio Romo, shot to death in the Cristero War, 1928. On the back of these cards, there's an Oración Por Immigránte. It's from the viewpoint of the people left behind. "... we ask through the intercession of Santo Toribio Romo for the caring and protecting of our family who have had to leave the house. . . . protect them from all evil and that they remain firm in faith, so they can soon return to our home, strengthened in the soul and body." *Regreso pronto.* Ken Chen and Jeff Chang were at the table too, but they weren't listening, talking to each other about logistics. I was among politicos, materialists, realists; even the comedians were realists. They aren't interested in the religion of the immigrants. I feel fuzzy-minded; I can't contribute anything practical. The comedians left the holy cards behind; I'd meant that they'd pass

* W. Kamau Bell, Nato Green, and Janine Brito. "Laughter Against the Machine: Guerilla Stand-up Comedy."

them along to migrants we'd meet. Realpolitik discounts the mythical and the mystical.

I read *Neighbor* for good arguments for free migration. Ben Daniel presents the Bible as a book of migrations— Exodus, the wanderings in the desert; the Good Samaritan and Ruth, aliens; Joseph and Mary, travelers on their way to pay their taxes. One of the comedians added: "Adam and Eve, migrants exiled from the Garden of Eden." "The journey north is a spiritual one," says Daniel, "it's a Christian pilgrimage." I would add that it's part of a Hopi pilgrimage; people who came from China across five rocks made sojourns east-west, west-east, gathering and mixing water from the Atlantic and the Pacific, and north-south, south-north, touching the jungles and the doors of ice.

(I'm having a horrible flashback of my interview on BBC Radio— not an interview but a debate, an unfair debate. The interlocutor had a producer, who prompted and fed him arguments—while I was speaking. I could hear his voice leaking from the interviewer's headphone. Two-against-one, punching at my pacifism. I wish I had stopped, on live air, and said, "Your earphones are too loud. Please turn them off. I want to talk to just one of you. Don't speak when I'm speaking. You have a coach;" I should have a coach.)

(Another memory: We learned from the Indians at the Pueblos and at the Grand Canyon that they have no myth about being exiled from Eden. They're still living on Isla Tortuga, Turtle Island. To the Chinese also, the continents are islands.)

After lunch, we went by bus to Tucson Federal Court. Jeff Chang drove, got lost, made a uey, slowed to look for the right streets. The Latino brothers teased him, "Driving while Asian." I am so proud of the Asian American Writers Workshop, leading this CultureStrike, and doing so with humility. We came to an immense new building, not quite brutalist architecture, airier; it was built especially for processing immigrants. Maribel Gomez briefed us: We're going to witness a judicial proceeding called "Stream-lining." Watch 70 immigrants be deported in 90 minutes. We waited and waited in the hallways. I met again Roberto

Bedoya, whom Earll says talks like a poet. The spectator seats are full; we'll have to take turns. But nobody was exiting. Let's go down to

Floor 2; maybe we can watch "initial processing." A guard said, "A lot of bleeding hearts here today." Waited and waited on Floor 2. There was a lit-up board like at the airport with names of people and their attorneys and judges, some lines labeled "Flipflop." Nobody could tell me what "Flipflop" means. Went back up to Floor 6. Maribel went inside the courtroom, got some of our group to leave, and I entered and took a seat in back.

A row of about ten men shuffled in; they were shackled hands and feet. Earbuds, for hearing translators? Mostly short men, brown skin, black hair, like Joseph, but Joseph sturdier, well fed. A Latino man seated on the outside of the railing turned around and looked at us, looked at me. I nodded, and looked away, but caught his nod back. Behind the shackled men were three or four officialspublic defenders? translators?—who would remove an earbud, and talk privately into a man's ear. The judge, a pretty blonde woman, asked a series of questions. Maribel had said that all of the accused will answer Yes to all of the questions. Yes is the correct answer; the court recommends Yes. I remember three of the questions. (I didn't take notes; getting pen and paper out of my bag, and writing things down would take too much concentration away from whatever was happening.) "Are you an alien? ... alien to the United States of America?" "Si." "Yes." "Si." "Si." "Yes." 10 "sies" and "yeses." "For detention of one hundred and five days, with credit for time served, do you agree to waive the right to a trial by jury?" "Yes." "Si." Etcetera. "Has no one forced you to plead guilty or made any promises to you other than what we've talked about here in this court?" "Si." "Yes." Etcetera. My naiveté is bottomless. I'm aghast that rights are like gaming chips; you're given so many chips— time, credits, jury trial— and you can trade them. And you swear that you were not coerced or pressured to play by these rules. The group of shackled men shuffled out, and a new group shuffled in. But this time there was a difference: A man answered "No" to waiving trial by jury. The judge asked him the question again, and asked if he understood it. (Maribel had said that this judge takes more time with prisoners than normal.) A lawyer took out the man's earbud, and spoke to him, told him the consequences of "No." The judge was giving him a chance to change his mind. He said again, "No." The Court finished the "streamlining." Shuffling out of the courtroom, many of the men kept their heads turned toward us spectators; I felt their eyes saying, "Help."

Next, we went to an amphitheater-like room, like a lecture hall classroom. A judge spoke from a table in front. Like every public official we met, he commended the state's treatment of illegal immigrants as "humane." "Operation Streamline is as humane as possible." Out of 1,000 people caught at the border, only seventy are put on trial and imprisoned. The rest are turned back. People with children are turned back. Those arrested are seen by the Mexican consulate, and given advice. The judge was very tired, a large, heavy, coughing man. He held what looked like a plastic unlit cigarette that he'd put in his mouth, and take out again. His other hand opened a matchbook, but he did not light up. Earll said, "He's going to die soon." Jessica Hagedorn said, "He's Shakespearean. He's tragic. I like him."

The judge suffered our group's questioning of him. One of the radical Latino guys asked whether the judge, a Mexican American, was going against himself— "betraying yourself"— and his own people. The judge gave his story, beginning with his grandfather's immigration. His family was "fortu nate," grandparents, parents, himself, all "fortunate." His grandfather fortunate to've come when the crossing was easi er. The family made money, got educations, served in wars. He himself in Vietnam. He'd been a public defender. ". . . not Mexican American . . . not this American, that American but American." He heaved himself up from weariness to the eloquence of the orating trial lawyer, barely coughing.

Teju Cole, who was sitting next to me, spoke respectfully. "Thank you for speaking with us. I know you don't have to do this, and we appreciate it." Carefully, he got around to asking how the judge feels seeing all this human suffering every day. The judge did not reveal his feelings, only told how he handles them: He has a time limit to his exposure to suffering. "I spend twenty-six minutes a day streamlining."

Someone observed that one of the streamlined men had grass in his hair. "Are they disoriented and wounded coming out of the desert into court?" The judge said, "I can't criticize a man's grooming habits. But they do not come straight from the desert to the courtroom. They are checked medically. They get fed; they get water, a place to sleep. Their consulate speaks to them. The lawyers speak to them. There are translators. At least two days of preparation before they come into the courtroom."

Jessica Hagedorn asked after the man who pleaded No. What's going to happen to him? The judge said, "He's basically screwed. He screwed himself. He could've gotten away with one hundred and five days in detention camp. Now he's going to get two to five years." (Somebody said later, "'Detention camp'? Immigrant Prison.")

I didn't even raise my hand to be recognized to speak. I just spoke up loud from near the back of the room. "What about the jury trial? What if he's found innocent? You'd have to let him go." I blurted out what I had to say before shyness overran me. And not only shyness, but fear of showing naiveté, ignorance of the law, and disingenuousness.

The judge said, "There's no way he will be found innocent." A judge said that! The judge pre-judged! He already knows: The man is guilty; he will get two to five. Patiently educating us, he reviewed the process: The Border Patrol picks up a group of immigrants, and sorts them out— You with the kids, you go back. You who've been seen entering the country without documents, you go to court. At court, you're offered a plea bargain; you can plead guilty to a misdemeanor, a small thing, not having papers. That man who pleaded No will be charged with a felony, illegal immigration. No way will he be found innocent; the Border Patrol witnessed him committing that crime. He broke the law the moment he stepped across the border. "Crimmigration," say the activists, who made up a word for criminalizing the attempt to cross the border. (It's hard— I've probably gotten a lot wrong— to make out legal-speak, what with its double, triple, quadruple negatives, and passive voices.) "So, why did he plead No?" said the judge rhetorically; "He's hoping. Hope is the last to die." Yes, I know what that man was hoping: He will have twelve men and women hearing him out. He can have more to say than Yes or No. He'll get to tell his whole story— his wife gone, his father ill, his children hungry. The listeners' hearts will melt, and they'll help him.

The streamlined people are locked up in private prisons run by CAA, Corrections Corporation of America. I know what these jails look like from the movie *The Witness*, which I chose for showing at the South Dakota Writers conference. Be on the lookout for anonymous, unmarked, no logo, nondescript buildings, camouflaged among shops, offices, storage facilities—they're jails.

We kept up our questioning of the judge—his sentencing, his applying the law, his following orders. Why can't he be an activist judge? Thrice, he pointed at us, and reiterated, "If you don't like it, you change it. It's up to you." He kept explaining that he doesn't make the law; we do. "I can't let one go, and not let all go. You may not believe it, but I am the easiest judge."

Somebody asked about NAFTA, whether it made things worse. The judge said, "No. NAFTA makes no difference."

"How open and free and efficient the crossing is," said the judge, "when we want something. We transport wild turkeys. And gray wolves. And money. And money. And tomatoes. And vegetables." His cigarette hand moved back and forth, indicating many things and creatures passing back and forth. "But we can't find a way to transport people. We want gray wolves, we transport gray wolves. We can't transport people."

The judge had an answer for every "but," an answer for everything, for every argument. All loop holes sewn up. The law is a bag around me, and there's no punching my way out. Talking with the judge is like talking with Bob Hayes or Corrinne, even Rachelle— lawyers all, as much as you love them and they love you.

We returned to the conference room at the hotel. Some students who just graduated from high school—a Latino boy, a Latina girl, and a Pakistani gir—did a power point presentation about trying to keep Mexican American Studies in the schools. Addressing us as "you guys," they charted Senate bills in the Arizona State Legislature. They'd memorized the many S.B. numbers, and explained how each bill harms immigrants. "It sucks," they said again and again and again. A bill "that really sucks": Amend the Fourteenth Amendment so children born to illegals are denied citizenship. They've taken direct action against the sucking S.B. that says "like Mexican American Studies is like illegal in the high schools." Senators are saying that Asian Americans don't need Asian American Studies to be successful; why should Mexican Americans need Mexican American Studies? Its curriculum is anti-American; it riles up discontent and revolutionary fervor. A picture popped up on the screen, and tears burst into my eyes. These kids had taken over a meeting of university officials, and chained themselves to a lectern. The action was futile; the bill passed, and Mexican American Studies is no longer a core requirement in colleges, and cannot be taught in high schools.

For dinner, we went to the Downtown Kitchen. People made jokes about Denny's. These young people have not forgotten Denny's. My own family forgets. Carmen and Bill waited 45 minutes to be served; racism did not occur to them.* Downtown Kitchen is a brick building; we came to it in the rain. Sharon lent us a black and pink beribboned umbrella. There was a long long table against the wall; Earll and I sat with our backs against the brick next to a man named José Lopez. Across from us was Jessica, who ordered a drink with an interesting name; the waiter brought a glass of pink tequila and a glass of beer. You mix the two; it tasted so horrible, she ordered wine. The food was mostly vegetable and vegan dishes served family-style. At the other end of the table, a Black man had a plate of fried chicken all to himself, very possessive of it, eating with an arm around his plate. José is a "coder"; he and the other young men, who were musicians and deejays, discussed programming and remote uploading and self-publishing and educating kids and indie everything. Jeff announced that he was driving the first van-load back to the hotel in fifteen minutes. The waitresses were handing out the bar bills, and ours wasn't there and wasn't there. Earll went to the back, found our bill, and paid it, including the bottle of wine we'd ordered for our end of the table.

The next morning after breakfast, we headed for the border. Jeff and Ken loaded the bus's luggage compartments with drums of water; plus we each had individual CultureStrike bottles. I remember the rule

* As a veteran, Joe's gotten free meals at Denny's. Also at Applebee's. And barbers have given him free haircuts.

for living at the Grand Canyon: Carry water at all times. But I didn't think we needed so much; were we taking water to the refugees? As we drove, Kat Rodriguez gave talks, and showed videos. Stadium lights illuminate eighty miles of border, and disrupt the night migrations of jaguars, and birds— hawks, hummingbirds— that navigate by the stars. No more darkness for bats. And jaguars, which have to travel north to mate. The Fence itself cuts through animal crossings, the migratory paths of snakes, turkeys, roadrunners, turtles. And, of course, people— the border goes through the land of the Tohono O'odham Nation, and five other tribes. They used to walk and drive easily across the reservations, but now they need passports and American citizenship, which Congress will not grant to the Indians on the Mexican side of the border. "We are driving to 'the corridor of death.'" Most crossings are attempted at the Sasabe Corridor. Fourteen Mexicans died there recently. "Death is part of Homeland Security's plan. The Fence is open at the worst, harshest part of the desert. The refugees are funneled there, and nature takes them out. As the judge said, the Fence isn't just a straight fence as you might think; it's an accordion."

The Homeland Security map of the U.S. divides our country not into states but Sectors. There are about a dozen Sectors. The one we live in is named Livermore. The head of Homeland Security, a non-elective office, can waive environmental protection laws. Eighty-five percent of the Arizona border is owned by the Federal government; they can build all the Fence they want without taking eminent domain.

Mike, the bus driver, could not restrain himself. He took the mic from Kat, and spoke about the "humane" programs for "the ... er ... people. Half-price fares to Mexico City. Fewer ... er ... people captured. NAFTA." (Later, Kat refuted every point. "I didn't kick him. Who'd drive the bus?")

There have been 6,000 deaths. 205 this year. 253 last year. Weather and animals eat up the bodies. Seventy-seven percent of the remains cannot be identified. D.N.A. testing is too expensive. "Recovered human remains" are tagged U.B.C., Unidentified Border Crosser. Humanos Derechos wants to change the label to Unidentified Immigrant, but the Feds' stance is that the found remains are not necessarily those of persons with the motive to immigrate. But then how can they say that the motive is border-crossing? Those in our group who forgot to bring their passports, or didn't have one, had stayed behind in Tucson, where they were touring the "medical facility," which is a morgue for recovered human remains.

Very rarely, a relative will come looking for a lost one. A father searched the desert for signs of his daughter, and found in the sand an arm and hand. The ring he had given her was on a finger.

Our bus passes "stock ponds," pools of muddy water. Cattle drink from them, and also poop in them. The migrants drink from the stock ponds, sicken in agony, and die.

We pass mines. Signs for "Mine Tour."

Much traffic going both ways. Many, many semis, carrying imports and exports. The closer we came to the border, the more big trucks, and fewer passenger cars. (Reminds me of Charlotte Painter counting the loaded lumber trucks driving out of Tibet every hour.) Somebody said that the Indians used to be generous giving rides; it was their custom to pick up hitchhikers. But they have been arrested and jailed for aiding and abetting illegal aliens. Someone else knew a woman who guiltily passed a man and a child thumbing for a ride; later on the news, she heard that they'd been killed.

Kat pointed out a hill. It's called Babakiway, which means Nipple. Babakiway is a god. The residents around here bemoan the awfulness, people dying in sight of the god. We saw Babakiway from many angles; I imagined her keeping an eye on us.

We would cross the border at Nogales. The bus parked at ugly chopped-up terrain. The chapparal crushed with drag roads. Sections of Fence here and there. It seemed unfinished, construction materials and machinery all about.

Cacti. Areas behind cyclone fencing. The border is not a line but a wide area, and the Fence is not continuous but staggered. You could get through or over or under one fence, and run into another one. Many rough cement structures.

Jeff said to use the bathroom in the bus. I got in line behind Jessica. We don't have to go, but just in case, we won't be sorry later. Jeff called,

"Maxine, hurry up." I'm the last one off the bus. Walking along a breezeway or gangway, I saw restrooms but they were locked. I passed piles of materials and equipment, and workmen, some Mexican-looking. Smile? Say hello? Hola? Eye contact? The Dalai Lama would've gone up to someone, and bow, smile, shake hands; they'd have an interchange that the chosen one would remember always. The workmen ignored me; I ignored them; nothing special our being here. I had my passport out, ready to present it, just as Ken and Jeff and Kat kept instructing. We walked and walked on a paved street with a yellow line down the middle, but no traffic. After quite a ways, we realized that we were on the other side; we were in Mexico. There had not been a point, a kiosk, a barricade where we had to stop and show our passports. Nobody checked them, nor stamped them, nor said Aloha. It's easy to leave the country.

Nogales, Mexico, is hardly a town. It's a barrio. But then, it's only part of a town; the other part is in Arizona. We came to a shed with a tin roof; the walls were cyclone fencing covered with posters and paintings. There's a huge picture of soles of feet, bloody from walking through the desert. The wounds of Jesus. I tucked a Father Toribio Romo holy card into the fencing; it fell out; I propped it up on a ledge inside the Fence. People behind me took photos. I heard someone ask, "What's that?" and Jessica answer, "That's Saint Romerio, patron saint of migrants." So, one person— sister poet— had listened to me, though she got the saint's name wrong. She asked me where I got the cards, and I proudly told her about the preacher in San José, and Earll and I finding them in bodegas on International Boulevard in Oakland. (I have since found Toribio Romo candles in the CVS store at Pleasant Valley. I have one on my altar, in gratitude for the safe passages of my mother and father. Also bought a Virgin of Guadalupe to stand with the other women and goddesses on my mantle.)

We went inside a *refugio.* Told not to take pictures of refugees unless we ask their permission. There weren't any refugees at the moment. We sat at three rows of picnic tables. On a smaller table were clean new white running shoes, some in boxes. Women were cooking in a tiny kitchen, like a closet; you could smell the rice warming, the good smell of home. I sat facing a long painting across the top of the fencing: The Last Supper but the people on either side of Jesus are women and children, and men who are brothers or fathers or sons. No Judas. Earll in tears.

Father Martinez spoke to us, Kat and Favianna translating. He looked like a regular sun-dark Mexican guy in blue jeans but is a Jesuit priest. Refugees being sent back come here. They're given food and water and shoes, and a bag that holds soap and toothpaste and a toothbrush and Q-tips. Hearing his voice say "Q-tips" was what brought me to tears. It takes so little to be of help. The *refugio* buys bus tickets for rides south; the bus station around the corner sells them at half price. Other helpers were an Ursuline nun, a college student, and four or five Anglos with white t-shirts that read "Samaritan." One of the volunteers, a woman, said how much they all love Father Martinez. The nun gave thanks to the migrants for allowing us to serve them. Everyone is humble. I think Father Martinez knew English but allowed himself to be translated. He's Jesuit but spoke practically, not intellectually / theoretically—food, water, half-price tickets.

Lots of questions from our group, which Father Martinez answered at length. There was a disagreement among the Spanish speakers over a correct translation —*quota*? *tolls*? *fines*? What about the drug cartels and the coyotes? Actually, the drug cartels have made this crossing place safe and orderly; they've organized it. They discipline the coyotes, make the coyotes behave. There's less trouble here because of the drug cartels. (The judge had said that he won't travel to Mexico because of the danger of the drug cartels. Wouldn't you think the cartels wouldn't want to call attention to themselves by harming a judge? Maybe he's afraid of revenge.)

I could hear a van or bus pull up, but focused on listening to the speakers. Migrant-sounding men were being dropped off or picked up. I did not turn around to rudely look.

Kat asked Earll for his hat; I thought she meant to donate it for the people having to travel under the desert sun. But she passed the hat for money. I contributed the packet of red St. Expedito candles and a handful of St. Romo holy cards. (Fred had re-gifted the candles, which

Jean had given him, for me to take to the immigrants.) We applauded Father Martinez and his crew, and left the *refugio*. Outside, I checked the ledge; the St. Romo holy card was gone. Someone told me that he saw the man who took it. I felt glad. I left another one, a special, more expensive card with gilt edges and a gold seal.

We walked back across the border, this time having to have our passports checked. We continued walking up a path, uphill toward the Fence, then alongside it. Through the stanchions, just far enough apart so you can't get your head through, you can see the town. It's right there, across the street. Kids are walking home from school, stopping in the candy store. A mother and daughter are waiting for the bus. Nobody looks across at us. You can hear their voices. You could talk to them. You can hear dogs barking and roosters crowing. We touched the Fence, the color of rust, rough as if rusty —so, I am touching material left over from Viet Nam; or this is newer section of Fence, and I am touching remainders for building airstrips in Iraq. There's a moat, which we can't see, below us, between the Fence and the street. People can't reach through and touch one another.

We walked further up, stood at the top of the hill, almost a mesa, and looked down at Nogales, Mexico. You can still hear voices, and barking, and crowing. At the Tijuana/San Diego border, you cross suddenly from desolation into wealth and greenery. Here, the lively town is on the other, Mexican, side; nothing on our side but dry grass, and people in uniform with guns. We have jailed ourselves. The people in our group who've been to Palestine say, This isn't too bad; it's worst over there; the soldiers carry more arms.

From our vantage on the hilltop, the Fence looked like the Great Wall of China, the way it curves up and down hills.

It looks solid, as if no openings. I looked higher, up into sky. It's a beautiful day. The sky is the gentlest, loveliest blue. Angel wing clouds in one direction, and puffs of clouds in another direction. More sky than clouds. Vast. Vast. Free. Free. I said, "Free" out loud. (Nobody heard; I didn't have to explain myself.) I must remember: Send my point-of-view high, and all is beautiful, all all right. The blue holds me in kindness. That good is always available.

Elizabeth Mendez Berry, a journalist, asked me what I was feeling. I told her I was feeling close to my mother and father, both illegal aliens. My father, a stowaway from Cuba, caught and deported, caught and deported, made it on the third try. My mother, jailed for three weeks on Angel Island, got a hearing all to herself, no streamlining, and entered the country with fifty pages of transcripts —a well-documented immigrant. (Fake papers, though, alias the woman whose visa my father won at the gambling table.)

We walked down the hill, and gathered at the Fence. There's a solid metal locked door. And another door made of bars. People took photos, instantly sending them. Colette Gaiter photographed great clouds rushing out of the mountains. And here's one of me near the Fence, my arms and hands hanging down, my mouth downturned; but I don't remember feeling sad. I felt exhilarated —I am at a border. Earll's at the other end of that picture; he's looking up at the Fence, eyes squinting; he's thinking, plotting, scheming. He's the only person looking up; the group, between us, is quiet, no one talking to another.

We returned to the wide area that is officially border. Followed pavement and dirt roads, past more Fence, parallel sections, which the workmen may connect. Three men were readying guns to shoot at targets —gray silhouette of a person, head and torso. The shooters have their backs to us; they'll shoot facing away from us and the road. The ground was bare but for a few shrubs, a cactus, and an old U.S. mailbox about to fall over. Also a large white cross, and a small one, stuck at angles into the ground. The small cross had the word *mujeres* on it. Surely not gravemarkers of women? Maybe picket signs taken from demonstrators. I heard someone say, "Poor taste, to have target practice right here."

Border Patrol checked our passports, and we got back on the bus. Eating our box lunches on our way to Sasabe.

Babakiway, mother goddess, appeared here and appeared there, different shape and height seen from different places. People identified her, and identified her again. There's Babakiway. It's Babakiway. A pair of impossibly tall horns or tusks came out of the desert. They're part of a gigantic steer skull —an ad, an entranceway to a business, restaurant, store, trading post, casino?

At Sasebe, we again crossed the border on foot, continued walking til we came to a row of hut-like structures. One was entirely painted orange —you couldn't miss it —Grupos Beta Instituto Nacional de Migración. We —about forty people, including the officials —crowded into the hut, smaller than the *refugio.* Some sat on the floor, some on tables, a few in chairs; many stood, as did our hosts, the officials. Grupos Beta is an agency of the Mexican government, the "consulate" that the judge said gives aid to border crossers. (But what about those who aren't Mexican, people coming from way south, Central America?)

The spokesman was a spectacularly good-looking man, a movie star of a man. Men as well as women referred to him as "that cute guy," "the good looker," "the handsome one."

Kat: "They always choose the good-looking one to talk. Don't tell my husband." There were about half a dozen of these agents / consuls; they wore orange shirts, orange like the building. The cute guy stood before us, legs apart, arms folded, then arms akimbo; a not-so-cute, older, shorter guy, who also spoke, stood next to him. The rest of them stood single file in a hallway. Kat, and Favianna, did the translating. Favianna in a low-cut sun dress, red hair long on one side, short on the other, tattoos, she and the cute guy looked like a scene in a Mexican soap opera. But they spoke seriously, listened carefully, smiled occasionally; the cute guy had a lovely smile. Quite a few Spanish speakers were too impatient for translation; I didn't catch all of the discussion.

The border was drawn during the Indian Wars. 1841. Cruzando Fronteras. Grupos Beta works the length of the border. They try to dissuade the migrants from continuing their journey; they tell them the laws, the dangers. They'll give help returning. They'll lend the use of the telephone to call families. But 90 percent of *los migrantes* choose to keep going. El Norte so close. So, Grupos Beta gives "orientation" lessons, warns about animal predators. Out of his pocket, the cute guy pulled a snake rattle. It was three inches long, at least. He'd killed the snake just today, and taken the rattle. The rattlesnake had bitten someone, who was treated for snakebite. Other animal predators are coral snakes, and scorpions. Women are warned about rape; 70 percent of the women are raped. But if you insist on traveling on, Grupos Beta will show you routes to water and openings in the Fence. Be warned: Nature. The heat. You will go through the worst of the desert. The weather will do the work of the Border Patrol. And there are drones. Look at the map. Covering a wall was a map of Mexico, the U.S. border on top, the Guatemala border on the bottom. Many immigrants are from southern Mexico, Oaxaca, the jungle —they're jungle people, and have no idea about the desert. We give them water and food, and legal support, advise them: Don't have confrontations with the authorities. We try to keep them from extortion. Every day, we encounter 25 to 50 persons trying to cross. Most of them are indigenous people; most speak Spanish. Twenty to 25 percent of those crossing are kids under eighteen. The 10 percent who turn back, we send on to another *refugio.* The bus company will transport them at half price, as far as Mexico City.

- What's your relation with the U.S. Border Patrol? We have good relations. We get calls about those lost. Their co-ordinates. 911 routed. G.P.S. Drones. Good co-operation with the Border Patrol and Borstar. Borstar is Homeland Security forces, U.S. Border Patrol special units.
- How are you funded?—Grupos Beta is paid with federal money, a section of the Mexican government.
- What about the coyotes? - The coyotes blend in with the rest of the people here, but we know from experience who they are. We give the people advice on coyotes. The desert at the openings in the Fence cannot be crossed without the help of coyotes.
- Earll asked, "Do you have trouble with drug cartels?" "No. No drug cartel problem."
- Are there abuses by the Border Patrol?—No, no abuse by the Border Patrol.
- Is there criminal activity involving the border crossers?—No crime reported, only migrant in need.
- Do more people die on this side or on the other side?—More people die on the U.S. side. Seven deaths lately. No water on the U.S. side.
- Why so many migrants from Chiapas?—Poverty. They want jobs. They have family in the U.S.; there used to be routes back and

forth. They have plans, families, destination. The American dream. Family. Work.
- Where do they go once they cross the border?—They head for Chicago.
- Do *you* (the cute guy) approve of the present immigration policies?—"They have made things harder."
- What is the Mexican government doing about poverty?—Work programs, working on ignorance, education, temp jobs.
- Is NAFTA good?—"*No mucho.*" "These problems have always existed, not because of NAFTA."

Lots of talk about conditions on our side. "Discri mination." "Disrespect." S.B. #1070 would make it a misdemeanor for an alien to be out and about without documents. Everybody —a citizen who *looks* illegal —has to carry papers. No jobs —a crime to hire aliens. It's the Pentagon that enforces immigration policy worldwide. One of the 9/11 terrorists came up from Mexico. "Failure of the nation-state." "U.B.C.", the tag on human remains, stands for Unidentified Border Crosser; it also stands for Undocumented Border Crosser.

As a parting gift, Grupos Beta gave each of us a booklet, "Cartilla de Derechos Humanos Para Los Migrantes." Tips and warnings for crossing the border. No, don't try to bribe the Border Patrol. No, don't try to cram yourself into an unventilated truck. Yes, you have the right not to be separated from your child. They used to hand out a comic book on how to cross the desert safely, but it has been banned.

On the door was a "death map." A red dot for each death. The border is almost solid red.

September 27, 2022 — Tuesday

*Jurassic Park* movies have been showing on tv. The fence for the dinosaurs looks like The Fence. When I see stanchions and construction sites and scraped earth, I get flashbacks of The Fence.

We walked back to the border at Saseb. Made to stand in line while the Border Patrol gathered passports, six at a time. They looked at a face, looked at the photo—then took the passports away. Probably looking people up on a computer. After a long wait, they called names. The named one, alone, walks over to the Patrol Agent, receives his or her passport, and is told to leave. (A much better world if we could but hear Welcome and Farewell at borders.) Before and after passports taken, standing all the while in the sun, our group of six walked over to a portico, a homey spot with chairs, shade, potted plants, where our hosts could've invited us to sit. A Border Patrol man came by, but not to chase us away; he visited, as if we were at a patio party. Somebody asked about the relations between him and Grupos Beta. He said that Grupos Beta "contributes" to illegal crossings; he didn't say "aids and abets," but had that tone. U.S. immigration policies are "humane," he said; "How else would you handle the situation?" I could not come up with alternatives on the spot. All that popped to mind was a question: Can't you patrol the border without killing people? Six thousand dead already. A Patrol woman called us away—"Kingston. Kingston. Two Kingstons."—gave us our passports, and told us to leave. Earll and I got to walk together. I hope our *comadres* and *compadres* could answer the question, What better plans for running the border?*

On the trip back to Tucson, the bus was stopped at checkpoints—three times! There are checkpoints! Within the U.S. Kat said, "Don't say anything." Soldiers boarded the bus, and asked if we were U.S. citizens. Everybody said Yes, except for Elizabeth, but she has a green card. A soldier carefully examined her document; the rest of us did not have to show our passports. Only twenty minutes later, at another checkpoint, a soldier, heavily armed, walked down the aisle between us silent passengers, and checked the restroom. Nobody hiding in the restroom. A few miles further, the bus had to stop again; a soldier talked to the driver, and waved us on. To not say anything means you

* Ken Chen remembers that Teju Cole and I were in a "very animated argument with a border guard carrying a large weapon." I don't remember any such scene. I fear and hide from confrontation with anybody. What must've happened: We had to cross back into the U.S. in small separate groups. Ken was probably at a distance, and saw Teju and me and the border guard talking with a lot of hand gestures. Teju recalls a "confrontational conversation."

can't ask for your Constitutional rights, can't ask to see *their* I.D. and warrant. Can't even be friendly. The many gregarious, funny people on the bus had to shut their natural friendliness down. Mustn't try to charm. (Years ago, British soldiers stopped our car on the way from Belfast to the airport. Jackie Kay said, "Don't say anything. Don't tell them we're going to the airport; they'll make you miss the plane." We said nothing as the soldiers went through the boot and our luggage.) There are checkpoints in California too, and New Mexico, and Texas. Georgia and Florida are modeling their borders after Arizona's. La Raza is planning a boycott of Georgia.

Dinner at Café Poca Cosa. Heavy food, even the vegetables, laden with cheese, huge portions. You had to go to the bar for drinks, long lines. Earll bought a bottle of wine to share with our end of the table. To my right, Sloe Poke, who's a D.J. with SoundStrike. (I should send him "Bonging Along.") He visited the Medical Examiner's Office instead of the border. The Medical Examiner's Office is not an E.R., where wounded and sick migrants could get help. It's the coroner's office, a morgue. Sloe Poke showed us pictures on his phone: Racks and shelves that look like the bunks at Angel Island and on slave ships, filled with bags of human remains, tagged "U.B.C." They are not human-size body bags; the weather and the animals get to the remains in days. If the examiners find a hand with fingers, they put it into a chemical solution until it puffs up, and they can take fingerprints. Sloe Poke wants the remains tagged "Immigrant," which honors the person having made it across the border. He talks as if on the radio, fast and smart; he does voices, paraphrasing the Judge carrying out "humane" laws: "I'll piss on your face so they won't shit in your mouth." All this while we're eating.

The next morning at 6 a.m., Sharon Zapata came to drive us to the airport. The sky was dawning pink. It was so early that we couldn't find a desk clerk. Let's go; she'll check us out later. In the passenger seat was a man who Earll says is an Arizona politician. Gustavo? Roberto? He offered to answer any questions we may have. So we're to work every moment.

I thanked them for getting up so early, but they are happy with the work they're doing, happy that we're with them. Tell me more about migrants once they get to an opening in The Fence. There are Predator drones flying over those openings. In the dead of night, infra-red detectors sense human movement, and transmit it to computers at Border Patrol. "The Border Patrol are lazy." They won't go out to the worst part of the desert. People do get through. Homeland Security is about to arm the drones. Has the boycott been called off? The boycott is NOT off. La Raza doesn't speak for us all. They have their headquarters in Washington, D.C. and tell the Obama administration—more deportations than any President—that there's no more need for a boycott. La Raza backs the corporations. "We hold La Raza in contempt." Saying goodbye at the airport, Gustavo/Roberto evinced the hope that "the human spirit is good and free; we'll be all right."

# The story of La Florida

## From Chapter One of *The Moor's Account*

### by Laila Lalami

It was the year 934 of the Hegira, the thirtieth year of my life, the fifth year of my bondage—and I was at the edge of the known world. I was marching behind Señor Dorantes in a lush territory he, and Castilians like him, called La Florida. I cannot be certain what my people call it. When I left Azemmur, news of this land did not often attract the notice of our town criers; they spoke instead of the famine, the recent earthquake, or the rebellions in the south of Barbary. But I imagine that, in keeping with our naming conventions, my people would simply call it the Land of the Indians. The Indians, too, must have had a name for it, although neither Señor Dorantes nor anyone in the expedition knew what it was.

Señor Dorantes had told me that La Florida was a large island, larger than Castile itself, and that it ran from the shore on which we had landed all the way to the Peaceful Sea. From one ocean to the other, was how he described it. All this land, he said, would now be governed by Pánfilo de Narváez, the commander of the armada. I thought it unlikely, or at least peculiar, that the Spanish king would allow one of his subjects to rule a territory larger than his own, but of course I kept my opinion to myself.

We were marching northward to the kingdom of Apalache. Señor Narváez had found out about it from some Indians he had captured after the armada arrived on the shore of La Florida. Even though I had not wanted to come here, I was relieved when the moment came to disembark, because the journey across the Ocean of Fog and Darkness had been marred by all the difficulties to be expected of such a passage: the hardtack was stale, the water murky, the latrines filthy. Narrow quarters made the passengers and crew especially irritable and almost every day a quarrel erupted. But the worst of it was the smell—the indelible scent of unwashed men, combined with the smoke from the braziers and the whiff of horse dung and chicken droppings that clung to the animal stalls in spite of daily cleanings—a pestilential mix that assaulted you the moment you stepped into the lower deck.

I was also curious about this land because I had heard, or overheard, from my master and his friends, so many stories about the Indians. The Indians, they said, had red skin and no eyelids; they were heathens who made human sacrifices and worshipped evil-looking gods; they drank mysterious concoctions that gave them visions; they walked about in their natural state, even the women—a claim I had found so hard to believe that I had dismissed it out of hand. Yet I had become captivated. This land had become for me not just a destination, but a place of complete fantasy, a place that could have existed only in the imagination of itinerant storytellers in the souqs of Barbary. This was how the journey across the Ocean of Fog and Darkness worked on you, even if you had never wanted to undertake it. The ambition of the others tainted you, slowly and irrevocably.

The landing itself was restricted to a small group of officers and soldiers from each ship. As captain of the Gracia de Dios, Señor Dorantes had chosen twenty men, among whom this servant of God, Mustafa ibn Muhammad, to be taken on one of the rowboats to the beach. My master stood at the fore of the vessel, one hand on his hip, the other resting on the pommel of his sword; the posture seemed to me so perfect an expression of his eagerness to claim the treasures of the new world that he might have been posing for an unseen sculptor. It was a fine morning in spring; the sky was an indifferent blue and the water was clear. From the beach, we slowly made our way to a fishing village one of the sailors had sighted from the height of the foremast, and which was located about a crossbow shot from the shore. My first impression was of the silence all around us. No, silence is not the right word. There was the sound of waves, after all, and a soft breeze rustled the leaves of the palm trees. Along the path, curious seagulls came to watch us and departed again in a flutter of wings. But I felt a great absence. In the village were a dozen huts, built with wooden poles and covered with palm fronds.

They were arranged in a wide circle, with space enough in between each pair of homes to allow for the cooking and storing of food. The fire pits that dotted the perimeter of the clearing contained fresh logs, and there were three skinned deer hanging from a rail, their blood still dripping onto the earth, but the village was deserted. Still, the governor ordered a complete search. The huts turned up tools for cooking and cleaning, in addition to animal hides and furs, dried fish and meat, and great quantities of sunflower seeds, nuts, and fruit. At once the soldiers took possession of whatever they could; each one jealously clutched what he had stolen and traded it for the things he wanted. I took nothing and I had nothing to barter, but I felt ashamed, because I had been made a witness to these acts of theft and, unable to stop them, an accomplice to them as well.

As I stood with my master outside one of the huts, I noticed a pile of fishing nets. It was while lifting one up to look at its peculiar threading that I found an odd little pebble. At first, it seemed to me that it was a weight, but the nets had smooth stone anchors, quite unlike this one, which was yellow and rough-edged. Then I thought it might be a child's toy, for it looked like it could be part of a set of marbles or that it could fit inside a rattle; it might have been left on the fishing nets by mistake. I held it up to the light to get a better look, but Señor Dorantes saw it.

Estebanico, my master said. What did you find?

Estebanico was the name the Castilians had given me when they bought me from Portuguese traders—a string of sounds whose foreignness still grated on my ears. When I fell into slavery, I was forced to give up not just my freedom, but also the name that my mother and father had chosen for me. A name is precious; it carries inside it a language, a history, a set of traditions, a particular way of looking at the world.

Losing it meant losing my ties to all those things too. So I had never been able to shake the feeling that this Estebanico was a man conceived by the Castilians, quite different from the man I really was. My master snatched the pebble from my hand.

What is this? he asked.

It is nothing, Señor.

Nothing?

Just a pebble.

Let me see. He scratched at the pebble with a fingernail, revealing, under the layer of dirt, a brighter shade of yellow. He was an inquisitive man, my master, always asking questions about everything. Perhaps this was why he had decided to set aside the comfort of his stately home in Béjar del Castañar and make his fortune in an uncharted territory. I did not resent his curiosity about the new world, but I envied the way he spoke about his hometown—it was, always, with the expectation of a glorious return.

It is nothing, I said again.

I am not so sure.

It must be pyrite.

But it might be gold. He turned the pebble around and around between his fingers, unsure what to do with it. Then, suddenly making up his mind, he ran up to Señor Narváez, who was standing in the village square, waiting for his men to complete their search. Don Pánfilo, my master called. Don Pánfilo.

I should describe the governor for you. The most striking thing about his face was the black patch over his right eye. It gave him a fearsome look, but it seemed to me his sunken cheeks and his small chin did not particularly reinforce it. On most days, even when there was no need for it, he wore a steel helmet adorned with ostrich feathers. Over his breastplate, a blue sash ran from his shoulder to his thigh and was tied with flourish over his hip. He looked like a man who had taken great pains with his appearance, yet he was also capable of the same coarseness as the lowliest of his soldiers. I had once seen him plug one nostril with a finger and send out a long string of snot shooting out of the other, all while discussing shipping supplies with one of his captains.

Señor Narváez received the pebble with greedy fingers. There was some more holding up to the light, some more scratching. This is gold, he said solemnly. The pebble sat like an offering in his palm. When he spoke again, his voice was hoarse. Good work, Capitán Dorantes. Good work.

The officers gathered excitedly around the governor, while a soldier ran back to the beach to tell the others about the gold. I stood behind Señor Dorantes, shaded from the sun by his shadow and, although I could not see his face, I knew that it was full of pride. I had been sold to him a year earlier, in Seville, and since then I had learnt how to read him, how to tell whether he was happy or only satisfied, angry or mildly annoyed, worried or barely concerned—gradations of feelings that could translate into actions toward me. Now, for instance, he was pleased with my discovery, but his vanity prevented him from saying that it was I who had found the gold. I had to remain quiet, make myself unnoticed for a while, let him bask, alone, in the glory of the find.

Moments later, the governor ordered the rest of the armada to disembark. It took three days to shuttle all the people, horses, and supplies to the white, sandy beach. As more and more people arrived, they somehow huddled around the familiar company of those closest to them in station: the governor usually stood with his captains, in their armor and plumed helmets; the commissary conversed with the four friars, all wearing identical brown robes; the horsemen gathered with the men of arms, each of them carrying his weapon—a musket, an arquebus, a crossbow, a sword, a steel-pointed lance, a dagger, or even a butcher's hatchet. Then there were the settlers, among whom carpenters, metalworkers, cobblers, bakers, farmers, merchants, and many others whose occupations I never determined or quickly forgot. There were also ten women and thirteen children, standing in throngs beside their wooden chests. But the fifty or so slaves, including this servant of God, Mustafa ibn Muhammad, were scattered, each one standing near the man who owned him, carrying his luggage or watching his belongings.

By the time everyone had congregated on the beach, it was late afternoon on the third day, and the tide was low. The waves were small, and a dark strip of shoreline was exposed. The weather had cooled; now the sand was cold and sticky under my feet. High clouds had gathered in the sky, turning the sun into a faint, distant orb. A thick fog drifted in from the ocean, slowly washing the color out of the world around us, rendering it in various shades of white and gray. It was very quiet.

The notary of the armada, a stocky man with owlish eyes by the name of Jerónimo de Albaniz, stepped forward. Facing Señor Narváez, he unrolled a scroll and began to read in a toneless voice. On behalf of the King and Queen, he said, we wish to make it known that this land belongs to God our Lord, Living and Eternal. God has appointed one man, called St. Peter, to be the governor of all the men in the world, wherever they should live, and under whatever law, sect, or belief they should be. The successor of St. Peter in this role is our Holy Father, the Pope, who has made a donation of this terra firma to the King and Queen. Therefore, we ask and require that you acknowledge the Church as the ruler of this world, and the priest whom we call Pope, and the King and Queen, as lords of this territory.

Señor Albaniz stopped speaking now and, without asking for permission or offering an apology, he took a sip of water from a flask hanging from his shoulder.

I watched the governor's face. He seemed annoyed with the interruption, but he held back from saying anything, as it would only delay the proceedings further. Or maybe he did not want to upset the notary. After all, without notaries and record-keepers, no one would know what governors did. A measure of patience and respect, however small, was required. Unhurriedly Señor Albaniz wiped his mouth with the back of his hand and resumed speaking. If you do as we say, you will do well and we shall receive you in all love and charity. But if you refuse to comply, or maliciously delay in it, we inform you that we will make war against you in all manners that we can, and shall take your wives and children, and shall make slaves of them, and shall take away your goods, and shall do you all the mischief and damage that we can. And if this should happen, we protest that the deaths and losses will be your fault, and not that of their Highnesses, or of the cavaliers here present. Now that we have said this to you, we request the notary to give us his testimony in writing and the rest who are present to be witnesses of this Requisition.

Until Señor Albaniz had arrived at the promises and threats, I had not known that this speech was meant for the Indians. Nor could I understand why it was given here, on this beach, if its intended recipients had already fled their village. How strange, I remember thinking, how utterly strange were the ways of the Castilians—just by saying that something was so, they believed that it was. I know now that these conquerors, like many others before them, and no doubt like others after, gave speeches not to voice the truth, but to create it.

At last, Señor Albaniz fell silent. He presented the scroll and waited, head bowed, while Señor Narváez signed his name on the requisition. Facing the crowd, the governor announced that this village would henceforth be known as Portillo. The captains inclined their heads and a soldier raised the standard, a green piece of fabric with a red shield in its center. I was reminded of the moment, many years earlier, when the flag of the Portuguese king was hoisted over the fortress tower in Azemmur. I had been only a young boy then, but I still lived with the humiliation of that day, for it had changed my family's fate, disrupted our lives, and cast me out of my home. Now, halfway across the world, the scene was repeating itself on a different stage, with different people. So I could not help feeling a sense of dread at what was yet to come.

• • •

MY FEARS WERE CONFIRMED early the next morning, when we heard a commotion behind the village storehouse. Señor Dorantes had wanted me to give him a haircut, and I had just begun to trim the edges of his thick, wheat-colored hair. His beard had grown, too, but he had not asked me to shave it. Perhaps he felt that he did not need to worry about matters of grooming now that he had reached the edge of the empire. Or he grew his beard because he could and the Indians, it was rumored, could not. I confess I did not ask him why; I was relieved to have fewer chores. But when we heard the cries of soldiers, Señor Dorantes shot to his feet, with the white linen cloth still tied around his neck, and ran across the square to see what had happened. I followed him, with the Sevillian scissors still in my hand. The soldiers, it turned out, had found some Indians hiding in the bushes and had captured four of them.

All four were men. All four were naked. I had seen Indians before, on the islands of Cuba and La Española, where the armada had stopped to purchase more supplies, but never at such close range. I was unused to seeing men walk about in their natural state, unashamed of their bodies, so my first impulse was to stare. They were tall and broad-shouldered, with skin the color of earth when it has rained. Their hair was glossy and long, and on their right arms and left legs, they had tattoos in shapes I did not recognize. One of them had a lazy eye, just like my uncle Omar, and he blinked in order to focus his gaze on his captors. Another was surveying the village, taking stock of all that had changed since our arrival: a large cross had been set up by the temple; the governor's standard hung from a pole in the square; and, along the perimeter, horses were tethered to newly built posts. The stories I had heard about the Indians had me expecting something incredible, fire-breathing jinns perhaps, but these men looked harmless to me—especially next to the Castilian soldiers. Still, they were tied up and brought to Señor Narváez.

From his pocket, the governor retrieved the pebble of gold I had found. Holding it up in his palm, he asked them about it. Where did you find this gold?

The captives looked at him levelly and two of them said something in their mother tongue. I could not detect a pattern yet to the stream of sounds that emerged from their lips—where did one word end and another one begin? My upbringing in a trading town like Azemmur had instilled in me a love of language and, if I may be forgiven for this moment of immodesty, a certain ease with it. So I was curious about the Indians' tongue, even though it had none of the clues that had been helpful to me when I learned new idioms: familiar sounds, a few words in common, a similar intonation. But, to my surprise, the governor nodded slowly, as if he understood the Indians perfectly and even agreed with them.

Still, he repeated his question. Where did you find this gold?

Behind him, the soldiers watched and waited. Up in the trees, birds were singing, determined in their trills despite the oppressive heat. The soothing sound of waves came from the beach nearby and I could smell smoke in the air—someone had already started a fire for the almuerzo. Again, the Indians answered the governor in the same way as before. At least, I assumed they were answering; it was just as likely that they were asking the governor a question of their own, or challenging him to a fight, or threatening him with death if he did not release them.

The governor listened politely to their answers and then he turned to his page. Lock them up in the storehouse, he said, and bring me a whip.

Señor Dorantes returned to his seat, and again I had to follow. Neither one of us spoke. I finished cutting his hair, handing him a small mirror and holding another one behind him. I saw both of our reflections on these opposing mirrors. My master looked satisfied with the haircut, nodding appreciatively as he turned his face this way and that. His beard nearly hid the scar on his right cheek, a scar, I once heard him proudly tell one of his dinner guests, he had sustained years earlier in Castile, when he had helped put down a rebellion against the king. As for me, my bondage had taught me to keep an impassive face, but in the mirror I noticed that my eyes betrayed my anxiety. I told myself that I had merely been curious about the kind of fishnets the Indians used. I had not been looking for gold. Yet the pebble I had found had caused these four men, men who had done me no harm, to be whipped. I had to pretend, like my master, not to hear the cries that had begun to emerge from the storehouse. Within moments, they had turned into howls, so long and so filled with pain that I felt they were echoing in the depths of my own soul. And then, interrupted by the periodic and terrifying crack of the whip, there was only silence.

Later, when I was helping Señor Dorantes into his boots, I overheard his younger brother, Diego, a quiet lad of sixteen or seventeen years of age, ask him about the governor's encounter with the Indians. Diego was so different from Señor Dorantes it was a wonder to me that they were blood brothers. Where one was shy and guileless, the other was bold and crafty. Where one was selective in his friendships, the other was quick to love and quick to hate. And yet Diego patterned himself after his older brother in whatever way he could. He wore his doublet unbuttoned at the top and his helmet tilted back, like a weary soldier. He had tried to grow his beard, too, but so far only scattered patches of hair had sprouted on his cheeks. Hermano, Diego said. When did Don Pánfilo learn their language? Has he been to La Florida before?

Señor Dorantes gave Diego an amused look, but he must have thought the question harmless, for he answered it presently. No, this is his first time here, just like us. But he has a lot of experience with the savages. He can make himself understood quite well by them, and he rarely fails to obtain the facts he seeks.

This made no sense to me, yet I remained silent, for I knew that my master would not take kindly to being challenged about the governor's fluency in the Indian tongue. The elders teach us: a living dog is better than a dead lion.

But why must he whip them? Diego insisted.

Because the Indians are known liars, Señor Dorantes replied. Take these four. They are likely spies, sent here to watch us and report on our movements. Slowly, almost imperceptibly, my master's tone had shifted from amusement to mild irritation. He stood up and ran a finger along the top edge of his boots, making sure his breeches were properly tucked in. "To get the truth," he said, "it is necessary to flog them."

THE GOVERNOR HAD WHIPPED the four prisoners until he was satisfied that they had given him the whole truth. Armed with it, he called a gathering of all the officers that evening. They met in the largest lodge in the village, a kind of temple that could have easily accommodated a hundred people, though only a dozen high-ranking men had been invited: the commissary, the treasurer, the tax inspector, the notary, and the captains, among whom was Señor Dorantes. Wooden statues of panthers, their eyes painted yellow and their arms bearing war clubs, had been removed earlier in the day, along with the hand drums that, I imagined, were used in heathen ceremonies. So the temple was bare now. But the ceiling attracted my eye: it was decorated with a multitude of inverted seashells that cast a faint gleam on the ground.

One by one, the Spanish officers took their seats on Indian stools that had been arranged in a circle. The governor's page had covered a long bench with a white tablecloth and placed lit candelabras on either end of it. Now he served dinner—grilled fish, boiled rice, cured pork, and fresh and dried fruit from the village storehouse. At the sight of the food, I felt hungrier than I had in many days, but I had to wait until after the dinner before I could eat my meager rations.

Standing before his officers, Señor Narváez announced that the pebble of gold came from a rich kingdom called Apalache. This kingdom was located two weeks' march north of this village, and its capital city had great quantities of gold, as well as silver, copper, and other fine metals. There were large, cultivated fields of corn and beans around the city, and many people who tended them, and it was also near a river filled with fish of all kinds. The Indians' testimony, which the governor asked Señor Albaniz to record, had convinced him that the kingdom of Apalache was as rich as that of Moctezuma.

This word had the effect of a cannon shot. It seemed to me that the entire party greeted it with awe, and I admit that I, too, gasped with wonder, for in Seville I had heard many stories about the rich emperor whose palace was covered with gold and silver. The captains' excitement was so contagious that I found myself daydreaming. What if, I thought, the Castilians conquered this kingdom? What if Señor Dorantes were to become one of the richest men in this part of the empire? The reckless hope came to me that he might, as a gesture of gratitude or goodwill, or even as a celebration of his gold and glory, free the slave who had set him on this path. How easily I slipped into this fantasy! I would be able to leave La Florida on a vessel bound for Seville, and from there travel back to Azemmur, the city at the edge of the old continent. I would be able to return home to my family, to hold them and be held by them, to run my fingers along the uneven edge of the tiled wall in the courtyard, to hear the sound of the Umm er-Rbi' when it is swollen with spring runoff, to sit on the rooftop of our home on warm summer nights, when the air is filled with the smell of ripening figs. I would once again speak the language of my forefathers and find comfort in the traditions I had been forced to cast aside. I would live out the rest of my days among my people. The fact that none of this had been promised or suggested did not dampen my yearning. And, in my moment of greed, I forgot about the cost of my dream to others.

The officers raised their glasses to the governor, to thank him for the good tidings he had brought, and the slaves, including this servant of God, Mustafa ibn Muhammad, refilled them with wine. (Reader, it is not easy for me to confess that I served the forbidden drink, but I have decided in this relation to tell everything that happened to me, so I must not leave out even such a detail.) However, the governor said, raising his palms to quiet the assembly, there was one complication. The armada was too large: four caravels and one brigantine, six hundred men and eighty horses, fifty thousand arrobas of supplies and weapons. It was not suitable for the mission at hand.

So he had decided to split it into two contingents, each roughly the same size. The first of these was the sea contingent, with the sailors, the women and children, and anyone who suffered from a cold or a fever or was otherwise too weak to continue. These people would sail along the coast of La Florida to the nearest town in New Spain, which was the port of Pánuco, at the mouth of the Río de las Palmas. There, they would set their anchor and wait. The second contingent, that is to say, the able-bodied men who could walk, ride a horse, or carry food and water, weapons and ammunition, would march inland to Apalache, secure it, and then send forward a smaller group to meet the sea party. The governor invited the captains to select the best men from among those who had traveled on their ships.

Silence fell upon the assembly. Then, all at once, several captains raised their objections to this plan, particularly a young man who was a close friend of my master's. His name was Señor Castillo and he had joined the expedition on a whim, after hearing about it at a banquet in Seville. His voice had a nasal tone that made him sound like a child, and indeed he was a slight man who looked barely out of his teenage years. I remember he stood up from his seat and asked if it was not too risky to send all the ships and supplies away while we went on a mission to the interior.

We have no map, he said. No means to resupply ourselves if the mission takes longer than we expect. And no agreement among our pilots about how far Pánuco is. Señor Castillo spoke with candor and without a hint of animosity; the others who had also objected to the plan were quiet now, tacitly allowing him to speak for them all.

We may not have maps, Señor Narváez replied pleasantly, but we have the four Indians. The padres will teach them our language, so that they can serve as guides and translators. As for the length of the mission, you have seen with your own eyes how poorly armed the savages are. It will not take us long to subdue them. The governor was not in his armor that night. He wore a black doublet, whose sleeves he periodically tugged and straightened. Now, he said, let us discuss how we will divide our numbers.

Señor Castillo ran his fingers through his mass of brown hair—a nervous habit. Forgive me, Don Pánfilo, he said. But I am still not convinced that we should send away the ships when the three pilots disagree about how far we are from New Spain.

We are not far from the port of Pánuco, the governor said. The chief pilot said it is only twenty leagues from here. The other pilots think it might be twenty-five. I would not call that a disagreement.

Surely you are not suggesting that we send the ships away, just like that?

Out of his good eye, the governor gave Señor Castillo a piercing look. That is precisely what I am suggesting.

What if the ships get lost on the way to the port? Some of us have invested large sums in these ships. We cannot afford to lose them.

I will not be lectured about the cost of the vessels, Castillo. I have put all my money in this expedition, too. The governor looked around him, enjoining all the officers who were present to share in his bafflement. Señores, my plan is simple. We march to the kingdom of Apalache, while the ships wait for us at a safe and secure port, where the crew can procure any supplies we might need. I used the same strategy in my Cuba campaign, fifteen years ago. Now the governor smiled nostalgically at the memory of his past glory and then, addressing himself only to Señor Castillo, he added: Probably when you were still a baby.

Señor Castillo sat down, his face the color of beets.

The governor's plan may have seemed bold to the young captain, but I knew that it had been tested. Before marching to Tenochtitlán to claim the riches of Moctezuma, Hernán Cortés had scuttled his ships in the port of Veracruz. And, seven centuries earlier, Tariq ibn Ziyad had burned his boats on the shores of Spain. In truth, Señor Narváez's plan was quite cautious, for he was only sending the ships to wait for us at the nearest port, where they could resupply. So I did not share Señor Castillo's fears, and a part of me even resented him for wanting to delay the journey to the kingdom of gold and thereby defer my dreams of freedom.

But Señor Castillo appealed to Señor Cabeza de Vaca, who sat across from him. Do you not agree that we are taking an unnecessary risk? he asked.

Señor Cabeza de Vaca was the treasurer of the expedition, charged with collecting the king's share of any wealth acquired in La Florida. Rumor had it that he was close to the governor, so most of the men feared him, even as they made jokes behind his back about his unusual name, calling him Cabeza de Mono, on account of his ears, which protruded like that of a monkey. Señor Cabeza de Vaca laced his fingers together; they were white and smooth and his nails were clean. He had the hands of a nobleman.

There is indeed a risk, he said. There is always a risk. But the Indians of this territory know about our presence now. We must start marching right away, before the king of Apalache can raise a large army against us or make alliances with any neighbors. We cannot squander a chance to take Apalache for His Majesty. Señor Cabeza de Vaca spoke with the innocence of a man in thrall to lofty ideas, ideas that could not be tainted by banal concerns about ships. Some of the captains nodded in agreement, for the treasurer was a thoughtful and experienced man who wielded a lot of influence among them.

The rest of the council was quiet now. Señor Narváez cleared his throat. I need someone to take charge of the ships while we march to Apalache. So if Castillo would rather not venture inland …

The insult in the governor's offer was barely hidden.

Don Pánfilo, Señor Castillo said, his manner completely changed. He stood up, ready to defend his honor. No, he said.

He will go, Señor Dorantes added, his hand on his friend's elbow, to stop him from saying anything to further damage his reputation.

So it was that the governor sent the ships to the port of Pánuco, while he led the officers and the soldiers, the friars and the settlers, the porters and the servants deep into the wilderness of La Florida—a long procession of three hundred souls looking for the kingdom of gold.

ALL AROUND US, the land was flat and dense. In places where the sunlight penetrated the canopy of trees, it was colored a faded green, or sometimes a sickly yellow. The sound of the horses' hooves was muffled by the soft ground, but the soldiers' songs, coarse and loud, the creaking of the officers' armor, the clanging of the tools inside the settlers' bags—all these announced the passage of our company in the lush sea of green. Behind the trees, a quiet swamp often awaited, surrounded by exposed roots and overhung with slimy branches. After each crossing, I emerged covered with gray mud, which caked on my legs and in between my toes, making me nearly mad with the urge to scratch.

Once, when we were crossing a large swamp, a slave by the name of Agostinho—a man like me, whom greed and circumstance had brought from Ifriqiya to La Florida—called for help with the heavy burlap bag he was carrying over his head. I walked toward him, past a clump of white flowers whose fragrance I found intoxicating. The swamp bubbled around us, as if it were taking a deep, restful breath. My hands were almost on the burlap bag when a green monster leapt out of the water and sank its teeth into Agostinho. There was a clear snap of bones breaking, a gush of blood hitting the surface, and Agostinho went down with a gasp. I ran out of the swamp as fast as my legs could carry me, my heart consumed with the same boundless terror I had felt as a boy, when my mother told the ghoulish tales she reserved for the early evenings of winter, tales in which, unfailingly, children who dared to go into the forest were eaten by strange creatures. I reached dry land and collapsed, in time to see the beast disappear, beating its tail in the muddy water.

In the language of the Castilians, as in mine, there was no word yet for this animal, no way to talk about it without saying, the Water Animal with Scaly Skin, a cumbersome expression that would not work for long now that the Spaniards had declared their dominion over La Florida. So they gave new names to everything around them, as though they were the All-Knowing God in the Garden of Eden.

Walking back to the edge of the swamp, the governor asked whose slave that was and what was in the burlap bag. Someone told him: the dead slave belonged to a settler; the bag was full of pots, dishes, and utensils. All right, the governor said, his voice tinged with annoyance. This animal, he announced, would be called El Lagarto because it looked like a giant lizard. It was not a name the expedition's notary needed to record. Everyone would remember it.

But the lagartos were not the only impediments to the governor's march. The rations he had assigned were not large: each man was given two pounds of biscuit and half a pound of cured pork, and each servant or slave, half that. So the men were always looking for ways to supplement their meals, particularly with hare or deer, but very quickly the governor forbade those who had bows or muskets from using them; he wanted them to save their ammunition in case the Indians of Apalache offered any resistance. I had no weapon; I had only my walking staff. With it, I could occasionally disturb a bird's nest and eat the eggs it held. Sometimes, I picked the fruit of the palm trees, which were smaller and thicker than those of my hometown, or I tried the berries of unfamiliar bushes, tasting only one or two before daring to eat them in greater quantities.

Señor Dorantes, of course, had no such troubles. Because he had invested some of his own money in this expedition, he and others like him received larger rations. He rode comfortably on his horse, Abejorro—a gray Andalusian with smart eyes, dark legs, and a good carriage—and tried to stave off the boredom by chatting with his younger brother Diego. On the whole, however, he seemed to prefer the company of Señor Castillo, often nudging his horse to keep up with his friend's white mare. As for me, I walked where Señor Dorantes had told me to: at all times, I was to be one step behind him. He was not satisfied just to travel through this wondrous land and to seek a share of its kingdom of gold, he wanted a witness for his ambitions; he felt himself at the center of great new things and so he needed an audience, even when there was nothing for him to do but march.

One fine morning, about two weeks into the march, we came upon a wide river. The sun glazed its surface a blinding white, but if you stood at the edge of the water you could see that it was very fast and so clear that you could count all the black pebbles at the bottom. The governor announced that this river would be called the Río Oscuro, on account of its multitude of black rocks, but the men barely paused to listen. Agua, por fin, they said, and Gracias a Dios and Déjame pasar, hombre!

Señor Dorantes dismounted, and I led Abejorro to the water, wading in myself to wash the gray mud off my legs and sandals. I thought we would rest on the riverbank for a while, but the governor ordered his carpenters to begin constructing rafts immediately, in order to transport those who could not swim—that is to say, most of the men—across the water. It was late spring and the days were longer, but sunlight had already begun to turn amber by the time the rafts were finally ready and the first groups of men crossed the river.

The other bank was flat and bare, with only a few tufts of grass jutting out here and there, but farther ahead a screen of green stalks showed where the wilderness began again. A cool breeze blew, rustling the edges of the pine trees in the horizon. I could feel it through the coarse fabric of my shirt as I adjusted the saddle on Abejorro and rubbed his neck. The officers and soldiers, who had been the first to be shuttled across the river, huddled together: the governor was having a long conversation with the commissary, his head inclined sideways toward the short friar, as if he could hear from only one ear; Señor Dorantes was showing Señor Castillo how to tie his cuirass so that it would not chafe against his skin; two men were arguing about a set of horse spurs.

Then a band of Indians emerged from behind the wall of trees, silently gathering on the field. Some were naked, but others wore, over their shameful parts, animal hides painted in patterns of blue and red. They held weapons made of animal bone and fire-hardened wood—lances, bows, or slingshots—but they did not threaten us. There were as many as a hundred of them. For a moment, each side regarded the other with the curiosity of a child who sees his reflection in the mirror for the first time. Then, unhurriedly, the governor climbed on his horse and the officers who had their mounts did the same. The page pulled the flagpole from the ground where it had been stuck and lifted it up; the standard of the governor whipped in the breeze.

Albaniz, the governor called.

In addition to being the official notary of the expedition, charged with the safekeeping of all its contracts and petitions, Señor Albaniz was also responsible for chronicling its progress for the next few months. His presence at this moment, our first encounter with an Indian nation, made me think of my father, who had dreamed of me becoming, like him, a notary public, a witness and recorder of major events in other people's lives. I felt as though my father's aspiration, which I had so easily and so carelessly brushed off many years ago, would never let go of me, that I would be reminded of it wherever I went, even here, in this strange land. But perhaps my father's dreams for me have come true in the end, for here I am setting down, for my own reasons, a relation of the Narváez expedition.

Tell the savages, the governor said, to take me to Apalache. He considered it beneath him to speak directly to the Indians.

With the look of a servant who has found himself chosen for a tedious chore, Señor Albaniz dismounted and stepped forward. This, he said, pointing behind him, is Pánfilo de Narváez, the new governor of this terra firma, by virtue of the bequest made to him by his Holy Imperial Majesty. He wishes to go to the kingdom of Apalache and to meet with its leader in order to discuss matters of great importance to our nations. He wants you to take him there.

Whether the Indians did not understand the notary's command or refused to comply with it, I could not guess. They remained silent. I looked for their leader, but I could not make out if it was the man who wore a headdress of stiff animal hair or the one who had the greatest number of tattoos.

Take us to the kingdom of Apalache, Señor Albaniz said, louder this time, his hands cupped around his mouth so that his voice could carry farther. One of the Indians sat on his haunches, enjoying the spectacle of this man in a metal costume and a feathered hat, crying and gesticulating before him.

Kingdom of Apalache! Señor Albaniz yelled again.

By then, the rafts had made another crossing, and more people disembarked—soldiers, settlers, servants, and captives. They joined our party without speaking; now we outnumbered the Indians.

You can stop, Albaniz, the governor said. He looked behind him. Bring me the captives. The order was passed down, and a foot soldier brought forth the prisoners. Because I was always with my master, near the head of our long procession, I had not seen the prisoners since our departure from Portillo, the fishing village. They shuffled forward now, their hands bound by a length of rope that was tied to the soldier's belt.

Their bodies were crisscrossed by lash marks and their limbs thinned down by the smallest of all the rations. One of the prisoners bowed his head in a way that struck me as unnatural until I noticed the hole where his nose should have been. Snot and blood caked at the edges of the gap. Flies darted around him relentlessly, but he could not swat them because his hands were tied. I averted my eyes from the horror, feeling as if I were witnessing something I should never have seen.

The prisoners came to stand next to Señor Albaniz, who spoke directly to one of them. Pablo, he said. Tell them to take us to Apalache.

The man Señor Albaniz had called Pablo, a lad whose long, glossy hair had been sheared and whose shoulders were covered with blisters, commenced to speak in his mother tongue, but almost immediately a lance surged in the air from the Indian side and the foot soldier who had been holding him by the arm lurched forward and tumbled to the ground, clutching his throat. An arrow had gone through his neck, its tip coming out on the other side. The soldier opened his mouth wide, but the only sound that came out was the bubbling of the blood inside. Now the Indians let out great howling cries, cries that sparked in me a nearly paralyzing fear.

My God, Señor Albaniz said, turning around and looking for his horse.

Ándale! the governor shouted.

Señor Dorantes nudged his horse forward and I felt Abejorro's tail swish across my chest as I turned to look for cover, though there was no place to hide. I tried to run back toward the river, but the crowd of Castilians who were moving forward pressed against me, their bodies bearing down on mine with such strength that I had no other choice but to sink to my knees. The air above me exploded with the sound of muskets. One of the soldiers next to me, a boy of no more than fifteen or sixteen years of age, raised his weapon and fired, but it was one of his own comrades who fell down. I could hear the Indian warriors advancing behind me, their unintelligible cries no longer in need of any translation.

Somehow, I made my way to a pack load, crates that held carpentry tools, and I cowered behind them. I would be safe here, I thought. Then I heard a labored grunt. Past a thicket of weeds on my left, not ten steps away from me, a settler was fighting an Indian. The settler had a trowel, which he was trying to land somewhere on the Indian. He missed. But the Indian's aim was unswerving and when he brought his hatchet down, he severed the settler's arm neatly at the elbow. Another blow to the head and the settler fell to the ground, eyes still open.

The Indian turned around, looking for another adversary. I flattened my back against the pack load. He seemed surprised when he saw me—a black man among white men. The color of my skin, so different from that of the others, made him pause. And I, as I said, had no weapon. He seemed unsure whether to leave me or kill me, but he decided on the latter, for he took a step forward with his hatchet raised. As he brought it down, I rolled to the side and he fell on top of me, his weight landing on my hip, his long hair falling on my eyes and blinding me. I could smell him—his sweat, his breathless anger, the snakeskin belt tied around his loins. We wrestled on the ground and I pressed the heel of my hand against his jaw, though my palm slipped against his hairless face. He punched me; I punched back. Still, he managed to right himself up and stand, with his hatchet drawn again. I thought my hour had come, but God willed that a stray musket ball brought him down. He fell forward and his hatchet grazed my leg, leaving a shallow cut along my shin. I cried out. I do not remember what I said, I imagine it was nothing at all, just a cry of relief at having survived the attack. Then I took the weapon by its handle and, trying to contain the fear inside me, I resolved to defend myself.

I raised myself upon my knees to peer over the stack of crates at the battlefield. Soldiers in armor were firing their crossbows and muskets, and the Indians were fighting back with their lances and arrows. Here and there, a few Indians had managed to inflict grievous harm—a Castilian in a rusty helmet tottered from his mount, his hands gripping the lance that had landed on his thigh; another had fallen from a slingshot strike—but more often, the Indians suffered injury. I remember that one of them, his bowels slipping out from his stomach, was holding on to himself with both arms. Another one screamed as a soldier straddled him and smashed his body with a mace.

I was not a man of arms and I knew nothing of battles, but I could see that this was not a fair match, that the Indians had no hope of winning. Soon, I found myself searching the dusty field for my master, the man to whom my mortal fate was tied. Where was he? Then I saw him, past the line of crossbowmen, riding on his horse. With his sword, he hacked an Indian on the shoulders until blood sprayed out from him. The man fell down to his knees, and Señor Dorantes trampled him as he moved on to the next. The other horsemen, too, had come upon the same solution; they crushed the Indians before them on the field in a savage stampede.

Then there came the sound of a horn and the Indians began to retreat. The sun had set now and it was difficult for me to make out the faces of all those who lay on the ground. As I walked, I was guided more by the sound of soldiers knocking the Indians about and the smell of dust and smoke than I was by sight alone. O Lord, I thought, what am I doing here in this strange land, in the middle of a battle between two foreign peoples? How did it get to this? I was still standing there, stunned and motionless, when torches were lit and names were called. Settlers and friars trickled in from wherever they had found some cover—a crate, a tree, or even a corpse. Behind us, the Río Oscuro rumbled, flowing unceasingly toward the ocean."

# Chapter One of *Homebase*

by Shawn Wong

## I

Back in the early fifties, when I was four, my father and mother drove from Berkeley to New York and back. The sound of the car's little engine is still buzzing and working away in my head. My sense of balance comes from lying asleep in the back seat of that car, my unsteady heartbeat comes from my father's night driving and my watching the chaos of passing headlights floating by on our car's ceiling and gleaming tail-lights reflected and distorted in the windows. In those nights, sleeping in the back seat of my father's car, I heard conversations my mother and father had, saw places I visited later, and remembered it all when I started driving. And the places I've never been to before were dreams, were whole conversations my father and mother had.

I will eventually travel to all the places I've dreamed about. I will meet my friends and know them as if I'd known them all my life.

I was named after my great-grandfather's town, the town he first settled in when he came to California from China: Rainsford, California. Rainsford Chan (Chan is short for California). Rainsford doesn't exist anymore. There's no record of it ever having existed, but I've heard stories about it. I've spent many days hiking and skiing through the Sierra Nevada looking for it. I've never found exactly where it was, but I'm almost sure I've seen it or passed by it on one of those days. I recognized it from a hill. It was one of those long, wide Sierra meadows. A place of shade. The sound of a stream reaches my ears. Dogwood trees make the place sound like a river when the breeze moves through the leaves.

My father knew all his grandfather's stories about the town or towns like it. Stories of how they survived there, of how they were driven out of the west and chased back to San Francisco. As they rushed back across the land they worked on, they burned their letters, their diaries, poems, anything with names. My father never told me these stories. He died too soon. He only taught me to sing "Home on the Range," and I'd teach him the songs I learned in school. But I knew all his stories because my mother told me all his stories and later I found stories he had written down and put away in an old shoe box.

The year before his death we moved from Berkeley to Guam. In 1956 my mother called the dirt road in front of our house on Guam "Ocean Street," and gave the only house on that street the number "25." We began to receive mail there from home. I was six and until we had moved to Guam I remembered only a few isolated events out of my childhood in Berkeley, where my parents were students. When we returned to Berkeley in 1957, Father was dead. And I remembered everything.

In 1956 my father taught me to sing "Home on the Range" on that island in the Pacific Ocean. Standing there in the heat of an ocean lagoon, I sang out for my father about our home on the range and my friends the buffalo and antelope. The sun was shining, it was raining, and the steam of the humid day filled my lungs. The waves washing up on the edges of the lagoon made the green grass seaweed between my toes.

I must have been calling my father "Bobby" for a few years before we arrived in Guam, but it was there that I actually remember for the first time calling him by that name. I had given him that name when, as a baby, I mispronounced "Daddy." That wasn't his real name, just my name for him, it made him the object of my play, a friend I learned my imagination from. When we lived on Guam, I got the last good look, the last clear view of my family at the age of six. On Guam, my world was a boy's paradise and I remember all of it and its memory is constant. In 1956, World War II was still on for me. If I dug beneath the fallen leaves and loose earth near the base of the tree, I always found gleaming brass bullet casings. And there was a fighter jet in the woods behind our house. It was a world of real aircraft carriers, destroyers, submarines, bombers, sunken ships, and palm-lined white sandy beaches. At night the humid animals of the day, the lizards, insects, and rodents, made a zoo of noises in my sleep.

On this island, the tropical night still hisses its hot breath against my ears. The day must cool into evening, Father. When you and I sat on the front porch, there was no movement to cool the day. I followed my father into the jungle behind our house, the boondocks, the name itself was myth and legend. The enemies of all our life were hiding in the grasses, behind the rubble, a jungle of blood. I knew Jap soldiers were hidden away in the tunnels against the hill, still fighting the war. The terror of my childhood was a crashed and charred fighter jet lying mangled amid the roots of the trees. Some nights I woke thinking I heard that jet crash into the trees with a noise so great that I knew it was a dream noise—it makes me deaf, but the dream still goes on. In the faint light of that humid night the fighter jet glowed, lifted itself in my eyes like silver smoke, and brought the taste of metal to my tongue. And I could not stop myself from peering down inside the cockpit, feeling the metal still warm from the burn, reaching down through the broken glass into that old air to brush away the smoke, and finding the broken body of a ghost.

When my father was a young man, he tried to climb Mount Shasta in California's north gold country, but was defeated by the wind rushing down the mountain face. My father said the wind was always the conqueror, not the cold, or the snow, or the heat, but the wind that makes you deaf, numbs your touch, and pushes blood into your eyes.

My father was sleeping in a stone cabin at the foot of Mount Shasta and was awakened by the sickening smell of rotting wood and the muted voices of Chinamen. His bed became soiled with the breath of poor men. He was getting sick in the pre-dawn night when a voice spoke to him, "Do you know me?" a woman asked, touching his ears with her hands.

"Yes," he lied, seeing the dim outline of her naked body. His eyes filled with smoke. He tried to breathe. The wood of the room smelled like burning dust as he reached for her.

"Are you afraid of dying with me?" she asked, drawing his hand to her stomach, putting her moist mouth in his ear, making him deaf, his throat ached for the moist moss of trees.

"Yes," he answered, knowing she was the nightmare that made China the bitterness of his grandfather's and father's life. He heard her heart beating in his stomach. He left tears on her breast.

In all the days I visited my father in the hospital when he was dying, I don't remember a single day in detail. I do not remember what I was doing when he died. I do not remember what day he went into the hospital, how many days he stayed there. What time he died. I never asked. I just knew one day in spring, 1957, it was all over. All I had left was a pile of pictures and some clothes my mother put away for me to wear when I got big enough.

My father is twenty-eight years old in the photo I carry of him. I remember him like that. He is seated in a wooden chair on a lawn somewhere, his legs are crossed, he is looking to his right. It is a settled look and if I try there's an ambitious feeling to the photograph. Perhaps that's because I'm his son. He is wearing a white shirt, dark V-neck sweater, heavy wool pants, checkered socks, and black shoes. The table at his right is also made of wood. It looks like a wooden box standing on one of its sides. There are heart-shaped holes cut in the two ends of the box table. A folded newspaper separates two empty coffee cups on the tabletop. A stone wall behind him divides the photo in half. Longleaf bushes spill over the top of the stone wall behind him. He is not yet a father. He will not be a father for four more years.

My father will always stay the same in that picture. April, 1945. And when I am twenty-eight we will be the same age. It is dangerous to honor your father. It is hard to really love your father. It is easy to respect him. When you are the same age, or even when you grow older than your father, like growing taller than him, your love changes to honor because you yourself would like to be honored. I must simply love him. When a son takes a risk of love, he naturally loves his father. He commits himself to his father. It is a dangerous risk.

In three more years we will be the same age and I will have been to all the places my father had been.

I remember you, Father, now with urgency. It is night and I am more like you than I have ever been. I hear the same sounds of a tropical night, the clicking of insects, the scrape of a lizard's claws on the screen door. Tonight I remember a humid night on Guam when I held your forehead in my small hands as I rode on your shoulders. My hands felt your ears, the shape of your chin, and the shape of your nose until you became annoyed and placed my hands back on your forehead and shifted my weight on your shoulders. It is April.

When I was a boy, my father whispered to me from his hospital bed, "Rainsford, I love you more and more." He cried and I thought he was singing. He was a father to me even when he was dying. He said, "Fathers should confess their youth to their sons. Confess the lovers of their youth."

My mother kept my father's love letters to her. I found the letters in an old box. I saw my mother and father in their youth. I see them as I see myself now. They are the celebration of strength for me.

I was left a father to myself after my father's death. When a son or daughter dies, the parents have another or adopt another child to raise and love. When a family loses a beloved dog, they go out and buy another quickly before the self-pity replaces that life. When a father dies, there is only violence. I am violent. I commit myself to love, saying it is there, but never going further to grasp loving. My real life eludes action. It leaves me a father to myself.

My mother died eight years after my father and it was then that I realized I was my great-grandfather's son and I knew why the label of orphan meant nothing to me. My great-grandfather had begun a tradition of orphaned men in this country and now I realized I was the direct descendant of that original fatherless and motherless immigrant. Now there was a direct line from the first generation to the fourth generation. I was not hampered by the knowledge of China as home. The closest I had come to China was my own mother, who was the daughter of a Chinese dentist, schooled by private tutors in Tientsin in English and Chinese literature, French, piano, ballet, and painting. She married my father in 1947 when she was a student in painting and he was a graduate student in engineering in Berkeley. His life had been the opposite of hers, and the realm of his history and tradition did not resemble hers in any way. But in America they were expected to notice each other and, in fact, to know each other. He was working as a dishwasher at the Blue and Gold Cafeteria when he did notice her, and he dismissed her with his own form of racial arrogance. His traditions and history were deeply rooted like scars, and he remembered only the bitterness of his father and grandfather, and he cultivated his sensibility from the lives of those lonely men. And he noticed her that day simply because she was the same color as he and she was good-looking. They did not meet again until she took a course in drafting, and he was the teaching assistant in the class. When they first met, she spoke to him in Chinese and he told her he didn't understand Chinese.

"You do not understand Chinese?"

"Nope."

The way he said "nope" was all she needed to prod him. She seemed to know what annoyed him. Young Chinese girls from China annoyed him. She was talking to the side of his face. When a man says "nope" it was time to move on, and my father was looking off into the distance, ready to move. She was slowly moving her head, then her shoulders, trying to make him look at her when she spoke.

"You were born here?"

"Yes," he said, looking at her, then looking away at a point in the distance.

"What generation are you?" she asked. Then she added, looking away from him at the same point in the distance, "I have an uncle who came from China to go to school in Pennsylvania and became a dentist in 1917." She paused, feeling him looking at her. "And another uncle who was a Methodist minister in California in 1850." It was a look of impatience.

"I'm third-generation Chinese," he said quickly.

"You are not Chinese." She caught him saying the word "Chinese" a little too forced, like a lie, just to dismiss her questions. And when they looked at each other finally he was half smiling and she was dead serious. She tested his patience.

A few months after they were married, my mother received a letter from her father telling her that China was closed to her, that it was no longer her home. She was now orphaned to this country and to my father. It would still be a few months before he told her about his history and the lives of his grandfathers because, among other things, he had to teach her how to cook.

When I started driving, I used to drive around at night through the hills, through empty streets, just drive around at night to keep from thinking about the pursuit of my own life. To keep from settling down into the dreams of Father and Mother. But in the end my life was nothing unless I pursued their lives, pursued the life of my grandfather, my great-grandfather. I mirrored them at the beginning, shaped everything behind them, told stories about them to myself, read yellowed letters from one to another. I knew more about them than they would have revealed to me if they were alive. I knew more about the love of my father for my mother than most sons know.

II

I am the son of my father, my grandfathers, and i have a story to tell about my history, about a moment in the Pacific when I heard myself saying "ever yours." "Ever" is a word that moves like a song, exposing the heart in its tone, never hiding, never patronizing. The word speaks directly, creates form, and has its own voice.

Great-Grandfather built the railroad through the Sierra Nevada in difficult seasons. Night was a time of peace. On warm nights Great-Grandfather would move away from camp to sleep, away from the night workers. There was a river nearby the camp, and farther upstream, the falls. He always walked beside the moonlit river at night, the cascading water glowing white with the reflection made his footsteps visible. And in the windless night he crossed warm pockets of night air, then cool dark spots, but as he moved closer to the sound of the falls, the night air became moist and only cool. His skin tasted the air. It was an uphill hike to the base of the falls and a steeper climb to the top, where he rested, looking down on the fires of camp. He climbed on large granite stones to reach the top of the falls. He began to sweat. The mist from the crashing falls soaked him and mixed with his sweat. The noise was relief from the railroad iron noise of the day. He rested for a moment, looking down into the river's valley. The water appeared vague, uncertain, it became the sound of moonlight, rather than the sound of water rushing through the valley. The moonlit mist carved valleys out of the granite, not the river. The moon made sounds in Great-Grandfather's eyes, made the mist from the falls look like gray smoke floating down the valley, washing out all the details of the canyon walls, losing its night walker in its movement, cooling his exhaustion, and leaving him dreaming a moan out of all his years of living. But he always woke from that easy rest, and demanded that the tradition he passed on be more than a dream and moan of breath. It was his own voice.

Great-Grandfather heard the last anger of his body in late summer, he craved for the violence of bare lighted rooms, that yellow glow to calm himself, that congestion of men without lovers, without families. He knew he was stuck here. In Wyoming, the thunderstorms moved in every day to bring afternoon showers. The raindrops made the dust rise from the ground, filled his nostrils with the smell of moist earth, he felt the ache in his body rise as the dust rises in the wide meadows. His giving in to America, here, was the violence of his soul and he felt it, chased it, and let it overcome him. After the rains, the humidity rose and moist air mixed with the dust the rain had raised. It was a good smell and he bared his chest to that air.

We do not have our women here. My wife is coming to live here. We are staying. Nothing was sweet about those days I lived alone in the city, unless you can find sweetness in that kind of loneliness. I slept in the back of a kitchen by a grimy window where the light and noises of the wet city streets were ground in and out of me like the cold. The bed was so small I could hardly move away from my dreams. And when I awakened with the blue light of the moon shining in, there would be no dreams. That one moment when I wake, losing my dreams, my arms and heart imagining that she was near me moving closer and I float in her movements and light touch. But the blue light and the noise were always there and I would have nothing in my hands.

"I left for San Francisco one month before my brother. In those days, ships were bringing us in illegally. They usually dropped a lifeboat outside the Golden Gate with the Chinese in it. Then the ship steamed in and at night the lifeboat came in quietly to unload. If they were about to be caught, my people were thrown overboard. But, you see, they couldn't swim because they were chained together. My brother died on that night and now his bones are chained to the bottom of the ocean. Now I am fighting to find a place in this country."

My father and I used to drive down a dusty road on that tropical island singing "Home on the Range," the dust pouring through the windows, collecting on the big furry seats of our Buick Super Eight. I followed him on his rounds, checking building sites, riding shotgun, wearing my Superman shirt and a white starched sailor's hat, and carrying a replica of a long-barreled Colt that made my arm ache whenever I lifted it to take aim. And when my father got sick and we had to fly home, I thought of all those jeep rides we went on, running down a dusty road, holding yourself on with both hands, and when we stopped, the dust would catch us and get in my hair and the corners of my mouth. And instead of making you feel dirty, it dried your back. Before we left, mother pulled the Buick into the garage, scraping the side, pinning us in. I crawled out of the window and went for help.

Great-Grandfather's wife was a delicate, yet a strong and energetic lady, insisting in her letters to Great-Grandfather to let her come and join him. The loneliness was overpowering him, yet he resisted her pleas, telling her that life was too dangerous for a woman. "The people and the work move like hawks around me, I feel chained to the ground, unable even to cry for help. The sun blisters my skin, the winters leave me sick, the cold drains us. I look into the eyes of my friends and there is nothing, not even fear."

Upon receiving his letter, Great-Grandmother told her friends that she was leaving to join her husband, saying that his fight to survive was too much for a single man to bear. And so she came and was happy and the hawks had retreated.

She lived in the city and gave birth to a son while Great-Grandfather was still working in the Sierras building the railroad. He wrote to her, saying that the railroad would be finished in six months and he would return to the city and they would live together again as a family.

During the six months, the hawks came back into his vision. "The hawks had people faces laughing as they pulled me apart with their sharp talons, they had no voices, just their mouths flapping open in a yellow hysteria of teeth." He knew that this was the beginning of sickness for his lover, he sensed her trouble and moments of pain, no word from her was necessary. "Your wounds are my wounds," he said in the night. "The hawks that tear our flesh are disturbed by the perfect day, the pure sun that warms the wounds, I am singing and they cannot tear us apart."

She saw the sun as she woke that morning, after waking all night long in moments of pain. The sun was so pure. She thought that this could not be the city, its stench, its noise replaced by this sweet air. She knew that this air, this breath, was her husband's voice. The ground was steaming dry, the humus became her soul, alive and vital with the moving and pushing of growth. She breathed deeply, the air was like sleep uninterrupted by pain, there was no more home to travel to, this moment was everything that loving could give and that was enough. She was complete and whole with that one breath, like the security of her childhood nights, sleeping with mother, wrapping her arms around her, each giving the other the peace of touch. There was a rush of every happiness in her life that she could feel and touch and as she let go, she thought of their son, and the joy of his birth jarred her and she tried desperately to reach out to wake, to hold on to that final fear, to grasp his childhood trust, but the smell of the humus, the moist decaying leaves struck by sunlight and steaming in her dreams was too much, and she was moving too fast into sleep.

Great-Grandfather had dreams and made vows to his son. "I shall take my son away from these hawks who cause me to mourn. My tears leave scars on my face. There is no strength in self-pity. I will take my son away and move deeper into this country."

For Great-Grandfather it was not enough anymore to say he was longtime Californ'. He had lost his faith in the land. He fell into deeper depressions, not from mourning his wife's death, but from his loss of faith in the country. He had been defeated when he vowed not to lose ground to the harsh land and cruel people.

The country that accepted Great-Grandfather and his son now rejected them. He sent his son, my grandfather, back to China. The railroad was finished and the Chinese were chased out of the mines. They were allowed to live, but not to marry. The law was designed so that the Chinese would gradually die out, leaving no sons or daughters.

Great-Grandfather stayed in Wyoming. After the transcontinental railroad was finished, the men in the work teams were cut loose to wander through the West. Thousands of Chinese men had no jobs. Some moved to other parts of the country to build the railroad networks, others became migrant farm workers until the unemployed white laborers forced the passage of laws prohibiting the Chinese from working at certain jobs, in certain areas, and finally with the Exclusion Acts, restricting them from entering the country. The Chinese laborers were rounded up and taken back to Chinatown, San Francisco. And if they couldn't be taken back to Chinatown to stay, they were buried where they stood their ground. Great-Grandfather was standing at the eastern edge of the mountains he had worked in, in every season and temperature, and he left a trail of friends lying in the mountains. Wyoming land was different from the Sierra, where he had started.

For Great-Grandfather and the other Chinese who worked through the Sierra seasons on the Central Pacific Railroad, the one conqueror, the one element they feared the most was the wind. The wind did not bring death, but the dread of it in any season was even more powerful than the freezing nights of winter that stiffened the limbs of the sleeping workers, or the summer heat that caused men to pass out, or the fury of the lightning and thunderstorms. After a few hours, the wind makes them deaf, and after a few days of the strong wind, they begin to lose their senses. Hearing goes first, so they talk to themselves while they work, listening to their own voices, just to listen to something that is not the wind, they wrap cloth around their ears. But the wind never lets up. And at night the men can't talk to themselves all night long, can't sing in their sleep. So the wind interrupts their only peace with the loud noise of trees. Their eyes are swollen from the blood pushed into the aching veins of their sight.

*Spring 1866*

Spring begins in the Sierras with the first thaw in late February, early March. These are months of apprehension for us. Those who are not laying track forward through the mountain passes move back along the track we laid in the hard winter, going from camp to camp, finding the frozen bodies of our lost friends, lost to the winter nights. Men who couldn't keep warm, or were caught in their sleep by the softly falling snow; thick snow that left us invisible by morning.

So we moved back along the tracks, picking up lost tools, lost friends. Spring was a time of mourning. We'd look for spots on the ground where the sun had melted the snow away and begun to thaw the earth. The ground was softer there, soft enough for a shallow grave. When we had walked back a winter season's worth of track, we would remove fallen trees, straighten the track, clear avalanches. The mountains were in a great stage of flux in spring. There were mud slides and avalanches, snow losing its grip in the warming sun. The sound of the earth was a constant dripping, the huge boulders were stained with melting snow, and each day the warm seepage soaked into the frozen earth, and each day our footfalls sank into mud.

The creeks of ice water began flowing now. The land in flux brought back its sounds of birds, leaves, waters, the land began to breathe and melt. Hairy beasts began to stir, awaken. Life was wet, cool. The train began to rust. When the railroad is finished, I will ride back home on a flat car during spring, pay homage to graves, camps, the whole rising of the earth.

My father wrote to my mother, his lover, said, "Dearest darling," like an old movie, an old radio show, out of the melodrama of their love before marriage. He sang it out in his mind as he wrote it down on the brittle onion-skin paper, "Dearest darling," each letter, each word drawn down from a fine point of ink, drawn out to her so that the heart speaks, not the voice. He whispers as in a dream.

Dearest darling,
Having read your letter of Jan. 8, my mind is rather mixed. My thought always follows your words which you told me in your last letter. I don't

know how to handle this if you really feel that way. I don't know even how the world seems to me if I lost you. Darling, don't think that way. It is no good for the both of us.

After I read your letter I went out to take a walk. I thought the cold air would do a little good for me. I staggered along the stone paved road. I did not know which direction I should go. I just followed a man whose name I did not know. I walked through the crowded streets. The darkness. I went into a restaurant finally. I drank a bottle of wine. I am not a good drinker. A bottle of wine is too much for me. All I wanted was to forget the present moment. Yes, it really did it. The earth went around before my eyes. I could feel it. I saw the jupiter.

I shall sail homeward at the end of the month. I saw him out there in the street. The jupiter was a vision of the heart, it was one man's love.

*Summer 1866*

Summer was the violent season. Everything was routine, every day was routine. And this dullness was what I reacted against, felt it overcoming my spirit, I let the days ride me. The heat made me sweat, and the sweat mixed with the dust we raised. I cannot tell you what we did each day, except to tell you what we did during the season. We laid more track than in other seasons, we cut more trees, we cleared more ground, built tunnels faster, while we grew weaker and weaker. In 1866 I discovered the sound of granite rock breaking away. We had reached a solid granite buttress and we chipped, blasted, and drilled at the rock day after day. I lost sight of the color of the day in the sun's heat reflecting off the gray granite mountain. We drilled at the rock until we heard a first warning, a low crack, almost a moan, short, quick, that could be heard even in a wind. If you were beneath that sound, that was your signal to move out of the way. The next sound was the shifting scrape of the granite block. The sun saps your energy, tires your muscles faster, facing the sun's glare in the granite rock, the sun's heat weakens your eyesight, but your hearing is centered on that dull sound of a shift, a scrape, just before the granite boulder breaks away from the cliff. It shatters the air with its bulk, hitting the slope a few times in an unobstructed fall toward the river, sometimes snapping off the tops of trees that stand in the way of its fall. There is so much force, weight, and destruction in its movement, yet that whole process occurs without any sound until it hits the river, and even when we see the splash, the sound doesn't reach us for several seconds. Then the sound is disconnected from the whole event. The granite laid bare by the part that broke away reveals its coolness. The air of its cavity smells old, still cold from its glacial years.

When they died, I needed more than my fifteen years to carry me through. There is more violence in forgetting at fifteen. I wanted to go out into the street, walk, drive, run, do anything to forget my love, not their memory. My father's love for my mother grew the longer they were separated by his job and her schooling. In a dark room at night I discovered the letters, blew dust from the envelopes, inspected the stamps, the date, the handwriting. My father spoke to a page, said what he wanted to say to his lover without embarrassment, without hesitation. Again he called her "Dearest darling" in his next letter, when I never heard him call her that in person. He spoke bravely to her heart, as he spoke bravely to their son twenty-five years later in a room alone.

Dearest darling,
This is the fourth letter I sent you from the beginning of the year. I have not heard from you for a long long time. How are you getting along? I hope you had a fine new year's celebration. Remember when we danced all night long at one party a few years ago? I was not a good dancer but you taught me how. I don't think I am a good dancer now. I don't know what I would do if we were invited to a party now. I lost a chance to learn dancing in my school days, because I was always playing ball. If I am not too old now, I hope I can learn to dance from you.

Enclosed is a snapshot which was taken a few days ago. It was in the evening of a winter day. It was unusually cold, you could feel it in the wind. You could see it in the trees and the natural colors of Wisconsin. Behind me is an old style 5-span bridge. It reminds me of a spot back home where we swam and dived into the cool lake. Those happy hours and laughter are still vivid in my mind. I shall leave here soon.

I feel lonely, darling. I keep myself busy, and try to forget my home and you and all the things of the past which make me lonely.

Sometimes I can't help thinking about those happy times and I feel so lonesome.

I will be home soon.

My letters will start somewhere in the Mariposa Grove of redwood trees, Big Trees, Yosemite National Park, where my father brought me and my mother and aunt and uncle. We camped there in the giant shade of those tall trees, counted steps around the base of those trees, drove through the tunnel redwood tree. My father took pictures of me in the driver's seat of that old black Ford. The car was parked in the giant opening of the tree tunnel, and I was standing on the seat with my two hands up high on the steering wheel, my mother was waving from the opposite window at the camera. And in the letter I will write I return there now, renew an acquaintance with cool earth, the smell of brown redwood leaves scattered on the forest floor. I will remember how my father showed me the stump of a once giant redwood tree, showed me its rings of growth. Like a blind man, he made me run my fingers over each year grain to feel the year of my great-grandfather's birth, my grandfather's birth, his own birth, and my birth. Out of all this I will see dreams, see myself fixed in place on the land, hear stories my father taught me.

*Late Summer and Fall 1866*

Late summer and fall were other seasons of change. Unlike spring, when the land is in a state of flux, late summer is the season when the air above the land changes. The weather rides over the land and for an instant brings relief to our sunburned backs, our aches from the heat, and our parched throats. The weather is mild and cool for an instant. The days grow shorter. The sunsets are more radiant, the mountains turn a brighter purple and red-orange when the sun begins to set. There are breezes and the dust of summer subsides from the air we breathe. The air grows moist at night. There is more dew at morning when we wake. The hint of water returning to a dry land, to the dry smooth stones in the creek. The clouds pass over our heads all day long in a steady parade of shade and light.

Then, as the days move from summer into fall, the clouds build up instead of passing overhead, build up against the mountain peaks that surround us, and the air grows heavy. Then we have thunderstorms in the afternoon, sometimes lingering into early evening, but it is relief to us, this short rain, it cools us, ends the long season of dust and heat. But it is a warning of winter. And we look ahead, all of us, down the long Sierra canyon to see where we'll be when winter hits us; we look until the sun moves lower in the sky and its rays wash the valley with light. Birds escape easily out of the canyon, flying south. Hairy beasts search for food in preparation for their long sleep. The movement of the land comes to a stop. Only the sky moves overhead, scraping the peaks in the afternoons. The sun is low to the ground. The days are shorter. We look again down the valley. There's no way home without walking out of the mountains. The train stays with us. Its soot clouds the sky.

*Winter 1867*

I spent a winter working on the summit tunnel. Stopped at the summit by more granite and another winter, we had to move trains, rails, tools overland, over the summit, and begin work on the other side while some of us labored at the tunnel. In 1867, the summit tunnel at Donner went into its second winter. I remember every day of winter.

The wind burns my face, throwing hot coals of ice against my skin, the ice wind that strips bark off trees. The white blurs my sight, absorbs all sound around me. I can barely hear my friends talking to me, my ears ache when they do. At night we fear the snowdrifts that cover us up while we sleep. The snow builds up in winter until we climb higher and higher on it, away from the earth that we labor at, carve at, beat our fists against, an immovable granite wall. So that winter we dug out a snow cave that led to the dark summit tunnel. We ate, slept, worked in that ice corridor out of reach of the sharp talons of the wind, but the cold still penetrates us all season long. Outside, needing firewood, we top trees sticking above the snow. The wind butchers my flesh, makes my whole body a wound, and my body's heat rushes to my face and hands to fight back the numbness, but only succeeds in melting the snow that is blowing into my face, and the water is turned to ice. The wet penetrates my skin, my entire body, like pins and every step requires so much effort I hold my breath, tighten my muscles and lift one leg forward, take a breath, and follow with the other leg.

The avalanche is a natural process, a natural occurrence in winter, just as a forest fire was a natural process before man ever stood up and walked around. The fire burned for days, weeks, months down to the edge of the lake, ocean, or desert. It cleansed the earth, and spring still arrived, and began working out of the fine ash. And when the snow gets too heavy for the mountain to hold, it breaks loose. Unlike the granite, the snow's sound shakes the ground, thunders down the trunks of trees, into the ground. Then the whole canyon is filled with its sound as it rips firmly rooted trees out of the earth, breaking others at their exposed tops, grabbing hold of boulders as large as railroad cars to race with them down the canyon walls, the whole slope transforms its expression into a watch until the mass hits the canyon bottom, shaking the frozen roots of trees, the fine bones of prehistoric beasts, lost ocean life. Then the whole canyon shifts into a fall, making rubble of its whiteness.

My strength, our strength combined, is nothing against this season. It is a selfish season. Each of us fights individually against the cold, working harder at night than during the day to fight off the cold of sleep. Each night I lie down exhausted, beaten, defeated, my hands and fingers numb and bleeding from moving cold granite, and the cold wetness covers my body and penetrates my bones as I fall uneasily into sleep. The last energies of the day we save for the night, for a restless sleep. And in the middle of winter, deep in the summit tunnel when the season is at its coldest and stormiest, we work at night and sleep during the day to keep from dying at night in our sleep. So for a few hours during the day, if the sun is out, we go outside and sleep soundly in the sun's brief warm light, baring our wounds to the warmth.

Winter is a season crueler than the men we worked for. All our energies are directed against the winter and to staying alive to greet the first thaw and perhaps the end of the railroad line. And finally, when the railroad is finished, I do not want the seasons to run over my back, letting the days and nights, the weather ride me, break me. I will find a piece of land to work where I can remain in one place and watch the seasons ease on that place, root down in this difficult soil, and nurture my land.

I want to give all the moments of my life the names of places I have been to before, categorize them so that I can lift them out of my memory, find the steady pulse of my life. Root down my life into the names of places. When I'm on the road at night I dream of places I've never been to before, I found places where my dreams joined like arteries out of the heart thick with blood, where my heart pulls at my breath.

# NON-FICTION

# Members Only: A Year in Zimbabwe

by Karla Brundage

I was a member of the largest gang in Zimbabwe, or I had the t-shirt at least.

In 2001, I set off on a journey to, amongst other things, reconnect with an inspiring college professor from South Africa and simultaneously to instill a deep love of and connection to unadulterated Blackness in my daughter, then seven.

Looking back on that version of me, I can finally have compassion. I was so full of love and fear. The love was completely channeled towards my daughter, Nia (purpose). She was and is my purpose. I had just split with her father and at that time I was wrestling with questions of Blackness (my own blood quantum being constantly called into question .) I felt, and continue to feel, like a traitor to the Black race just by my very existence. In fact, one could go as far as to say those of us born in the 60 s, love children of interracial Black/white parents, were traitors to both races. To exist in this body, not out of force such as rape or violent consummation, but by choice, the middle of the Civil Rights and Black Power movements. My parents chose free love. Since my conception, I've been trying to undo my very existence, but that is not this story.

This is the story of when I found love: Love of my daughter, Nia. Nia's skin tone is much darker than mine, and much like her father, her hair falls in tight curls around her face. My quest to connect her to her Black roots, and in doing so, possibly shed some light on my own quest, set me on a path to Zimbabwe.

It was a misguided path, because like many people, I saw the Motherland, or Africa, as one amalgamate whole. My drive was so passionate that getting there became the driving force. I was not educated about the absurdity of my quest.

My college friend, who is a white American, tried to warn me, but I needed to know for myself. She had moved to Mali, fresh out of college and married a Malian man. A week before the time of my departure we had a significant disagreement (or argument in the purest form of argument). The parallels are uncanny. At the time of the argument, she had just given birth to her first child, a mixed race Black/white child, but not African American— just African and American. Would she identify as Black American? Simultaneously I was raising my daughter to not identify as mixed. Why should she? However, Nia has just begun to see herself as dark skinned and to see me as different from her— this was a source of unbearable pain for me.

Again, looking back at this self that I was, I can now understand that the skin color is way too weighted in our society as an indicator of difference. As my daughter grew into her adult self, there would be many more instances of her self-assertion and self-definition.

But I could not see that then. Losing her was my greatest fear, after a series of losses: my father to divorce, the failed relationship with her father, my ex-partner, my grandmother's recent death, and the closeness I sought with my own mother and step-family (although things are much more repaired now).

You are wondering, I suppose, about the gang and my promise of gang violence.

Well it is ZANU PF (Zimbabwe African National Union -Political Front). What I did not know when we stepped off the plane and felt our feet touch African soil, was that I was bringing Nia into great danger of a kind with which I had little experience.

## Chapter 2

The Fulbright application process was fraught with errors, miscalculations and miscommunications, but we were finally there—Zimbabwe.

We had not intended to land in Zimbabwe, but here we were. It was 2001 and Zanu PF War Veterans had been rumored to have killed four white Zimbabwean farmers in an effort to reclaim colonized land. The US was pulling out all its diplomatic programs, including the Peace Corps, but here I was with my seven-year-old daughter heading into the heart of the country, four hours away from the capital of Harare. We would live in a growth point called Zhombe with the wife and four children of my teaching exchange partner for a year. While Nia attended the village school, I would be teaching at the local high school. Rio Tinto Zhombe High School was a boarding school, built by the RioZim Foundation supported by [then] Rhodesia's lucrative gold mining interests. The nearest town by bus, called KweKwe, was thirty kilometers away.

Tension had been rising. When we first arrived the exchange rate of Zimbabwean dollars to US dollars was 40z to $1, by the middle of the year, Mugabe had frozen it at 140z to $1. I could buy US dollars on the black market at a rate of 200z to $1. Eventually the rate would fall to 400z to $1 and I would walk around town with backpacks full of money. Some would roll money around in a wheelbarrow.

I have not lived through a war on home territory, but I have felt the collective tightening and silencing, the growing mistrust. Elections were coming up and Mugabe's tightened grip on the last vestiges of his power could be felt throughout the country. It was 2001 and the AIDS epidemic was at its unacknowledged peak. We now know that as many as one in four Zimbabweans contracted HIV/AIDS in that time period, but still, Mugabe, like many African presidents, denied its existence. We did not say "the word" but instead spoke in code, so and so died of a "short illness" just after his/her partner died of a "long illness," and so it went.

As the elections got closer, Mugabe and ZANU PF began to hold rallies, bussing in audience members to gain more media attention. There were rumors that major actors in the opposition party, Movement for Democratic Change (MDC), said to be supported by the West, were being detained, arrested and searched, beaten or worse. This escalated my fears disproportionately as an outsider as I did not know what I would do if something would happen. Who would I call? Would Nia be safe? We did not have cell phones. And the only two landlines in the village of Zhombe were in the Post Office, which kept an irritatingly irregular schedule, and one in the school Head Master's house. Moreover, the *Daily News*, considered the mouthpiece of MDC and western influence, had been bombed in January.

I am not sure when it happened but neighbors had ceased visiting. Laughing and joking abated. More and more people began to gather in language groups. The geography of Zimbabwe carries the history. Bulawayo is the southern capital in the Matabeleland region, home to the Ndebele people who descend from the great Zulu warriors. Harare, home of Mugabe, and the official state capital, is historically Shona. Mugabe, a Shona, is estimated to have been responsible for the deaths of approximately 20,000 Ndebele during his rise to power. In the 1980s after defeating the Rhodesian army in the civil war of independence along with Joshua Nkomo, the war shifted and Nkomo fled the country, ceding power to avoid being killed. Twenty years later as the election loomed, once again talk of mass graves in Matabeleland became common. Many supporters of MDC were Ndebele, including the family that hosted me.

We lived in the very middle of the country in African Homelands set up to house indigenous black Zimbabwean people during the Apartheid era where generally both Ndebele and Shona were spoken equally, sometimes simultaneously, by all. But as Mugabe's desperation became apparent and old wounds were reopened, language became both a safe and a divisive force.

**Imagine a sponge**

The way Europeans tell it, Mugabe was a fist squeezing all the liquid out of that sponge. But in reality, the colonial west (Europe, the U.S.A.) World Bank, IMF sanctions, tariffs are the collective fist squeezing every last drop out of the sponge which was Zimbabwe. We were all just droplets.

One Monday I arrived at the school where I was teaching. "M is gone. He was at the beer hall talking about MDC," said a colleague after our traditional greetings. "A war criminal (which is how some referred to Mugabe's army composed mainly of ex-soldiers, criminals, and veterans from the war of independence) was also in the bar. They beat him. When he returns he will be with ZANU PF."

I thought with some shock and dismay about the slight, bespectacled computer science teacher. We had had our differences because he had been raised to believe in traditional gender roles. It had taken a lot of convincing to encourage him to allow any women, much less girls, in the computer lab, but he had finally conceded to nighttime hours. We were making progress. After his brief disappearance, it took weeks for the teachers to enter the computer lab. When he had been kidnapped, he had the lab keys with him. Plus, we wanted to show some respect to his position.

Not long after, Mrs. Z, joined the ZANU PF Youth League, known for their violence. Mrs. Z was a slight, brown, mousy woman, in her twenties and rumored to be HIV positive. Her husband had passed away recently to a long illness, leaving her with a newborn. She found it difficult to refuse the small stipend offered to help "recruit" new members to the party.

It wasn't long after these two incidents that our Headmaster called that fateful meeting. He trembled as he stood at his lectern in our crowded staff room. Papers were piled high on the shared tables where we often worked, windows shut against the winter cold. He would deliver this message three times. First in English for my sake, then Shona, his home language. Finally, Mr. K would repeat it in Ndebele.

This was the first time I realized that, as a westerner, I could have put the entire school in danger. I did not see it then. After the Peace Corps rep left, we were some of the only *murungu* (foreigners) left in Zhombe. My exchange partner had gone to Honolulu to teach. As suspicions rose, our school was suddenly under fire.

"Good morning esteemed colleagues," said the headmaster in his most formal tone. This was the same voice he used when we had to set up a signup sheet to attend funerals. There had been so many deaths (AIDS-related) during the school year, it was difficult to cover classes. So the traditional observations had to be renegotiated.

His tone was not tempered with humor, such as when earlier in the year he had assigned me to the discipline committee so that,

"Our American friend might learn about corporal punishment in Zimbabwe." Everyone laughed.

No, this was his most firm, patriarchal and caring but unwavering tone. "I would like to announce formally that this morning, in a meeting, (he paused), I was encouraged, and accepted, (pause), an invitation…" he looked meaningfully at the group, "on behalf of us all. Together, as a faculty, to join ZANU PF."

An outburst arose and he placed his one, well timed joke, "Yes, even our American friend, Karla. You will join ZANU PF too. I have purchased a shirt for each one of you. You will *all* sign the register."

There was a hush.

"This is not a debate. Later on M. will collect your dues and you will sign." He looked at me again. "All teachers."

It seemed to get a bit colder in the room as he closed. "I do not. May I repeat, *do not* want to hear your opinion. It is my job as caretaker of this school to help you to understand the importance of my message. Are there any questions?"

It was completely silent. A sudden cold breeze blew through the cracked windowpane like an omen. Nia had, months before, transferred to an international school thirty kilometers away. She was staying with another family during the after-school hours as she awaited my return. My thoughts flitted to her. What was Nia to do if war broke out? Why did I come here? I berated myself. But as I looked around the room at my friends and colleagues who had no choice, I hushed myself again.

"Good. That's how I like it. The walls have ears."

You may go to class.

# James Baldwin and The "Black-Italian Nexus"

by Nancy C. Carnevale

In his memoir, *Born to Run*, Bruce Springsteen provides a sober assessment of his fabled friendship with saxophonist, Clarence Clemons:

> ". . . no matter how close we were, I was white. We had as deep a relationship as I can imagine, but we lived in the real world, where we'd experienced that nothing, not all the love in God's heaven, obliterates race." (244)

While Springsteen— son of Adele Zerilli—does not discuss his relationship with Clemons within the context of African American/Italian American relations, the topic is of increasing interest to scholars of Italian America across disciplines. As the quote above suggests, African American and Italian American relations—within the lived experience as well as the imaginaries of each group—have been complicated and necessarily influenced by the context within which they developed, the "real world" Springsteen recognizes. They have been marked by both hostile confrontations as well as affinities that have sometimes led to racial crossings. African American writers going back to the early 1900s have also referenced this conflicted relationship, most notably James Baldwin (Skerrett).

Italian American violence against African Americans was emblazoned on the national consciousness with the 1989 murder of Yusef Hawkins in the then largely Italian neighborhood of Bensonhurst in Brooklyn. The locals' racist taunting of African American protesters was widely reported in the media "who positioned Italian Americans as the most racist of whites." (Guglielmo and Salerno, 6-7). Such violence was not new; it extends back to the earliest encounters between the two groups who often shared urban and sometimes suburban spaces. (Carnevale) It may be difficult then to consider that relations or understandings between the two could also be more agreeable.

In his recent book, John Gennari explores the "black-Italian nexus" which he describes as "a complicated intersection between Italian America and African America, a space of hopeful encounter and wary suspicion, dangerous, sometimes violent collision, and magnificent, joyous collusion." (Gennari, 9;8). Baldwin's Black and Italian American characters in *Another Country* seem to confirm this assessment, illustrating the ways in which the two groups overlapped and yet often remained at odds.

The two literal countries referenced in the title are France and the U.S. Most of the story takes place in New York. Within the city, the setting shifts between 1950s Harlem, Greenwich Village, the Upper West Side, and Brooklyn, neighborhoods which then might as well have been different countries. The title also appears to reference the social divides of race and class, as well as the separateness of the individual within a couple, heterosexual or homosexual, each person his or her own country. Baldwin sums up the fundamental mystery of the journey to reach that other country in a question posed early on in the novel: "What *do* two people want from each other . . . when they get together?" (426)

At the center of the novel are two African American characters—Rufus, a jazz drummer, and his sister, Ida who works as a waitress while pursuing a singing career. Both are connected to Vivaldo Moore, an aspiring writer whom Rufus describes as "an Irish wop," (386). Indeed, Vivaldo plays a pivotal role in the novel; he is connected to varying degrees with all of the other main characters and a good portion of the book is told from his perspective. Although Vivaldo is able to form relationships with Rufus and later with Ida, we watch him struggle with their deep-seated suspicion of him as a white man, no matter how liberal his views or how marginally white his class and ethnic origins.

Baldwin is attuned to the barriers Italian Americans have faced as a group that was racialized far beyond the early years of the out-and-out racial nativism of the early 1900s. In addition to their proximity to Blacks and others at the margins of mainstream white society, their liminal status was linked to their prolonged climb out of the working class, a social position they maintained in the aggregate well into the postwar era. The two groups intersect in other ways, such as styles of self-presentation and performance (Gennari, 12), cultural crossovers and borrowings that have been especially pronounced in music, from jazz (Celenza) to doo-wop (Cinotto) to hip hop (and "hip wop") (Sciorra). They have also shared stereotypes regarding criminality, intelligence, and sexuality, to name a few. And Southern Italians had their own history of racialization in their home country that influenced how they were perceived in the U.S. Immigrants from southern Italy were commonly singled out by native born Americans including government officials for their color ("swarthy") as well as other physical features that suggested Black ancestry. At times, it may have been these very commonalities that fueled Italian Americans' desire to distinguish themselves from African Americans once they absorbed the racist narrative of their adopted country.

Given this history of racialized overlap, it should not be surprising that African American authors have incorporated Italian American characters into their work. According to literary critic, Samuele F. S. Pardini, African American authors including Baldwin have used the ambiguous racial positioning of Italian Americans to interrogate notions of race. Focusing on the literature of the Jim Crow era, what Pardini calls the "invisible blackness" of Italian Americans allowed Black authors to de-center and subvert racial essentialism and its consequences:

> Gradually, the African American literary investment in the invisible blackness of the Italian Americans allows the credible dilution and the seeming hiding of color from the black subject and reorients the discourse about race from a color-dominated issue to questions pertaining to twentieth-century America . . . the question of who is white and what is whiteness. Whiteness, not blackness, tied together a political system and a social order." (Pardini, 82).

In *Another Country*, Baldwin's attention to Italian American difference extends beyond the character of Vivaldo. In describing Vivaldo's walk through his Greenwich Village neighborhood, Baldwin sardonically recognizes the ostracism of the immigrant generation by the white mainstream that stoked the animosity of the former towards Blacks:

> He walked along MacDougal Street. Here were the black-and-white couples, defiantly white, flamboyantly black; and the Italians watched them, hating them, hating in fact, all the Villagers, who gave their streets a bad name. The Italians, after all, merely wished to be accepted as decent Americans and probably could not be blamed for feeling that they might have had an easier time of it if they had not been afflicted with so many Jews and junkies and drunkards and queers and spades. (631).

Elsewhere, Baldwin writes of the immigrant generation as more tolerant of African Americans than their Americanized children who had imbibed the racism of the larger society. This understanding was based on his experience as a longtime resident of Greenwich Village. In one instance, he took shelter from a group of threatening whites in an Italian-owned restaurant where he had previously been unwelcome:

> I was *in*, and anybody who messed with me was *out*—that was all there was to it, and it happened more than once. And no one seemed to remember a time when I had not been there. I could not quite get it together, but it seemed to me that I was no longer black for them and they had ceased to be white for me, for they sometimes introduced me to their families with every appearance of affection and pride and exhibited not the remotest interest in whatever my sexual proclivities chanced to be. They had fought me very hard to prevent this moment, but perhaps we were all much relieved to have got beyond the obscenity of color.* (Baldwin, quoted in Guglielmo & Salerno, 2).

In *Another Country* as well, Baldwin presents moments of possibility between the immigrant generation—"the Italians"—and African Americans. In one scene, Vivaldo's ex-girlfriend who is white taunts him about his Black girlfriend in full view of groups of Blacks and Italians. Vivaldo observes:

---

* In the novel *Tell Me How Long The Train's Been Gone*, Baldwin similarly characterizes the Italian immigrant owners of a pizzeria as sympathetic to the African American main character, even as their children are becoming acclimated to American racism.

> The blacks now suspected him of being an ally—though not a friend, never a friend!—and the whites, particularly the neighborhood Italians, now knew that he could not be trusted. . . And laughter rang down the street . . . the suppressed, bawdy laughter of the Italians—for, after all, Vivaldo was one of them, and a male, and apparently, a gifted one—and the delighted, vindictive laughter of the Negroes. For a moment, behind him, they were almost united—but then, each, hearing the other's laughter, choked their laughter off. The Italians heard the laughter of black men; the black men remembered that it was a black girl Vivaldo was screwing. (633-4).

Here Baldwin hints at some common ground, or at least its potential, between the two populations that is stifled by the social realities of race.

For his part, Vivaldo wants to identify with Blacks; he relates his past life in "a tough neighborhood" in Brooklyn, to Ida's home in Harlem which he finds "so familiar." (464-6) According to Vivaldo, in his neighborhood " . . .you had to be tough, they'd kill you if you weren't, people were dying around us all the time, for nothing . . . You had to be a man where I come from, and you had to prove it, prove it all the time . . . Most of the kids I knew are dead or in jail or on junk. I'm just a bum; I'm lucky." (464-466).

Vivaldo's relationships with Rufus but even more particularly with Ida force him to confront his past, leading him to emphasize the similarities over the differences between himself and Ida. Walking through her Harlem neighborhood, Vivaldo tells his white friend, Cass:

> 'I walked through that block and I walked in that house and it all seemed—I don't know—*familiar* . . . there were the same kids on the block that used to be on my block—they were colored but they were the same, really the same—and hell, the hallways have the same stink, and everybody's well, trying to make it but they know they haven't got much of a chance. The same old women, the same old men—maybe they're a little bit more *alive* . . . I kept thinking, They're colored and I'm white but the same things have happened, really the *same* things, and how can I make them know that?' (465-466)

Yet Cass—ironically, the high WASP wife of Vivaldo's friend and mentor, Richard— contradicts him—" 'But they didn't . . . happen to you *because* you were white. They just happened. But what happens up here . . . happens *because* they are colored. And that makes a difference.'" (466). Ida too reminds Vivaldo of all the ways that the kids on his block are not the same as the kids in Harlem. All Vivaldo had to do was leave Brooklyn and its ethnic and class markers. But even though Rufus and Ida leave Harlem for the bohemian life of Greenwich Village, they cannot leave their blackness behind. Indeed, racial oppression is a palpable, inescapable presence throughout the novel as we watch its corrosive effects on Rufus and Ida though they come to very different ends in their struggle to deal with it. The quotidian experience of racism is a burden that Vivaldo, for all of his sympathy and affection for Rufus and Ida, cannot fully share.

There are moments when Baldwin highlights Vivaldo's own class/ethnic oppression to which he seems strangely oblivious (as he is to his own bisexuality). In describing Vivaldo's thoughts about getting together with a blonde woman, Baldwin writes:

> And he was abruptly very excited, as he had been years ago, at the prospect of making it with a chick above his station, a chick he was not even supposed to be able to look at. He was from the slums of Brooklyn and that stink was on him, and it turned out to be the stink that they were looking for . . .The blonde reminded him of Cass. And this made him realize—for the first time, it is astonishing how well the obvious can be hidden—that when he had met Cass, so many years ago, he had been terribly flattered that so high-born a lady noticed such a stinking boy. (634-5)

Of his white mixed ethnic, working-class family, Vivaldo displays conflicting feelings of disdain and love: "They should, really, all of them, still be living in stables, with horses and cows, and should not be expected to tax themselves with matters beyond their comprehension. He hated himself for the sincerity of this reflection and was baffled, as always, by the particular and dangerous nature of its injustice." (614)

Of his mother, Vivaldo thinks after hanging up the phone too quickly on her: "Yet, he had loved her once, he loved her still, he loved them all." (615)

Baldwin—through his characters—recognizes that Italian Americans like Vivaldo can enjoy the privileges of whiteness even if the cost is a negation of roots. That whiteness contributes mightily to the gulf that Vivaldo desperately wants to bridge between himself and his African

American lover, a gulf that was presaged by his strained friendship with her brother.

The book ends on a note of tentative optimism as lovers are reunited across continents and more cautiously, in the case of Vivaldo and Ida, across the racial/ethnic divide. Yet, just as in the real world, there is no easy resolution to be had. As Ida cautions:

"'Our being together doesn't change the world, Vivaldo.'

'It does,' he said, 'for me.'

'That,' she said, is because you're white.'" (656)

## References


James Baldwin, *Another Country* in *Baldwin: Early Novels & Stories* (New York: The Library of America, 1998)

— *Tell Me How Long The Train's Been Gone* (New York: Dial Press, 1968).

Nancy C. Carnevale, "African American and Italian American Encounters in the City and in the Suburb" *Journal of Urban History* 40:3 (May 2014): 536-562.

Anna Hardwell Celenza, *Jazz Italian Style: From Its Origins in New Orleans to Fascist Italy and Sinatra* (Cambridge, UK: Cambridge University Press, 2017).

Simone Cinotto, "Italian Doo-Wop: Sense of Place, Politics of Style, and Racial Crossovers in Postwar New York City," in *Making Italian America: Consumer Culture and the Production of Ethnic Identities*, ed. Simone Cinotto (New York: Fordham University Press, 2014), 163-177.

John Gennari, *Flavor and Soul: Italian American at its African American Edge* (Chicago: University of Chicago Press, 2017).

Jennifer Guglielmo, "Introduction" in *Are Italians White? How Race is Made in America*, eds. Jennifer Guglielmo and Salvatore Salerno (New York: Routledge, 2003).

Samuele F. S. Pardini, *In the Name of the Mother: Italian Americans, African Americans & Modernity from Booker T. Washington to Bruce Springsteen* (Hanover, New Hampshire: Dartmouth College Press, 2017).

Joseph Sciorra, "The Mediascape of Hip Wop: Alterity and Authenticity in Italian American Rap," in *Global Media, Culture, and Identity: Theory, Cases, and Approaches*, eds. Rohit Chopra and Radhika Gajjala (New York: Routledge 2011), 33-51.

Joseph T. Skerrett, Jr., "James Baldwin Imagining Italians and Italian Americans: *Giovanni's Room*, *Another Country*, and *If Beale Street Could Talk*," *Voices in Italian Americana* 18:2 (Fall 2007): 79-108.

Bruce Springsteen, *Born to Run* (New York: Simon & Schuster, 2017).

# The Savage City

by T.J. English

*The Savage City: Race, Murder, and a Generation on the Edge* was published in 2011. That was three years before the uprisings in Ferguson, Missouri following the fatal police shooting of Michael Brown; three years before the asphyxiation of Eric Garner in Staten Island, leading, in retaliation, to the execution of two NYPD officers (Rafael Ramos and Wenjian Liu) in Brooklyn; four years before the killing of Freddie Gray in Baltimore that led to violent riots; five years before a series of police killings of young black men in various states led, in retaliation, to the execution of five police officers in Dallas by a crazed gunman; eight years before the police asphyxiation murder of George Floyd, witnessed by the world, led to protests and destructive uprisings around the U.S.; eleven and a half years before, in January 2023, the police beating death in Memphis of unarmed, twenty-nine year-old Tyre Nichols…

And so on and so forth.

I wrote the book hoping it would bring attention to some specific antecedents in America's violent, ongoing hostilities involving urban law enforcement and the country's African American population. The origins of this go back to the earliest formations of urban police forces in the United States, but, in the book, I focused on a period in the late 1960s and early 1970s—in the wake of the Malcolm X and MLK Jr assassinations—when the fault lines became exposed. I was seeking to dramatize this exposure through the lives of three people who lived it at the time. The hope was that by revisiting this history, dragging it into the light of day, we could acknowledge the flash points and examine the structural defects.

The book was a work of narrative non-fiction. It was not a polemic or an extended essay or a veiled editorial designed to spoon feed righteous conclusions to the already converted. I thought that by dramatizing the lives of these three men it would show not only the costs for them as individuals but also for all of American society. I believed then—and still do—that the United States will rise or fall based on its ability to address this racial chasm within its system of criminal justice.

By the time you read this, there may have been further notorious instances of police abuse and institutional injustice that result in riots and more killings of citizens and cops. There will likely be still more in the future.

Reactionary explosions in the media, with opinionating on all sides of an issue masquerading as discourse, is not the same as "dealing with it." The national press, social media, and public officials will only be brought to bear when the citizenry makes it so. "Defund the police" and "Black Lives Matter" are rhetorical flashpoints designed to lob smoke bombs into the discussion. White folks retreat into the belief that urban police forces are only there to protect them from crime; they remain incapable of acknowledging systemic issues that have been baked into American policing and criminal justice since at least the period of Reconstruction.

Works of literature—or art—can serve an important function by contributing to a body of knowledge that a nation ignores at its own peril. It takes a special kind of racial psychosis and denial to stare into the face of recent history and not see the warning signs.

* * *

Prison can be a state of mind. The walls close in, the day is regimented by force of arms, dreams wither and die. A convict can be crushed by the institutionalized monotony, whether the sentence is one year or twenty. And then there are the bars. As Malcolm X expressed it in his autobiography, "Any person who claims to have deep feelings for other human beings should think a long, long time before he votes to have other men kept behind bars—caged. I am not saying there shouldn't be prisons. But there shouldn't be bars. Behind bars, a man never reforms. He will never forget. He never will get completely over the memory of the bars."

Dhoruba Bin Wahad had been behind bars for four years, and in that time he had received exactly one visitor—his mother, who came to see him at Coxsackie. The Bureau of Prisons made it so difficult and costly for a person of limited means to navigate the prison bureaucracy and get to the facility that visits were rare to nonexistent. While Dhoruba was behind bars, his past and future disappeared; there was only the present, a world of cement walls, cold floors, Caucasian authority, and chain-link fences topped with barbed wire.

It was not part of Dhoruba's makeup to see himself as a victim. Therefore, his time in prison was sometimes contentious. He fought with guards, stood up to the authorities, and showed little contrition when called before the parole board. Though his extensive reading in prison had raised his consciousness, the gang mentality was just as present in prison as it was on the streets of the Southeast Bronx. At Comstock, Dhoruba took part in a yard-gang rumble that got him thrown in the Box for an extended period. In late 1965, the prison administration decided to transfer him to a maximum-security facility. Dhoruba was inching closer to completing his five-year bit, but he was also sinking deeper and deeper into the system.

Green Haven Correctional Facility is located near the town of Poughkeepsie, eighty miles north of New York City, not far from the New York–Connecticut border. Dhoruba was initially housed in the orientation compound, a kind of quarantine for new inmates. After a month, he was released into general population. He had been circulating among the other convicts for less than a week when a guard told him, "Hey, there's somebody in the yard who wants to see you."

It was a gray and drizzling day. When Dhoruba went out to the yard, he saw a man huddled under an awning to stay out of the rain. The man was his father.

Dhoruba had never had any real relationship with the man who had brought him into the world—though back when he was still little

Richard Moore, that had never seemed like a major issue. Collins Moore, known to his friends and associates as Cokey, was a bona fide street character, a neighborhood fixture Dhoruba referred to as a "slickster." Out on the street, his hair was conked, and he wore the zoot suits of his youth. He was a talented dancer, popular with the ladies. But he was also a heroin addict whose habit diminished his status in the underworld, making him more of a street hustler than a full-fledged player.

Pops Moore was only in his mid-forties when Dhoruba found him in the prison yard, but he seemed withered. The father looked at the son and blinked; it took him a moment to recognize his own blood. Dhoruba remembered:

> The meeting was kind of routine. That's the odd part about these abnormal encounters; they can sometime seem mundane. We just started talking about simple stuff, like what did you get busted for, when are you getting out, et cetera. I believe he was in there for boosting, probably to support his habit. Eventually the conversation swung over to family matters, my grandfather, cousins, and all that.

In childhood, Dhoruba's view of his father had been colored by the constant negative comments made about him by his mother's family. "That man is no good," his aunts and grandparents would say whenever the name of Collins Moore was mentioned. As a boy, Dhoruba sometimes saw his father working the streets or coming out of a bar, a shadowy figure with a bebop strut. Young Dhoruba wanted to approach the man and ask, "Pops, why they talk so bad about you?" But he was just a kid, without the courage to approach this unfamiliar street hustler they said was his father.

Dhoruba didn't bring it up now, either. It was Cokey Moore who broached the subject with his son. "You a young man now," he told Dhoruba. "So let me explain why I wasn't around much when you was little."

Over the course of three days in the prison yard at Green Haven, Old Man Moore told Dhoruba how he met his mother in Harlem. The mother's family were hardworking immigrants, "old-school West Indians, very clannish and family oriented." Moore was from Georgia, the southern slave tradition, with its legacy of bullwhips, lynching, and familial decimation. To the mother's family, Moore was a lazy malcontent with the heart of a hustler. "They never could accept me," he told Dhoruba.

The breaking point came in 1944, right around the time Dhoruba was born, when Collins Moore decided to join the army. He was motivated in part by a desire to show his wife's family that he could be somebody. The wife's family came from a military tradition: her father had been in the merchant marine and her brother—Dhoruba's uncle—had been a war hero who died in combat during a rescue mission. The uncle's death had been a touchstone event in the family history; a plaque commemorating his service and death during the Second World War was on a wall in the house.

In 1945, however, Collins Moore went AWOL. To his wife's family this was a disgrace to the memory of Dhoruba's heroic uncle, and it was one of the factors that led to his separation from Dhoruba's mother. From that point on, they acted as if Collins Moore had never existed—except when they wanted to curse his name.

Hearing this side of the story for the first time, Dhoruba felt an unexpected emotional connection with his father. The surroundings only added to the sense of intimacy: it took a prison encounter for Dhoruba to learn his family's secrets, the undercurrents that had shaped his African American family and set him off on his own rebellious course.

"I'm glad you told me," Dhoruba said to his father. "I never knew the whole story."

"Well, now you know," said Pops.

Their time together was brief. Three days after Dhoruba first met Collins Moore in the yard at Green Haven, he got into an altercation in the mess hall. It wasn't a serious incident—there weren't even any punches thrown—but Dhoruba's disciplinary record was so bad that any small event was enough to get him hauled off to the Box. He would spend the remainder of his sentence there in isolation, with no library, limited rec time, and only one hour a day outside the unit. He was a twenty-year-old male entering into manhood, a manchild serving out his time as ward of the state. He would spend the remainder of his sentence fixating on one thing: his release date.

George Whitmore was also in prison. Since his last legal proceeding he'd been housed at the Brooklyn House of Detention, with easy access to the courts. That was the cycle that defined his weekly routine: prison to court, court to prison. Like Dhoruba bin Wahad, Whitmore found himself surrounded by mostly African American inmates and white guards, escorted from one institution to another by court officers and armed marshals, handcuffed, searched, told to "sit right there" or "stand right there" until further notice. Unlike Dhoruba, though, George had no release date to look forward to. Not even his lawyers knew for sure how his future would play out. He was told not to lose hope, which was, of course, the battle cry of the era. Martin Luther King Jr. and other civil rights leaders implored their followers to "keep hope alive." Hope had become the placebo of an entire generation.

In the public arena, Whitmore's case had become a potent symbol of injustice. In May 1965, as the New York State Senate legislators prepared to vote on whether to abolish the death penalty, one legislator declared: "This is the year of Whitmore."

Bertram L. Podell, the Brooklyn assemblyman and attorney who spearheaded the initiative to outlaw capital punishment, used the Whitmore case as Exhibit A. In introducing the bill, he told his fellow senators: "A sixty-one page, completely detailed confession was manufactured and force-fed to Whitmore. On the basis of this confession, this defendant not only could have been, but probably would have been executed. I don't have to highlight the terrible effect Whitmore's execution would have had if the falsity of his confession and the tactics used in securing it had come out after the switch had been pulled, instead of before."

It was a watershed moment in the history of capital punishment in New York. State legislators had introduced legislation to do away with the death penalty ever since it was introduced in 1948, but every year the bills had failed. With the story of George Whitmore in the ether, though, the State Senate dramatically reversed its position, voting 47–9 to eradicate capital punishment in New York. In June, the bill was signed into law by Governor Nelson Rockefeller.

In another bill, legislators challenged the state's practice of employing well-heeled Blue Ribbon juries, which tended to find against impoverished defendants. Using the Minnie Edmonds murder trial as an example, proponents of the bill argued that Blue Ribbon juries "perpetuate a systematic exclusion of women, Puerto Ricans and Negroes . . . thereby making it a near-mathematical certainty that a defendant would be tried by a lily-white, all male jury." The bill was approved later that year, and Blue Ribbon juries became a thing of the past.

The Whitmore case was like a virus that had entered the system through the usual channels but could not be easily expunged. Whitmore now had advocates who were altering the way he was perceived by the general public. The young man scorned as a "nineteen-year-old pimple-faced hoodlum" a year and a half before was now "the most celebrated wrong man in the history of the city," according to the *Herald Tribune*. For groups like the NAACP, CORE, the American Civil Liberties Union (ACLU), and others, Whitmore was a cause célèbre, routinely cited in the press as a symbol of injustice. The newspapers, some of which had helped to frame Whitmore in the eyes of the public, took up his case on the editorial pages. When the NYPD announced it was launching an investigation into the circumstances surrounding the Whitmore confession, *The New York Times* asked, "Can the police be relied on to investigate alleged misconduct by their own department?" It was a fair and logical question, but also a revolutionary one: at the time it was unheard of for a newspaper to challenge the authority of the police.

* * *

Dhoruba bin Wahad never got the chance to say good-bye to his father. On May 2, 1967, he was released directly from the Box at Green Haven prison into civilian life, leaving his old man behind. Dhoruba had spent his last fourteen months in isolation. Having served the full five years of his term, Dhoruba would not be required to report to a parole officer or a bail bondsman; he would no longer be beholden to the system in any way. He was free and clear.

The Bureau of Prisons gave Dhoruba ten dollars' meal money and a one-way ticket to New York City. No one met him at the gate upon release. He took a bus from Poughkeepsie to the Port Authority terminal in Manhattan, then hopped a subway to the Bronx.

While he was away Dhoruba's mother had remarried. She now lived with her new husband, Louis, in a two-bedroom apartment on the seventeenth floor of the St. Mary's Housing Project, a huge new complex at 159th Street and Third Avenue in the South Bronx. When her prodigal son arrived home, she wept.

So much had changed. On that first day back, Dhoruba walked the streets of Morrisania, trying to take in the new topography. While he was away, the Third Avenue elevated subway line had been completely demolished; the area was now dominated by two massive new housing projects, St. Mary's and the Grant housing projects.

The streets were teeming with people, more Puerto Ricans than Dhoruba remembered, and a new generation of young Negroes—teenagers and older—who seemed ready to seize the day with a kind of restless energy, all of it set to the music of James Brown, Aretha Franklin, Smokey Robinson, and other soul and R&B singers whose music would become the soundtrack of a rising consciousness.

That night, Dhoruba met his stepfather; the two eyed each other warily over the first home-cooked meal Dhoruba had had in five years. Later, after everyone else had gone to bed, he sat alone in his mother's apartment in the St. Mary's projects and pondered the past and the future.

> I'll never forget this shit—my mother lived on the seventeenth floor in the project. She was high up. She had this magnificent view south of the Bronx and over into Manhattan. It was a crystal clear spring evening, and I sat up in the living room with the lights out. Everybody had gone to bed. I sat up there, just looking at the city. Maybe four hours, just looking at the city, watching it grow darker and darker. Everything in my life before then was like a dream. Now, I was another person in another place and time.

He may have been a new person, but Dhoruba was back in the old neighborhood. "Hey, did you hear? Torch is back," cried his old gang-banging homies in the Sportsmen Disciples. It wasn't long before he was back running with the gang.

> It happened fast, maybe a few weeks after I got out and was back in the Bronx. The simple fact was, I needed money. I had no job, nothing coming in. And I was back with my old cronies. And these brothers weren't jitterbugging no more; they were now full-fledged gangsters. Somebody came up with the idea to stick up this after-hours club in the Bronx. Being back in the hood, running with the boys again, I was down for that.

One of those who accompanied Dhoruba on this would-be robbery was a neighborhood kid named Augustus Qualls, who would play a major role in one of Dhoruba's later entanglements in the criminal justice system.

It was the middle of the afternoon on a Sunday. The after-hours club they targeted was known for selling liquor illegally on Sunday. Dhoruba and three others entered the club and pulled out weapons. "Nobody move!" somebody shouted. One of the gang members fired a shot into the ceiling; that caught everyone's attention. Dhoruba and the others loaded up a pillowcase with cash from behind the bar, then fled out into the street.

Someone in the neighborhood must have heard the gunshot and called the cops, because a police cruiser drove up almost as soon as Dhoruba and the others hit the street. "[The cops] didn't even say halt," remembered Dhoruba. "They just started shooting at us." He and his fellow robbers fled across the street into a vacant lot; the police car drove in reverse, with one of the cops leaning out the window firing off rounds.

Dhoruba and the others disappeared into the projects. For days afterward, Dhoruba hid out at an old girlfriend's apartment. Since none of the robbers had worn disguises during the stickup, many people knew that Dhoruba was involved, and that the cops were after him. Anxious that someone might snitch to the cops, Dhoruba had to get out of the neighborhood.

On a Saturday morning, he pulled his hooded sweatshirt tight around his head and took to the streets for the first time in days.

He hopped on the subway and headed for his grandfather's house in Queens. To Dhoruba, Queens was like another country; he figured the cops would never find him there.

On the subway, he pondered his predicament. He was disappointed to find himself on the run after being out of prison only a few weeks. The gangbanger Torch might have thought it was cool, but his new self did not. He'd already lost five crucial years to the penitentiary; he didn't want to go back. His prison studies had convinced him there was more out there for him than robbing after-hours joints and counting cadence with the gang. He vowed to lie low for a while and stay out of trouble.

He holed up in his grandfather's basement in the neighborhood of South Jamaica, in the outer reaches of Queens. To Dhoruba, South Jamaica was the suburbs, but in fact it was a ghetto—a Queens version of the South Bronx. As with many neighborhoods in the outer boroughs and in Harlem, South Jamaica was struggling to deal with a huge influx of poor blacks from the South. And, just as in these other neighborhoods, a true race consciousness was beginning to take shape among its black residents.

Within days of his arrival in Queens, Dhoruba came across a modest Pan-African cultural center run by the Shakur brothers, Lumumba, Mutulu, and Zyad. Dhoruba had learned about black nationalism in prison, but the Shakur brothers were intense; they were members of Revolutionary Action Movement (RAM), a group dedicated to armed insurrection and to securing land for people of African descent in the United States so that they could establish their own state.

Having only recently been let out of prison, Dhoruba was more interested in his newfound freedom—with its promises of sex, drugs, and sweet soul music—than he was in enlisting in the Republic of New Afrika. Yes, he had changed his name, learned some Swahili, and begun a process of racial self-actualization, but Dhoruba wasn't yet nearly as radicalized as the Shakur brothers. He did, however, pick up some vinyl 45 rpm recordings of Malcolm X's speeches at the Uhuru Cultural Center, along with the book *Malcolm X Speaks: Selected Speeches and Statements*, with its cover photo of Malcolm in midspeech, finger raised, virtually spitting fire.

Down in his grandfather's basement, Dhoruba listened to "The Bullet or the Ballot" and "The Black Revolution," seminal speeches he had read in prison but was hearing in Malcolm's own voice for the first time. Dhoruba was mesmerized by Malcolm's crisp articulation and his ability to think on his feet. The speeches dealt with history, but they also addressed the contemporary situation: Martin Luther King Jr., LBJ, integration, the escalating war in Vietnam, and so on. Dhoruba was especially startled by the transcript in *Malcolm X Speaks* of a symposium Malcolm had taken part in the year before his assassination. When asked about a series of articles in *The New York Times* that quoted police sources alleging there existed an antipolice youth gang called the Blood Brothers, Malcolm said he didn't know whether the group actually existed—but that if it did, they were justified. "If we're going to talk about police brutality," he said, "it's because police brutality exists. Why does it exist? Because our people in this particular society live in a police state. A black man in America lives in a police state. He doesn't live in a democracy, he lives in a police state."

Elsewhere in the book, Malcolm was quoted putting the issue of police treatment of black people in a Pan-African context. "Recently, three students from Kenya were mistaken for American Negroes and were brutally beaten by New York police. Shortly after that, two diplomats from Uganda were also beaten by the New York police, who mistook them for American Negroes. If Africans are brutally beaten while only visiting in America, imagine the physical and psychological suffering received by your brothers and sisters who have lived here for over three hundred years. . . . It is not a problem of civil rights but a problem of human rights."

It was almost too much for Dhoruba to absorb: Malcolm's words were like a synaptic laser. He was putting the issue of police repression at the center of the struggle for human rights—in New York, Africa, and around the world.

In Dhoruba's head, as in the world beyond his basement hideout in Queens, something was happening. The civil rights movement had been under way for more than a decade, and conditions in the ghetto had gotten worse. The frustration of an older generation of Negroes was now being subsumed by a new generation waiting in the wings—people like Dhoruba, not yet fully engaged, but primed and ready for action.

The assassination of Malcolm X left a void, but in Afrocentric cultural centers and among political activists—who were less motivated by integration with whites than by the free expression of black nationalist pride—the movement was gaining steam and taking on a whole new slant.

* * *

The Newark riot might have seemed unsurpassable in its violence until two weeks later, when an uprising in Detroit proved even worse. Again, the inciting incident involved police activity, in this case a special police squad shutting down a "blind pig"—an after-hours club—that hadn't been making its regular payoffs to the local precinct. The Detroit riots resulted in 43 dead, 467 injured, 7,200 arrests, and 200 buildings being burned to the ground.

In New York City, the reverberations were immediate. People watched the images on the nightly news, with shell-shocked reporters on the scene struggling to make sense of the carnage.

Bill Phillips read about the Newark riot in the papers. As with most cops, the level of civil disobedience displayed was beyond his comprehension. Phillips came from a time and place where lawmen were respected or at least feared. The fact that idiot street hoodlums were now fighting back was a source of concern, as were reports of snipers shooting at police from windows and rooftops, an urban legend that had preoccupied police ever since the Rising of the Negroes first began. Phillips knew enough about ghetto psychology to know that the effects of the Newark riots would likely send their ripple effects into the streets of New York.

On the night of July 23—the very night the Detroit riots began—Phillips was riding in a squad car with his partner when a call came over the radio of a huge disturbance brewing in East Harlem.

> My partner and me pulled up to 110th Street and Third Avenue, four hundred people around, right? All those cocksuckers all over the roofs with bricks and

> bottles and shit. We get out of the car. OK, you fucks, break it up. Before we got back into the car, we were devastated with bricks and bottles and every other fucking thing they could throw at us. . . . We got back in the car. I emptied my gun at the fucking roof. . . . I could have killed four, five people. Who the hell knows? I didn't give a shit at this time. I was looking out for my own ass. There's two of us on the corner now and we're deluged with bricks and bottles. Windows in the radio car are busted. We have three fucking flat tires now from all the broken glass in the street. We drove on the rims. Get the fuck out of there, right? We go back and get our forces together now. Call for help. Radio cars come. We get another car, we're going down the block at Lexington Ave and 112th Street and they build a fire in the street and we can't go through. Holy shit! We start to back up and here comes a fucking garbage can from a roof, full of bricks. It comes right through the windshield. We're now covered with glass from head to foot. . . . Fucking garbage can still sticking out of the head of the car.

To Officer Phillips, the most frustrating aspect of the riot was the response of the police brass:

> Our bosses told us, do nothing, just make them move along, don't lock anybody up, don't shoot anybody. There were about ten of us seasoned guys. We decided the first chance we get we're going to get a hold of [the rioters] and beat the shit out of them. . . . I don't give a fuck now because I can be a statistic in the morning. I'm going out and break heads and I'm going to break everybody's fucking head I come across because I know these people hate us up there now and they're looking to knock me and everybody else off. . . . We chased them into the 23rd Precinct and up on a roof. There was about twenty of them. We beat the living shit out of everybody. I mean beat their fucking heads, knocked their teeth out. I left them all up there for dead. Came down, no more riot. It was all over.

The city of New York considered itself lucky. The damage from the East Harlem riot was minimal compared to Newark and Detroit. The Lindsay administration claimed credit for managing the disturbance, keeping it from exploding into an urban street version of the End of Days.

Their sense of relief was misplaced. What was happening in New York was more like a slow-motion riot—a schism buried deep within the contours of city life that would rumble and spew for much of the next decade.

* * *

In the spring of 1968, Dhoruba bin Wahad took a part-time job at a small printing plant in lower Manhattan. He was still selling weed on the side, throwing occasional parties at his loft on East Third Street, and educating himself on the symbiosis between black liberation and anticolonial struggles around the world. Among the books he devoured was *Soul on Ice*, a collection of essays on race, revolution, and criminal justice by Eldridge Cleaver. With Huey Newton locked up in prison, Cleaver was coming into his own as the most famous and visible leader of the Black Panther Party. On TV to promote his book and at rallies, Cleaver was articulate and attractive. With his neatly trimmed goatee, tinted sunglasses, and fierce street patter (*can you dig it?*), Cleaver appeared to Dhoruba and a whole generation of young black men as a kind of street prince, the epitome of Panther chic. More than a hustler, he brought a level of philosophical insight to his politics that was exciting to likeminded, would-be revolutionaries.

In *Soul on Ice*, Cleaver identified the revolution as a conflict between personal liberation and the repressive forces of "the white mother country." Just as Malcolm X had noted that the relationship between the police and people in the ghetto was at the core of the struggle, Cleaver framed the issue of police repression in an international context:

> The police do on the domestic level what the armed forces do on an international level: protect the way of life for those in power. The police patrol the city, cordon off communities, blockade neighborhoods, invade homes, search for that which is hidden. The armed forces patrol the world, invade countries and continents, cordon off nations, blockade islands and whole peoples; they will overrun villages, neighborhoods, enter homes, huts, caves, searching for that which is hidden. The policeman and the soldier will violate your person, smoke you out with various gases. Each will shoot you, beat your head and body with sticks and clubs, with rifle butts, run you through with bayonets, shoot holes in your flesh, kill you. They each have unlimited firepower. They will use all that is necessary to bring you to your knees. They won't take no for an answer. If you resist their guns, they call for reinforcements with bigger guns. Eventually they will come in tanks, in jets, in ships. They will not rest until you surrender or are killed. The policeman and the soldier will have the last word.

Dhoruba was hooked. Not since Malcolm had someone expressed the "truth" so vibrantly, in terms immediately recognizable to "a brother from the block." Dhoruba's social consciousness, long since hotwired in prison, had just been waiting for an incident that would push him over the edge into action. That incident occurred on April 4, 1968.

He spent most of that morning making deliveries for the printing plant. He'd just returned to the plant when a fellow worker asked, "Hey, did you hear the news?"

"What news," said Dhoruba.

"Martin Luther King was assassinated."

Dhoruba took the news like a kick to the groin. He left the building, walked across the street, and sat down in a small park. Someone nearby had a transistor radio, and as he listened, he learned more about King's shooting in Memphis. Police believed the assailant was a white man named James Earl Ray, who was still at large (Ray would be captured two months later). The killer had shot King while he was standing on the balcony of the Lorraine Motel; the civil rights leader was dead before he reached the hospital. He was thirty-nine years old.

The fact that Dhoruba had mixed feelings about King's campaign of nonviolent protest only added to the shock. For many young men of Dhoruba's generation, King had become a kind of symbol of appeasement. To allow black protesters to be hosed down and beaten by cops, to be spat upon while they engaged in peaceful sit-ins at some lunch counter in Alabama or Mississippi, was anathema to Dhoruba and almost everyone else he knew growing up in the Bronx. To black men like Dhoruba, nonviolent protest meant getting beaten by your oppressors and just standing there and taking it; at the most fundamental level, it was an affront to their manhood. As the Black Power movement increasingly dominated the headlines, King was receding from the front lines of the civil rights struggle. The idea that he, not one of them, had been violently gunned down was almost beyond belief.

*They killed that dude?* Dhoruba thought to himself. *He wasn't even a threat. And they killed the man.*

When Dhoruba returned to work, he was met with a surprising development: the white workers at the plant all started apologizing to him. *Why do they feel the need to apologize on behalf of that cracker who pulled the trigger?* he wondered. *Do they feel complicit in the act?* The apologies only depressed him further.

That day, he quit his job at the printing plant. Within forty-eight hours of hearing about the assassination, he headed out to Brooklyn, to what he heard was the new headquarters for the Black Panther Party in New York, an Afrocentric bookstore at 780 Nostrand Avenue in Bed Stuy. In the window was a poster, soon to be iconic, of Huey P. Newton sitting in a wicker chair, a modern-day African warrior with a spear in one hand and a rifle in the other. Dhoruba entered the store.

"Where do I sign up for the Black Panther Party?"

The young brothers and sisters in the store, Dhoruba remembered, were sporting black berets, goatees, and Afros. One brother identified himself as the officer of the day. "Well, my brother, it ain't like that," he said. "You can't just join. We have to educate you first. You have to know the party's ten-point program and platform by heart. Also, you have to attend PE classes."

"PE classes," said Dhoruba. "What's that?"

"Political education—learning history from a black perspective. All the things they don't teach us in school, you dig?"

Dhoruba nodded. "Where do I take the classes?" "They're held twice weekly at Long Island University in Brooklyn." The Panther officer handed Dhoruba a couple of pamphlets and an application form. "Fill this out. You have to report for class every week in Brooklyn till you're accepted into the party."

Dhoruba looked at the list of Panther reading material in a pamphlet: Frederick Douglass, Du Bois, Baldwin, *Crisis of the Negro Intellectual* by Harold Cruse. "I've read some of these books already," he said.

"Yeah?" said the officer. "That puts you ahead of the game. Where did you attend college?"

"Oh, various penal institutions upstate," he replied. "That was my college."

The officer of the day reached out and shook Dhoruba's hand. "All power to the people, my brother. You've come to the right place."

George Whitmore was in the second-floor rec room at Sing Sing when the news came that King had been gunned down in Memphis. Like everyone else, he was stunned. When the network news showed footage of King giving his speech before the National Mall, George choked up. He remembered sitting in the empty catering hall at the Ivy Hotel in Wildwood that day—August 28, 1963—watching the March on Washington play out on television. If it hadn't been for the magnitude of that day and King's speech, Whitmore's coworkers might not have remembered that he'd been there watching TV at just the moment when detectives claimed he was in Manhattan raping and eviscerating Janice Wylie and Emily Hoffert.

King's speech had become Whitmore's alibi. Martin Luther King Jr. had literally saved his life.

That night, the penitentiary was put on lockdown. Worried about riots or acts of revenge by black convicts against white convicts, authorities kept the inmates in their cells twenty-three hours a day for five straight days. Mealtime was doled out in shifts, to ensure only minimal interaction between prisoners. An eerie quiet descended upon Sing Sing in those days, and it lingered until the guards lifted the lockdown and allowed prisoners to circulate in general population.

As he had after Malcolm X's assassination, George made a few dollars painting portraits of King and selling them to inmates. Sometimes, as he sketched out the contours of King's face and then painted in the details, George felt like he wanted to cry.

As with most cops, the first thing Bill Phillips wondered after the King assassination was, When would the rioting start? In New York City, the hours and days immediately after the assassination were tense. There were sporadic disturbances around the city, with some looting, broken windows, and candlelight vigils that occasionally turned unruly. The threat became much worse on the night of April 6, as news came of full-fledged rioting in more than one hundred cities. The National Guard was sent in to restore peace in Chicago, Baltimore, Washington, D.C. Before the riots were over, thirty-seven to forty-six people were killed, with thousands of injuries and property damage of more than $50 million.

In New York, Mayor Lindsay took to the streets in an attempt to quell the growing, restless anger. There would ultimately be rioting in New York, some of it destructive and costly, but nothing like what Phillips and the NYPD had experienced the previous summer, when police cars were shot at, torched, and showered with brick-filled garbage cans from tenement rooftops. Still, the toll from rioting in New York after the King assassination was one dead, seventy police and civilian injuries, and 428 arrests. Property damage was estimated at $5 million.

One week after King was buried in a nationally televised ceremony, Phillips was cruising in a squad car with his latest partner, Eddie Lawrence. Lawrence was what was known in the department as a "hair bag," a veteran cop with close to twenty years on the job, slow, cautious, with one eye on his retirement date and dreams of suburbia.

At Park Avenue and West 122nd Street, in the shadow of the elevated tracks of the New York Central railroad, a Latina in her midtwenties came fleeing out of a building and flagged down Phillips and Lawrence.

"I've been robbed, I've been robbed!"

"When did it happen?" Phillips asked the woman.

"It's happening right now. He's still up there in the apartment."

Phillips thought about that: How likely was it that a robber was waiting up there for cops to arrive? "He's not up there," said Phillips.

The woman was taken aback. "Yes he is. He's still there."

Phillips sighed and got out of the car, followed ten steps behind by his partner. He opened the front door of the building, a run-down four-story tenement at 1743 Park Avenue. In the narrow hallway, Phillips saw a man carrying shopping bags in each hand. The man was short but well-built, black, mid-thirties, wearing jeans and a loose cotton shirt.

"That's him," said the woman. "Look, he's still got my things in the bag. That's my radio."

Phillips stepped forward and said to the man, "Okay, you fuck, drop the loot and get against the wall."

The man's name was Calvin McCoy. He had an extensive police record, twenty-five arrests on charges ranging from disorderly conduct to possession of narcotics to burglary. He was a junkie, likely robbing the woman's apartment for items to pawn so that he could buy smack. He had the skittish mannerisms of a junkie but looked like an athlete.

McCoy's eyes darted here and there, looking around the hallway; he had nowhere to run. He put down the bags and faced the wall. When Phillips stepped forward to frisk the suspect, McCoy elbowed him square in the solar plexus and knocked him off balance. McCoy bolted down the hallway and out the front door.

Standing outside the building, Officer Lawrence looked up to see a black dude come running frantically out the front door, with Phillips close behind.

"Grab him, Eddie!" shouted Phillips.

Lawrence tried to stop the robber but was knocked flat on his ass. He did, however, slow McCoy down enough that Phillips managed to catch up and grab him. Phillips and McCoy tussled on the street. The fabric of McCoy's shirt ripped and the shirt was torn completely off. McCoy pulled out a switchblade, and Phillips froze. The robber lunged at Phillips. The cop raised his left hand to block the attack, and the blade sliced the meaty part of his palm, sending blood spurting everywhere. Phillips jerked back his hand, pulling away. McCoy bolted down Park Avenue underneath the elevated railway tracks, a shirtless black man on the run. Phillips took off after him, his hand dripping blood. He recalled:

> Zip! The guy's running like a deer under the el. He's got some body on him, looked like a weight lifter. I'm chasing him and he's gaining on me every step. I hear Eddie yell, shoot him, shoot him. Good fucking idea, right? He's now about fifteen, twenty yards away. I whip out my gun and fire two shots up in the air under the el. . . . On the corner there's a traffic stanchion. I rest my hand on it, cock the gun and fire one shot. Get him right through the back. He doesn't fall down, but he stops running. When I get to him he's bleeding from the nose and mouth. The bullet severed the lung artery. I says, holy shit, this guy's going to die. Jesus Christ almighty, I killed this fucking guy.

Police cars with sirens wailing flocked to the scene as local residents gathered on the street. Also among the first responders were representatives of a special Urban Task Force that Mayor Lindsay's office had established after King's assassination for exactly this purpose—to arrive at the scene of potentially explosive incidents and try to maintain the peace. As people milled about, uncertain what to do, a few angry comments were shouted at the cops.

Phillips was taken to the same hospital as the robber. While his hand was being stitched up, he was informed that Calvin McCoy had died.

"What did you have to shoot the guy for?" one of the mayor's task force members asked Phillips. "Can you account for this shooting? You may be in a lot of trouble."

Phillips wasn't in any trouble. The investigation of the shooting, treated as a routine inquiry by the NYPD, found that the suspect was killed in the line of duty. Phillips was given a special commendation for valor, but he wasn't especially proud of the shooting.

> A police officer is supposed to understand that any time he shoots at a guy he intends to kill him. But I think, most of us think, that most of these guys that get shot don't die. As a matter of fact, them guys are hard to kill. Shoot these people in the fucking head and they live, I swear to Christ. So when I'm shooting at the guy, I figured the guy isn't going to die for chrissakes. . . . I didn't think, I'm going to kill him. I didn't aim at his head. I just aimed at his general body. It's really hard to hit a guy with a handgun at that distance.

Several weeks later, a man came into the Twenty-fifth Precinct station house in Harlem and said, "I want to report a murder."

He was sent up to the second floor to see a detective. He walked into the squad room and repeated his refrain, "I want to report a murder."

"Yeah?" said a detective. "Who was murdered?"

"My brother was murdered. By Patrolman William Phillips."

The detective glared at the guy and said, "Get the fuck out of here."

There was no rioting after the shooting of Calvin McCoy. His long criminal record, and the fact that his death took place while he was in the midst of committing a crime, seemed to mitigate whatever reaction the community might have felt. Everyone breathed a sigh of relief. McCoy's death raised all kinds of theoretical issues: Does a burglar caught in the act deserve to die? Was shooting a fleeing perp in the back an act of "valor," as the department would proclaim? But this was the sort of encounter that took place regularly in the ghetto, where a cop had to make a hair-trigger decision about the use of deadly force, and the residents were left to decide if the results were outrageous enough to justify burning down their neighborhood.

A few months after the shooting of Calvin McCoy—after Phillips had been presented with his medal of valor by the NYPD—the officer was at a grand jury hearing about the shooting. In the hallway of the courthouse, he happened to walk by the mother of the man he shot. Weary beyond her years, in tremendous emotional distress, the woman looked at the cop and said, "You killed my son."

The normally loquacious Phillips had no comeback.

(Excerpt from *The Savage City: Race, Murder, and a Generation on the Edge*, published by William Morrow/HarperCollins. 

# "Sharing the Darkness: An Essay on Ukraine"

by Carolyn Forché

February 24, 2022. I wake with a start at midnight. A nightbird striking the window? A bat in the eaves? Maybe someone in the theater of my sleep gave me a nudge—someone I don't know in waking life. It is cloudy and warm this night, so the waning moon isn't visible through the window beside me, nor the bright star Antares to the right of it. There is no wind. There have been no sharp knocks on the door as I seem to hear sometimes, and no imaginary bell. A stillness has descended on everything: the pile of books on the bedside table, the water glass lit from within, and across the room, a gallery of people looking out from their photographs as if through windows in the past. Nothing moves. *Something has happened*, is what the darkness says. It had to do with the maps I had been studying in recent days, with the drawings of tanks and the arrows pointing at Ukraine. At one time, I would have reached for the Grundig shortwave radio and spun the dial through frequencies of music, languages and white noise. Now I reach for my cell phone and begin to scroll, tenting the light with a bedsheet so as not to disturb my husband's sleep. At first the world seems quiet. Kyrgyzstan's President has signed a decree banning the slaughter of cattle during funerals. Anti-war protesters have gathered outside the Russian Embassy in Berlin. Singapore reports a record number of Covid cases. I solve the Wordle puzzle and the mini-Crossword, and then I play the game of guessing how many words can be made from the same seven letters, using the same single letter in each of them. I learn that it will rain tomorrow. I hear the water heater turn on then off again. Car lights from the road pass over the walls. Maybe in the distance a raccoon is opening a garbage can. It is all very normal, but something bothers the mind. *This has to do with the war that is coming* is what the darkness is saying, and it is right. The country on the map is now ringed by battalions and tanks, convoys with their missiles pointing at the clouds. The Russian military forces are arrayed along the borders of Russia, Belarus and occupied Crimea.

The air raid sirens sound just after dawn in Kyiv, and some minutes later in Lviv. Blasts are heard in the cities of Dnipro, Mariupol, Kramatorsk and Odesa. *This has to do with a city near the sea, city of wheat and light, city of limestone soft enough to cut with a hatchet.* Poems sometimes whisper in the dark like this. They sometimes appear in the dark like lights when the eyes are closed. Within hours, I would know what woke me up. In Kyiv it was already morning and it was clear that a full-scale war against the people of Ukraine had begun, a war to destroy kindergartens and libraries, theaters, farmer's markets, hospitals, filling stations; a war on universities and maternity wards, factories and shopping malls, apartment blocks and playgrounds, a war on a language spoken for five hundred years, on the history of a people, on folk songs and dances, fairy tales, literature, and food; a war, as I saw it, upon *an opera house, a madhouse, a ghost church with wind for its choir/ where two things were esteemed: literature and ships, poetry and the sea.* These lines are from a poem I wrote for the Ukrainian-born poet Ilya Kaminsky after our journey to Odesa two decades ago, when it seemed fortuitous for him to go back, to see once again the city of his childhood, the city he left with his mother and father in the years just after the collapse of the former Soviet Union.

This was not my first trip there. A decade earlier, I had driven through Belarus toward Ukraine to document the conditions for people living in the exclusion zones surrounding the damaged reactor at Chernobyl: the elderly people who refused to leave, and refugees from the war in Chechnya, who found safety in the peace and quiet of the place. In memory, the giant blue cabbages growing in their radiated gardens are visible through a scrim of acacia trees lining the streets of Odesa. The passage of time has caused these journeys to happen all at once, the images flickering like photographs in a kaleidoscope. We are walking in the cold wind toward the Potemkin steps when Ilya interrupts this reverie by playfully inviting me to dance, as instructed by the title of his first volume of poems, *Dancing in Odessa*. And so we waltz down Prymorskyi Boulevard, and later, over a samovar of black tea in the Hotel Londonskya, he tells me that emigration is death. "You must die when you board the plane and walk into your resurrection as you disembark in the new land. If you are unable to do this, you remain a corpse. I'm not sure I can say now that emigration is a good thing."

That trip was the first of many for him. He even went back after the invasion this year, in part to visit his ailing uncle, to bring whatever aid and comfort he could to his relatives and friends, the poets he had come to know in the decades since that first journey, poets he had been translating and publishing, and now was trying somehow to rescue in whatever way he could. Most Ukrainian poets had chosen to stay behind when millions of women, children, and elderly men boarded the trains, piled into cars, or walked to the country's borders. Like everyone else in the west, I was confined in my knowledge of this exodus to photographs and video footage: arms reaching through train windows, crowded platforms, children in snowsuits, house cats and small dogs tucked into winter jackets, roller boards, rucksacks, wheelchairs. Some had packed believing they would only be away a short time. I wondered what they had chosen to bring with them and tried not to think about all they had left behind. I did, however, understand that the images before me did not transmit how cold it was, how raw the air, how painful the boots and shoes, did not convey the desperate hope for a toilet, a sip of water, a place to dry out the mittens and socks. In the photographs, the black smoke pouring from burning apartment blocks doesn't sting the eyes or burn the throat; there is no stench of cordite and no overpowering petroleum odor of war.

Soon after the invasion began, the writer Askold Melnyczuk asked me to join a Zoom gathering of Ukrainian poets, sponsored by the PEN-American Center. Despite our far-flung locations, in the computer screen, it was as if we were all in the same apartment house, looking out from our different windows. In Ukraine, it was already dark. The mood in our dimly lit poetry building was solemn. Vasyl Makhno was in New York, Ostap Slyvynsky and Halya Kruk were in Lviv, Oksana Lutsyshyna was in Austin, Texas; Iryna Shukalova in Beijing, and Oksana Zabuzkho tried to join us from Warsaw, but was unable to get the technology on her borrowed computer to work. **Askold welcomed us.** There were greetings and sad smiles, shrugs and knowing looks. I knew that I would share a poem I wrote for Ilya, titled "Exile," but in the hours leading up to our meeting, I also composed a message in the form of a poem, an urgent message written quickly and read in its raw state. In the days that followed, the message was published, translated into Ukrainian, and letter-pressed as a broadside in both languages against a field of sunflowers.

**If there is ink**
If there is ink for this hour if there is
something to say to write that would
send the tanks the convoys and transports
into reverse on the roads they have rutted
send them back to the borders they crossed
send them back, and the hours too that have passed
since dawn on the twenty-fourth day of the second month
send those hours with them, and the enemy
soldiers dragging with them their crematorium
and the corpses of their fellow soldiers they have left
behind and their own wounded send them back if there is ink
if there is something to write that would raise the cities
from the ruins the apartment blocks hospitals schools
that would put the cities back as they were
I would give everything to fill my pen with it

Якби існувало чорнило
Якби існувало чорнило для цих часів якби існувало
таке що можна розповісти написати що би змусило
танки конвої транспорти

повернути назад на шляхи на яких вони залишили ритвини
погнати їх геть до кордону який вони перейшли,
і прогнати часи що минули
від світанку двадцять четвертого дня другого місяця
прогнати часи оці а за ними ворожих солдатів
що волочать свої крематорії
і прогнати покинуті трупи і прогнати
поранених гнати їх якби існувало чорнило
якби можна було словами написати таке що підніме міста
із руїн і будинки квартали лікарні і школи
щось таке що відродить міста відсотворить їх тими
що перше я віддала б усе щоб наповнити ручку таким чорнилом

tr. by Переклад Оксани Луцишиної

This was before Mariupol was razed to the ground, before its theater was bombed, killing six hundred people who had taken refuge within it; before the discovery of the torture chambers and the corpses of Bucha; the aerial bombing of Vinnytsia, Chernihiv, Kyiv, and Izium, a litany of cities and towns; the siege of the steelworks; a child photographed lying dead beside a baby carriage; a mother in labor carried on a litter from a burning maternity ward. It was possible in those first weeks and months to imagine myself to be following "the news," especially by reading *The Kyiv Independent*, just as it was possible to hope that the sanctions would work, that the courage of a besieged people could prevail against despotic aggression, that the largest land war in Europe in almost seventy years would not end in thermonuclear war; that Ukraine would somehow survive this onslaught against significant odds. After all, hadn't the Russian warship been sunk off the coast of Snake Island? Hadn't the farmer's tractor towed the broken tank out of a field? Didn't they put these on postage stamps? The warship and the tractor-towed tank?

I lie in the dark most nights, aware that at that very moment, on the other side of the world, a rocket had struck a power plant and the lights had gone out. In those hours, I was lying again on a basement floor in Beirut many years ago, listening to the thunderous shelling of

Ras Beirut from the Maronite east. Almost every journalist posted to Beirut was in that hotel basement, along with a handful of people from neighboring apartments. There were thirty or so of us. Beside me was a young Lebanese girl lying under her coat, whispering to me about her life, and wondering if there would be anything left in the morning. "Of course, there will," I reassured her, "they can't destroy everything." I wanted now to remember this particular fear: that our building would be hit and we would be crushed beneath it. "We have to sleep," I said to the girl. In the morning we would wake up, and it would be over. I said things like that until she fell asleep, and then I lay there, keeping myself awake to keep the world intact. That is how one thinks in a make-shift shelter under bombardment.

As I scroll through photographs taken in Kherson or Nikopol, I want to remember , not only the stench, but the deafening sounds of detonated ordnance, acrid dust and debris, the screeching of metal on metal, the coughing of the mortars and shattering of glass. In the morning, the streets of Ras Beirut were covered with broken windows, green, jagged scraps that made it look as though the streets were iced. It was hard to walk. And there is so much else one can forget: how for hours or even days nothing happens, and it seems safe to come out because after all it is necessary to find food and water, to prepare meals and wash up, to think about where to go next. I remembered the young boy who every day ran from doorway to doorway with a tall stack of pita bread he balanced like plates in a circus act. He sometimes had to dodge rifle-fire, but he never dropped the bread, and people watching from a slight distance cheered him on as if he might not die at any moment.

Sometimes in the early hours, I discover my friend, Edward, awake in Odesa. I ask him if he is somewhere safe, in a shelter or basement. "No," he replies. Then: "Around 20:00 hours, two heavy shots sounded right next door to our house. It was our defense firing. I now live not far from the restaurant where you and I dined. My wife and three animals and I do not lose heart. We are not afraid." And: "A few hours ago there were ten shots, very loud, so my head ached but we are not discouraged. We think it will be over soon." And: "Thank you for being with us. In

Odesa there were several volleys from the sea and the air. In the city for a long time a siren and a distant cannonade were heard. My wife and I and our three pets—Santa, Puma, and Charlie—are calm and confident in our victory. We are waiting for the end of the war."

Lying awake at night I insist to myself that yes, this is happening again, now, in the heart of Europe, a genocidal war to eliminate a people. What the Polish poet Czesław Miłosz wrote is true: "If a thing exists in one place, it will exist everywhere." There is nothing that cannot happen. Nothing impossible where humanity is concerned. War is an old story. As for human survival and civilization, there are no guarantees. In our times, everything senses that an end might come, that annihilation is possible and, as the poet Nazim Hikmet wrote: *This earth will grow cold one day /not like a block of ice/ or a dead cloud even/ but like an empty walnut it will roll along in pitch black space. // You must grieve for this right now /—you have to feel this sorrow now—/ for the earth must be loved this much/ if you are going to say "I lived."*

"The poetic act changes with the amount of background reality embraced by the poet's consciousness," Miłosz also wrote: "What surrounds us, here and now, is not guaranteed. It could just as well not exist—and so man constructs poetry out of the remnants found in ruins." Awareness of that *background* reality demands vigilance, this very wakefulness, and is sustained through the faculty of the empathetic imagination, by our ability to respond to hidden forces, to disturbances in the cosmos, the way horses run back and forth across a pasture before a storm, or migratory birds sense an early winter. The background reality for those who live far from the war zone is the war itself. It shares the darkness with us, the moment of night.

Before the invasion the artist Ashley Ashford-Brown had begun a large painting in his studio in Basse-Normandie, France. He had been working on a series of interiors—rooms emptied and swept, no longer inhabited except by a palpable stillness, painted partly in pigmented concrete, the material he had used in the past when making paintings of dolmens and cairns.

One of these interiors he recognized as a room in Aleppo, Syria, where he'd had an exhibition of his work before that city was destroyed.

He does not know what happened to the paintings, offering that they were now possibly *somewhere under the rubble*. Unlike most of Aleppo, the room in the painting is nearly intact, but for a cracked floor and some fallen plaster. Through the doorway, we glimpse the balcony, and beyond its arches, a city painted from memory.

In the painting begun just before the invasion of Ukraine, we are looking through a hole in a blown wall. It is dark. There is another wall blown open beyond it, with pieces of wall on the floor. Through this opening, there is another in the shape of a doorway with no door. The light enters here, washing over the floor to where we stand in a pile of fallen plaster. There is a tree growing in the distance, but it is leafless. He was puzzled by this painting at first, as it emerged on the canvas, and then realized that the room was in Ukraine, a place he had never been. A demolished room in Ukraine had come to him, presaging the invasion. "That is how it happens with painting sometimes," he said.

Carolyn Forché<br>Homer, Alaska, September 2022

# Preface to *Colored People*

by Henry Louis Gates, Jr.

Dear Maggie and Liza:

I have written to you because a world into which I was born, a world that nurtured and sustained me, has mysteriously disappeared. My darkest fear is that Piedmont, West Virginia, will cease to exist. If some executives on Park Avenue decide that it is more profitable to build a completely new paper mill elsewhere than to overhaul one a century old. Then they would close it, just as they did in Cumberland with Celanese, and Pittsburgh Plate Glass, and the Kelly-Springfield Tire Company. The town will die, but our people will not move. They will not *be* moved. Because for them, Piedmont—snuggled between the Allegheny Mountains and the Potomac River Valley—is life itself.

I have written to you because of the day when we were driving home and you asked your mother and me just exactly what the civil rights movement has been all about and I pointed to a motel on Route 2 and said that at one time I could not have stayed there. Your mother could have stayed there, but your mother couldn't have stayed there with me. And you kids looked at us like we were telling you the biggest lie you had ever heard. So I thought about writing you.

I have written for another reason, as well. I remember that once we were walking in Washington, D.C., heading for the National Zoo, and you asked me if I had known the man to whom I had just spoken. I said no. And, Liza, you volunteered that you found it embarrassing that I would speak to a complete stranger on the street. It called to mind a trip I'd made to Pittsburgh with my father. On the way from his friend Mr. Ozzie Washington's sister's house, I heard Daddy speak to a colored man, then saw him tip his hat to the man's wife. (Daddy liked nice hats: Caterpillar hats for work, Dobbs hats for Sunday.) It's just something that you do, he said, when I asked him if he had known those people and why he had spoken to them.

Last summer, I sat at a sidewalk café in Italy, and three or four "black" Italians walked casually by, as well as a dozen or more blacker Africans. Each spoke to me; rather, each nodded his head slightly or acknowledged me by a glance, ever so subtly. When I was growing up, we always did this with each other, passing boats in a sea of white folk.

Yet here were certain Negroes who would avoid acknowledging you in this way in an integrated setting, especially if the two of you were the ones doing the integrating. Don't go there with those white people if all you're going to do is Jim Crow yourselves— Daddy must have said that to me a thousand times. And by that I think he meant we shouldn't *cling* to each other out of habit or fear, or use protective coloration to evade the risks of living like any other human being, or use clannishness as a cop-out for exploring ourselves and possibly making new selves, forged in the crucible of integration. Your black ass, he'd laugh, is integrated already.

But there are other reasons that people distrust the reflex—the nod, the glance, the murmured greeting.

One reason is resentment at being lumped together with thirty million African Americans whom you don't know and most of whom you will never know. Completely by the accident of racism, we have been bound together with people with whom we may or may not have something in common, just because we are "black." Thirty million Americans are black, and thirty million is a lot of people. One day you wonder: What do the misdeeds of a Mike Tyson have to do with me? So why do I feel implicated? And how can I not feel racial recrimination when I can feel racial pride?

Then, too, there were Negroes who were embarrassed about *being* Negroes who didn't want to be bothered with race and other black people. One of the more painful things about being colored was being colored in public around other colored people, who were embarrassed to be colored and embarrassed that we *both* were colored and in public together. As if to say: "Negro, will you *puh-lease* disappear so that I can get my own white people?" As if to say: "I'm not a Negro like other Negroes." As if to say, "I am a human being—let me be!"

For much of my adolescence and adulthood, I thought of these people as having betrayed the race, I used to walk up to them and call them *Brother* or *Sister*, loud with a sardonic edge, when they looked like they were trying to "escape." When I went off to college, I would make the "conversion" of errant classmates as a serious project, a political commitment.

I used to reserve my special scorn for those Negroes who were always being embarrassed by someone else in the race. Someone too dark, someone too "loud," someone too "wrong." Someone who dared to wear red in public. Loud and wrong: we used to say about each other. Nigger is loud and wrong. "Loud" carried a triple meaning: speaking too loudly, dressing too loudly, and just *being* too loudly.

I do know that when I was a boy, many Negroes would have been the first to censure other Negroes once they were admitted to all-white neighborhoods or schools or clubs. "An embarrassment to the race"—phrases of that were sort of bandied about. Accordingly, many of us in our generation engaged in strange antics to flout those strictures. Like eating watermelon in public, eating it loudly and merrily, and spitting the seeds into the middle of the street, red juice running down the sides of our cheeks, collecting under our chins. Or taking the greatest pride in the Royal Kink. Uncle Harry used to say he didn't *like* watermelon, which I knew was a lie because I saw him wolf down slices when I was a little kid, before he went off to seminary at Boston University. But he came around, just like he came around to painting God and Jesus black, and all the seraphim and cherubim, too. And I, from another direction, have gradually come around, also, and stopped trying to tell other Negroes how to be black.

Do you remember when your mother and I woke you up early on a Sunday morning, just to watch Nelson Mandela walk out of prison, and how it took a couple of hours for him to emerge, and how you both wanted to go back to bed, and then, to watch cartoons? And how we began to worry something bad had happened to him on the way out, because the delay was so long? And when he finally walked out of that prison, how we were excited and teary-eyed at Mandela's nobility, his princeliness, his straight back and unbowed head? I think I felt that there walked the Negro, as Pop might have said; there walked the whole of the African people, as regal as any king. And that feeling I had, the gooseflesh sense of identity that I felt seeing Nelson Mandela, listening to Mahalia Jackson sing, watching Muhammad Ali fight, or hearing Martin Luther King speak, is part of what I mean by being colored. I realize the sentiment may not be logical, but I want to have my cake and eat it, too. Which is why I still nod or speak to black people on the streets and why it felt so good to be acknowledged by the Afro-Italians who passed by my table in the café in Milan.

I want to be able to take special pride in a Jessye Norman aria, a Muhammad Ali shuffle, a Michael Jordan slam dunk, a Spike Lee movie, a Thurgood Marshall opinion, a Toni Morrison novel, James Brown's Camel Walk. Above all, I enjoy the unselfconscious moments of a shared cultural, intimacy, whatever form they take, when no one else is watching, when no white people are around. Like Joe Louis's fights, which my father still talks about as part of the fixed repertoire of stories that texture our lives. You've seen his eyes shining as he describes how Louis hit Max Schmeling so many times and so hard, and how some reporter asked him, after the fight: "Joe, what would you have done if that last punch hadn't knocked Schmeling out?" And how ole Joe responded, without missing a beat: "I'da run around behind him to see what was holdin' him up!"

Even so, I rebel at the notion that I can't be part of other groups, that I can't construct identities through elective affinity, that race must be the most important thing about me. Is that what I want on my gravestone: Here lies an African American? So I'm divided. I want to be black, to know black, to luxuriate in whatever I might be calling blackness at any particular time— but to do so in order to come out on the other side, to experience a humanity that is neither colorless nor reducible to color. Bach *and* James Brown. Sushi *and* fried catfish.

Part of me admires those people who can say with a straight face that they have transcended any attachment to a particular community or group . . . but I always want to run around behind them to see what holds them up.

I am not Everynegro. I am not native to the great black metropolises: New York, Chicago, or Los Angeles, say. Nor can I claim to be a "citizen of the world." I am from of a time and place—Piedmont, West Virginia— and that's a world apart, a world of difference. So this is not a story of a race but a story of a village, a family, and its friends. And a sort of segregated peace. What hurt me most about the glorious black awakening of the late sixties and early seventies is that we lost our sense of humor. Many of us thought that enlightened politics excluded it.

In your lifetimes, I suspect, you will go from being African Americans, to being "people of color," to being, once again, "colored people." (The linguistic trend toward condensation is strong). I don't mind any of the names myself. But I have to confess that I like "colored" best, maybe because when I hear the word, I hear it in my mother's voice, and in the sepia tones of my childhood. As artlessly and honestly as I can, I have tried to evoke a colored world of the fifties, a Negro world of the early sixties, and the advent of a black world of the later sixties, from the point of view of the boy I was. When you are old enough to read what follows, I hope that it brings you even a small measure of understanding, at long last, of why we see the world with such different eyes...and why that is for me a source both of gladness and of regret. And I hope you'll understand why I continue to speak to colored people I pass on the streets.

Love,
Daddy

*Piedmont, West Virginia*
*July 8, 1993*

# Joy Harjo

## Two excerpts from *Catching the Light*, Yale University Press



Every poem is a prayer, a supplication in the cacophony of humanity. There are more words now than ever, and there are so many so fast on the internet and being texted that they have lost their innate power. They are not cared for, and so many are lost and scattered. I am lonely for lullabies sung at night, I am lonely for the man singing beautifully out of tune on the street up to the window framing a beloved, I am lonely for the first words of the baby and the toothless smile of accomplishment that follows, lonely for the speaker bringing us all into the circle together by clan and ceremonial ground, lonely for the voice of a mother who plants poetry in her children, lonely for the sound of wind in the corn plants that have been sung to as they rise up from seedlings to god figures beneath the sun.

There are some words I would like to call back. There are words that have been knives of separation, words of treaties that stole land and children, words of contracts that have taken the last cents from the poor, demeaning words, cutting words, words meant to destroy, words that took you so far away from me, my beloved.

I will use words to call my spirit back. These words are made of mists of myth, made of architectures of restorative history, made of ancient songs of coming together that lift us over and through to beauty, so that nothing or no one can ever be lost or uncared for again, now, or forever.

49

Every place has guardians whose responsibility it is to tend that person or place. There are guardians of cities, mountains, plants, and animals, for all beings and states of mind on this planet Earth. These guardians are real and in healthy societies they are active. When the guardians, or keepers, of these lands are forcibly removed, massacred, and their lifeways stolen through the theft and warehousing of children, when female power is no longer standing equal with male power, then the lands suffer. We all suffer. The waters become polluted, fires are out of control, storms become massive and aggressive, and the Earth trembles. There is confusion and destruction among all those who inhabit the land, these times.

But we can change the story—and that is done by the artists, the thinkers, and the dreamers, those who can envision from within this immense field. Indigenous artists must be part of the leadership in the revision of the American story. We can change the story of a violent hierarchy that follows in the wake of the papal bulls proclaiming indigenous peoples as non-humans for land and resource theft and slavery, to Manifest Destiny, which opened the West and the world for the taking and set in place a caste system that places value according to skin color, culture, sexual identity, and economic standing. We can turn to honoring female power, without whom there is no life. Rivers, mountains, lands, other animals, and elemental inhabitants will be respected co-inhabitants.

Time, experience, and the ancestors have taught me that it is while practicing our arts and in ceremony that we come closest to who we really are, as individuals, as part of a family, a generation, a country, a planet, a timeless point of experience. It is then we come into close contact with our ancestors, the origin. We must feed that place, honor it.

I bow down to the story keepers, to the keepers of poetry. I am reminded of the water spider, who when the Earth was covered with water, carried an ember on her back so we could make fire to keep the story going. Everything is a prayer in the becoming as she approaches us, swimming through time.

# "The Displaced"

## Introduction to *The Displaced: Refugee Writers on Refugee Lives*, an anthology

by Viet Thanh Nguyen

I was once a refugee, although no one would mistake me for being a refugee now. Because of this, I insist on being called a refugee, since the temptation to pretend that I am not a refugee is strong. It would be so much easier to call myself an immigrant, to pass myself off as belonging to a category of migratory humanity that is less controversial, less demanding, and less threatening than the refugee.

I was born a citizen and a human being. At four years of age, I became something less than human, at least in the eyes of those who do not think of refugees as being human. The month was March, the year 1975, when the northern communist army captured my hometown of Ban Me Thuot in its final invasion of the Republic of Vietnam, a country that no longer exists except in the imagination of its global refugee diaspora of several million people, a country that most of the world remembers as South Vietnam.

Looking back, I remember nothing of the experience that turned me into a refugee. It begins with my mother making a life-and-death decision on her own. My father was in Saigon, and the lines of communication were cut. I do not remember my mother fleeing our hometown with my ten-year-old brother and me, leaving behind our sixteen- year-old adopted sister to guard the family property. I do not remember my sister, who my parents would not see again for nearly twenty years, who I would not see again for nearly thirty years.

My brother remembers dead paratroopers hanging from the trees on our route, although I do not. I also do not remember whether I walked the entire one hundred eighty-four kilometers to Nha Trang, or whether my mother carried me, or whether we might have managed to get a ride on the cars, trucks, carts, motorbikes, and bicycles crowding the road. Perhaps she does remember but I never asked about the exodus, or about the tens of thousands of civilian refugees and fleeing soldiers, or the desperate scramble to get on a boat in Nha Trang, or some of the soldiers shooting some of the civilians to clear their way to boats, as I would read later in accounts of this time.

I do not remember finding my father in Saigon, or how we waited for another month until the communist army came to the city's borders, or how we tried to get into the airport, and then into the American embassy, and then finally somehow fought our way through the crowds at the docks to reach a boat, or how my father became separated from us but decided to get on a boat by himself anyway, and how my mother decided the same thing, or how we eventually were reunited on a larger ship. I do remember that we were incredibly fortunate, finding our way out of the country, as so many millions did not, and not losing anyone, as so many thousands did. No one, except my sister.

For most of my life, I did remember soldiers on our boat firing onto a smaller boat full of refugees that was trying to approach. But when I mentioned it to my older brother many years later, he said the shooting never happened.

I do not remember many things, and for all those things I do not remember, I am grateful, because the things I do remember hurt me enough. My memory begins after our stops at a chain of American military bases in the Philippines, Guam, and finally Pennsylvania. To leave the refugee camp in Pennsylvania, the Vietnamese refugees needed American sponsors. One sponsor took my parents, another took my brother, a third took me.

For most of my life, I tried not to remember this moment except to note it in a factual way, as something that happened to us but left no damage, but that is not true. As a writer and a father of a son who is four years old, the same age I was when I became a refugee, I have to remember, or sometimes, imagine, not just what happened, but what was felt. I have to imagine what it was like for a father and a mother to have their children taken away from them. I have to imagine what it was that I experienced, although I do remember being taken by my sponsor to visit my parents and howling at being taken back.

I remember being reunited with my parents after a few months and the snow and the cold and my mother disappearing from our lives for a period of time I cannot recall and for reasons I could not understand, and knowing vaguely that it had something to do with the trauma of losing her country, her family, her property, her security, maybe her self. In remembering this, I know that I am also foreshadowing the worst of what the future would hold, of what would happen to her in the decades to come. Despite her short absence, or maybe her long one, I remember enjoying life in Harrisburg, Pennsylvania, because children can enjoy things that adults cannot so long as they can play, and I remember a sofa sitting in our backyard and neighborhood children stealing our Halloween candy and my enraged brother taking me home before venturing out by himself to recover what had been taken from us.

I remember moving to San Jose, California, in 1978 and my parents opening the second Vietnamese grocery store in the city and I remember the phone call on Christmas Eve that my brother took, informing him that my parents had been shot in an armed robbery, and I remember that it was not that bad, just flesh wounds, they were back at work not long after, and I remember that the only people who wanted to open businesses in depressed downtown San Jose were the Vietnamese refugees, and I remember walking down the street from my parents' store and seeing a sign in a store window that said, ANOTHER AMERICAN DRIVEN OUT OF BUSINESS BY THE VIETNAMESE, and I remember the gunman who followed us to our home and knocked on our door and pointed a gun in all our faces and how my mother saved us by running past him and out onto the sidewalk, but I do not remember the two policemen shot to death in front of my parents' store because I had gone away to college by that time and my parents did not want to call me and worry me.

I remember all these things because if I did not remember them and write them down then perhaps they would all disappear, as all those Vietnamese businesses have vanished, because after they had helped to revitalize the downtown that no one else cared to invest in, the city of San Jose realized that downtown could be so much better than what it was and forced all those businesses to sell their property and if you visit downtown San Jose today you will see a massive, gleaming, new city hall that symbolizes the wealth of a Silicon Valley that had barely begun to exist in 1978 but you will not see my parents' store, which was across the street from the new city hall. What you will see instead is a parking lot with a few cars in it because the city thought that the view of an empty parking lot from the windows and foyer of city hall was more attractive than the view of a mom-and-pop Vietnamese grocery store catering to refugees.

As refugees, not just once but twice, having fled from north to south in 1954 when their country was divided, my parents experienced the usual dilemma of anyone classified as an *other.* The other exists in contradiction, or perhaps in paradox, being either invisible or hypervisible but rarely just visible. Most of the time we do not see the other or see right through them, whoever the other may be to us, since each of us—even if we are seen as others by some—have our own others. When we do see the other, the other is not truly human to us, by the very definition of being an other, but is instead a stereotype, a joke, or a horror. In the case of the Vietnamese refugees in America, we embodied the specter of the Asian come to either serve or to threaten.

Invisible and hypervisible, refugees are ignored and forgotten by those who are not refugees until they turn into a menace. Refugees, like all others, are unseen until they are seen everywhere, threatening to overwhelm our borders, invade our cultures, rape our women, threaten our children, destroy our economies. We who do the ignoring and forgetting oftentimes do not perceive it to be violence, because we do not know we do it. But sometimes we deliberately ignore and forget others. When we do, we are surely aware we are inflicting violence, whether that is on the schoolyard as children or at the level of the nation. When those others fight back by demanding to be seen and heard—as refugees sometimes do—they can appear to us like threatening ghosts whose fates we ourselves have caused and denied. No wonder we do not wish to see them.

When I say *we*, I mean even those who were once refugees. There are some former refugees who are comfortable in their invisibility, in the safety of their new citizenship, who look at today's hypervisible refugees and say, "No more." These former refugees think they were the good refugees, the special refugees, when in all likelihood they were simply the lucky ones, the refugees whose fates aligned with the politics of the host country. The Vietnamese refugees who came to the United States were lucky in receiving an American charity that was born out of American guilt about the war, and resulted from an American desire to show that a capitalist and democratic country was a much better home than the newly communist country the refugees were fleeing. Cuban refugees of the 1970s and 1980s benefitted from a similar American politics, but Haitian refugees of the time did not. Their blackness hindered them, just as being Muslim hurts many Syrian refugees today as they seek refuge.

From everything I remember and do not remember, I believe in my human kinship to Syrian refugees and to those 65.6 million people that the United Nations classifies as displaced people. Of these, 40.3 million are internally displaced people, forced to move within their own countries; 22.5 million are refugees fleeing unrest in their countries; 2.8 million are asylum seekers. If these 65.6 million people were their own country, their nation would be the twenty-first largest in the world, smaller than Thailand but bigger than France. And yet they are not their own country. They are instead—to paraphrase the art historian Robert Storr, who was writing about the role that Vietnamese people played in the American mind—the displaced persons of the world's conscience.

These displaced persons are mostly unwanted where they fled from; unwanted where they are, in refugee camps; and unwanted where they want to go. They have fled under arduous conditions; they have lost friends, family members, homes, and countries; they are detained in refugee camps in often subhuman conditions, with no clear end to the stay and no definitive exit; they are often threatened with deportation to their countries of origin; and they will likely be unremembered, which is where the work of writers becomes important, especially writers who are refugees or have been refugees—if such a distinction can be drawn.

The United Nations says that refugees stop being refugees when they find a new and permanent home. It has been a long time since I have been a refugee in the definition of the United Nations: "someone who has been forced to flee his or her country because of persecution, war, or violence." But I keep my tattered memories of being a refugee close to me. I cultivate that feeling of what it was to be a refugee, because a writer is supposed to go where it hurts, and because a writer needs to know what it feels like to be an other. A writer's work is impossible if he or she cannot conjure up the lives of others, and only through such acts of memory, imagination, and empathy can we grow our capacity to feel for others.

Many writers, perhaps most writers or even all writers, are people who do not feel completely at home. They are used to being people who are out of place, who are emotionally or psychically or socially displaced to one degree or another, at one time or another. Or perhaps that is just me. But I cannot help but suspect that it is from this displacement that writers come into being, and why so many writers have sympathy and empathy for those who are displaced in one way or another, whether it is the lonely social misfit or whether it is the millions rendered homeless by forces beyond their control. In my case, I remember my displacement so that I can feel for those now displaced. I remember the injustice of displacement so that I can imagine my writing as attempting to perform some justice for those compelled to move.

What is unjust about the lives of refugees, of stateless people, of asylum seekers, of all those who are no longer at home? When it comes to justice, it does not matter whether those in a host country think they have no obligation to refugees. Keeping people in a refugee camp is punishing people who have committed no crime except trying to save their own lives and the lives of their loved ones. The refugee camp belongs to the same inhuman family as the internment camp, the concentration camp, the death camp. The camp is the place where we keep those who we do not see as fully being human, and if we do not actively seek their death in most cases, we also often do not actively seek to restore many of them to the life that they had before, the life we have ourselves.

We should remember that justice is not the same as law. Many laws say that borders are sacrosanct, and that crossing borders without permission is a crime. Unpermitted migrants are thus criminals and the refugee camp is a kind of prison. But if borders are legal, are they also just? Our notions of borders have shifted over the centuries, just as our notions of justice and humanity have. Today we can usually move freely between cities within a country, even if those cities were once their own entities with their own borders and had fought wars with each other. Now we look back on those times of city-states—if we remember them—and I doubt few of us would want to return to such a condition.

Likewise, we should look at our current condition of national borders and we should imagine a more just world where these borders would be markers of culture and identity, valuable but easily crossed, rather than legal borders designed to keep our national identities rigid and ready for conflict and war, separating us from others. The dissolution of borders is the utopian vision of cosmopolitanism, of global peace and of a global place where no one is displaced, of humanity as a global community that is allowed its cultural differences but not the kind of differences that lead us to exploit, punish, or kill. Making borders permeable, we bring ourselves closer to others, and others closer to us. I find such a prospect exhilarating, but some find this proximity unimaginably terrifying.

If this global community has not been achieved, it is not because it is a wholly utopian fantasy, a nowhere not marked by any boundary. There have been moments in our history—and many times in our writings and our folklores and our theologies—where we have achieved the best of ourselves in our ability to welcome the other, to clothe the stranger, to feed the hungry, to open our homes. This is what we need to remember as we hope and work for a future where borders do not matter, but people do. This is the kind of memory, the memory of our own humanity, and our inhumanity, that writers can offer.

We need stories to give voice to a writer's vision, but also, possibly, to speak for the voiceless. This yearning to hear the voiceless is a powerful rhetoric but also potentially a dangerous one if it prevents us from doing more than listening to a story or reading a book. Just because we have listened to that story or read that book does not mean that anything has changed for the voiceless. Readers and writers should not deceive themselves that literature changes the world. Literature changes the world of readers and writers, but literature does not change the world until people get out of their chairs, go out in the world, and do something to transform the conditions of which the literature speaks. Otherwise literature will just be a fetish for readers and writers, allowing them to think that they are hearing the voiceless when they are really only hearing the writer's individual voice.

The problem here is that the people we call voiceless oftentimes are not actually voiceless. Many of the voiceless are actually talking all the time. They are loud, if you get close enough to hear them, if you are capable of listening, if you are aware of what you cannot hear. The problem is that much of the world does not want to hear the voiceless or cannot hear them. True justice is creating a world of social, economic, cultural, and political opportunities that would allow all these voiceless to tell their stories and be heard, rather than be dependent on a writer or a representative of some kind. Without such justice, there will be no end to the waves of the displaced, to the creation of ever more voiceless people, or, more accurately, to the ongoing silencing of millions of voices. True justice will be when we no longer need a voice for the voiceless.

To become a refugee is to know, inevitably, that the past is not only marked by the passage of time, but by loss—the loss of loved ones, of countries, of identities, of selves. We want to give voice to all those losses that would otherwise remain unheard except by us and those near and dear to us. In my case, I remember the losses of my parents, and I remember their voices. I remember the voices of all the

Vietnamese refugees that I encountered in my youth, hoarse from telling their stories over and over again. But I do not remember my sister's voice. I do not remember the voices of all the refugees who shared the exodus with me and did not make it, or did not survive. But I can imagine them, and if I can imagine them, then maybe I can hear them. That is a writer's dream, that if only we can hear these people that no one else wants to hear, then perhaps we can make you hear them, too.

# Excerpt from "Plague Diary"

by Margaret Porter Troupe

April 4, 2020

By the time I start this diary, I've been sheltering in since March 20th. The last person who's visited us inside the apartment was Monique Clesca. She came to lunch here. We sat apart and neither of us wore facemasks. We elbow bumped and didn't shake hands or kiss. I waited 14 days to see if I had symptoms of Covid-19.

The police arrived yesterday and made the people who hang out in A. Phillip Randolph Square Park, (formerly Dewey Square), drinking, loitering, littering, and just being an eyesore and nuisance, leave the park. This little triangular park is directly across the street from Graham Court and where Miles Davis and other beboppers playing at Minton's during the 1940s used to come to shoot up or do whatever they did there in-between sets. Minton's is around the corner on 118th Street between 7th Avenue and St. Nicholas. The police or parks people removed the benches too and put up a chicken-wire fence at the entrances to keep people out.

Now those people come across the street and congregate under the scaffolding in front of Graham Court. There's a lot of drug dealing going on too. It feels quite a bit more unsafe around here lately. Must keep antenna raised for trouble.

Woke up today thinking about my friend Cynthia, who was sounding scary to me yesterday as we discussed how we're both feeling. I've been having congestion the last eight days and she has been having symptoms too but don't know whether to attribute them to her blood pressure medication, pollen (it's Spring now and everything's bursting in bloom) or the novel coronavirus, Covid-19. She said yesterday she had a terrific headache, cough, and I was sure she said a fever. She hadn't been able to sleep the night before and she sounded weak. I told her about the hair dryer treatment that's been circulating on Facebook and which I admitted I'd tried even though I knew the woman in the video was lying. But I am scared and desperate to get this congestion out of my head and chest and practically willing to do anything, and her treatment kind of sounded reasonable, since they said that heat kills the virus. So I tried it and honestly I felt better afterwards, but I can't be certain the hairdryer had anything to do with it, since I've been taking ampicillin for the last week, and doing all the rest of the advisories like drinking hot teas, gargling with warm salted water, having Quincy give me the chest therapy procedures demonstrated on another video that someone else had sent me on Messenger. Even though I don't have a fever, or a cough, shortness of breath, or any of the scary symptoms I've read about, all I keep thinking about is the fact that no one knows what or how or whatever about this virus and so I figured why not.

Yesterday, when I heard about Patricia Bosworth, after having heard about David Driskell dying the day before and then Bill Withers, and the day before that Ellis Marsalis, and the day before that Wallace Roney and the week before that my niece Tammy in Detroit who dropped dead in one day, without knowing she'd had any symptoms whatsoever, it was just too much, and I yelled out my pain in a Facebook post. I hate posting intimate details of my life on Facebook but somehow I couldn't resist the urge. It just felt like the best way to express my fear and grief. I've had so many family members and friends, people I love, die recently that I just gave in to the impulse and bared my feelings on fucking Facebook. Oh my god. Not that I knew Patty that well. Honestly, I've only known her just a few months, having met her at the marriage celebration of a mutual friend in Upstate New York last summer. Patty and I sat next to each other at his wedding celebration, and she regaled me with stories about her ex-husband the photographer, Tom Palumbo, who'd had a session with Miles Davis and shot one of the most beautiful pictures of

Miles Davis I'd ever seen. Clear-eyed and healthy, Miles was standing behind a plastic sheet, staring directly into the camera, so young and innocent, so vulnerable. Patty told me the photo had been taken in Miles' home while he was building himself an indoor gym so he could do his boxing. He was off drugs and totally clean, which is why he looked so healthy. I think she said Miles must've been in his late 20s or early 30s.

Patty was such a great storyteller and she had me spellbound the entire luncheon telling me about herself and the people she'd known and written about during her lifetime, including Montgomery Clift, Marlon Brando, and Diane Arbus. So I asked her if she'd do a salon. I told her that she was so interesting I'd love to have her as a guest at my Harlem Arts Salon, and to my surprise she readily accepted. "I'd be happy to," she'd said brightly. I don't know what it is, but I have the best luck meeting the most wonderfully engaging people. After the luncheon, I started to have doubts that it was such a great idea to have Patty because as ignorant as I was about her and her life story, I figured everybody else was too and doubted that I could attract enough of an audience to justify the expense of having her solo as the special guest even though I realized she was an important historical figure that would bring cache to my program. Also, I couldn't find any of her books anywhere, which was really weird. They were all out of print. So I procrastinated and ruminated about how to deal with the invitation. Then it hit me, *Of course! Miles Davis is the connection, so center the invite around a discussion about him.* Miles was a subject that always brought in a good crowd. People were endlessly fascinated about Miles and any and everything to do with him.

A few weeks later after the luncheon at Stanley Cohen's, I learned that Stanley Nelson's film *Birth of the Cool* was finally being shown in New York at the Film Forum and the Brooklyn Academy of Music. And I thought, *Aha! Maybe Patty and Stanley Nelson* would be a good pairing since Patty's husband's photo of Miles was included in that documentary. I called Patty to see if she'd object to being on a program with Stanley and true to form, she was gracious and open to the idea. I checked with Stanley Nelson's team to see if they were open to the idea and bingo! I had my program set.

I don't know why Patty's death brought me to tears yesterday. I had been unable to cry over Joe Overstreet, or Steve Cannon. No tears for Tammy or Wallace or Driskell, which wasn't surprising since I had no real emotional connection to Wallace or David Driskell, nor Bill Withers and Ellis Marsalis. But Tammy was my niece and she'd died so young and tragically, having just lost both her father, my brother Wash to whom I was deeply connected, and her mother Dorothy with whom I had no particular connection. But somehow Patty, an eighty-five-year-old white woman I'd met a little over a year before (was it that long?) brought my composure, my grief, all crashing down.

Maybe it also had to do with the times we're in. This modern day plague and the incessant sounds of ambulance sirens, the half-deserted streets, the closed shops and mask-covered faces, the discarded rubber white, purple, blue gloves strewn about the streets, the lines of grocery shoppers standing six-feet apart now made to wait outside the supermarkets until allowed entry by a store sentry when it's deemed permissible to allow another few inside to preserve the social distancing now mandated by Governor Andrew Cuomo and Mayor Bill de Blasio. Maybe it's also the pent- up rage, frustrated anger at Donald Trump and his agency of nincompoops, his confederacy of incompetents who mismanage this health crisis at every opportunity in their craven desire to benefit politically, financially, and the impotence it lays on my soul that caused me to cry out on Facebook.

April 5, 2020

Warnings today to cease and desist going to the supermarket and the pharmacy at least for the next two weeks. What is abundantly clear is that those in authority issuing these directives haven't a clue what's happening with this plague. Read a tweet from Charles Blow that a relative of his who's in the health care industry advised to wear glasses, goggles, or some kind of eye protection, because the virus can enter the system through the eyes. Decided to call close friends and neighbors today in addition to taking a stab at housecleaning. Kali called from DC to say that Louise Meriwether has been hospitalized. Annoyed that I didn't know this already; the person I know who knows Louise closest didn't call to tell me. So I started calling friends and finally reached Cheryl to ask about Louise, who I learned has Covid-19 and was taken to St Luke's last Thursday (April 2nd ). I really wanted to yell at Cheryl since she'd been avoiding me anyway but I didn't. Decided to call other people instead of waiting for people to call me. Don't know why I feel like people should call me. But I do. So I started with my neighbor Sidney who had also posted a photo on FB with several of her closest friends that included Gayle. Sidney told me that Gayle has been hospitalized with Covid-19, but her family wants to keep the news private; then she told me about another friend's mastectomy. Shocked, I called my friend. She sounded cheerful but didn't share the news about her own health. I figured she didn't want me to know.

April 6, 2020

Scanned Facebook today looking for the names of friends and loved ones and discovered that Patty's male friend whom I didn't know died the day after she did. I wrote Patty's assistant, Jaime, to express condolences. She replied that she was heartbroken at Patty's death and so I'm sure she's feeling a double whammy right now. Like Davis, Tammy's brother and my nephew. I see he's posting a lot of his thoughts on Facebook and pouring out his grief there. I comment sometimes but often don't because I don't want to put my feelings out like that so publicly. My niece, Kendra, called yesterday to ask if Tammy had died. I felt terrible because I realized I hadn't thought to let her know beforehand. Another indication of how disconnected we are as a family, in spite of the fact we always thought we were so close. Our family is like a forsaken garden, no tending, no nurturing, no replanting. Everything going to seed. As the older generation passes away, we younger ones are dying one by one alone and out of touch with one another, which is brought into high relief by this plague. Especially for me. I really am feeling it.

Sometimes I wonder if it's because I am one of the youngest of my mother's fifteen children, so that at soon-to-be seventy-one years old, I still feel like a child. Growing up I've always felt emotionally isolated.

By the time my mother gave birth to me, she was so overwhelmed with all those other children she depended on them to help raise the rest of us and they themselves needed mothering. I was thinking also that my mother gave birth to nine boys and six girls and, with the exception of her firstborn Dorothy, the rest of us girls came in-between all those males, Betty had four boys ahead of her, Barbara only had one, I had three boys ahead of me and Jackie had none. Dorothy never had an older brother. I think my mother really liked her girls who were almost like firstborns in a way.

The call came in just about the time I'd decided to check. Louise Meriwether is holding on. She's been moved to a rehab center on the East Side, a very good place according to Cheryl, and she's breathing well. Her fever has gone down, but she's very tired and weak. She's only eating pureed foods, no solids. Sleeping a lot. Trying to regain her strength. But Joan Sandler died today. Joan and Louise were very close friends. When I met them, they were a circle: Joan Sandler, Louise Meriwether, Maya Angelou, Vertamae Grosvenor, Jayne Cortez, and Rosa Guy. Joan was an absolutely stunningly beautiful woman to me, made more so because she was extremely cultured and sophisticated. I remember Quincy in his attempt to get me to start writing told me to interview Joan. I did, but nothing ever came of it. I never felt confident about writing and I was hopelessly shy and underexposed. I was just a country girl in the big city and didn't have a clue about all these people I was meeting at the time. I think I wrote something about Joan and gave it to Thomas Johnson who was one of my mentors at *The New York Times*. He was very critical of my writing. I'd always been told I could write well, but I never believed it. Nor did I have any ambitions to become a writer. Come to think of it, I've never had a real passion for any one thing it seems. I am so easily distracted and flit from one thing to the next, never really dedicated to just one goal, one mission. No in-depth attention to any one thing. Flit like a butterfly. Always a quick learner, new ideas attract me, like a bee to honeysuckle.

Those women —Louise, Rosa, Joan, Vertamae —were so strong and powerful. They were quite a bit older than I; I was just a fly on the wall. Nobody cared what I thought and my whole job was to stay out of their way, blend in, don't bring too much attention to myself. Their egos were enormous, almost as large and overwhelming as their accomplishments. They were always kind to me, or shall I say tolerant, and I was with a most domineering and dominant personality who was jealous of his position. So I stayed on the sidelines as much as possible. What did I have to offer? A nice smile. But nothing threatening that would cause me to be unwelcome in their presence. Then again there was so much going on, it was hard to retain everything. It was hard to find a niche when I didn't know who I was or what I wanted. Just being there among them was enough. They all lived in Dark West Village (the apartments on Central Park West from 96th Street to 100th Street, between Central Park and Columbus Avenue). Those were kind of luxury apartment buildings, probably the first upscale apartment buildings on the park where a lot of professional blacks lived and many had terraces.

I listened today for the sirens and I can't really tell if they're more frequent now than before this plague. But they tell me on the television that the calls to 911 have doubled or tripled since the plague. Living in Harlem, close to two major hospitals, actually three if you count Harlem Hospital, I'm used to hearing ambulance sirens, so I can't really distinguish whether there's been an uptick. St. Luke's is just across Morningside Park and Mt. Sinai is half a mile down 5th Avenue. Harlem Hospital is about a mile or so north on Lenox Avenue (Malcolm X Blvd) at 135th Street. Louise Meriwether is at St Luke's I've been told, I think I ought to call but I don't really want to since I imagine they're overwhelmed there with all the Covid-19 patients. Also imagine Louise doesn't have a room with a telephone and that she's probably unable to talk anyway if she has difficulty breathing.

April 7, 2020

Today I took a quick look on Facebook for the dead but I didn't find any people I know and love. Neither did I receive a call or news of a death. I was kept busy all day typing up a list of poems Quincy wants to include in *Duende*, his new book of poems to be published by Seven Stories Press in Spring of 2021. Despite doing the work in front of the television,

I didn't pay attention to the news about the most recent developments during this day of the plague. It seems the number of deaths are subsiding, but the warnings to stay inside were being repeated by almost everyone. Not only stay inside, but if one does go out, one is cautioned to wear eye goggles, a face mask, and gloves. To cover completely in other words. Received an email from Karole offering to bring me turkey soup and homemade bread. I turn her down, despite wanting to ask her to bring me some fresh garlic. Then Chandra calls later in the day. I was sure she'd tell me about Joan Sandler's death. Turns out she didn't know about it herself, so I'm the bearer of that bad news. Chandra was about to make her last trip to the grocery store before sheltering in for the next week or so. I desperately want to ask Chandra to bring me some fresh vegetables, peppers, garlic, and a few other produce items, but I resist the urge.

I spent the day in the bedroom, which is in the rear of the apartment and therefore was unable to hear the sirens. Oh, Julie Park died. She was in the fashion industry and lived in House 3 of the Graham Court. Julie was Korean, and I found out about her death on the Graham Court Tenants Association's Facebook page. I met Julie in the 1980s through Lester Hyatt, a fashion designer with whom Julie worked. Lester gave me three of his designs because he wanted me to model them at work. I worked at that time at *The New York Times*. I never had much contact with Julie, not one that I can recall. Lost touch with Lester when we moved to La Jolla. I think he died of the AIDS virus. When I try to conjure his face, it is a blur, a blank. I will Google him to see if there's a photo. I can't remember how I met Lester. So after doing the Google search I see that he was a native of Panama who moved to NYC at age eighteen and enrolled at Parsons, where he won the Butterick Vogue Young Designer Award during his first year. He interned with Giorgio di Sant'Angelo, and designed for Lady Madonna (a maternity label) for years prior to opening his namesake boutique in NYC. He lived in House 3, so perhaps I met him through Terry Williams, who also lives in Graham Court's House 3 or Jan Williams, Terry's sister, who's since died. We all used to be very friendly back in the 1980s. Harlem was in the middle of the crack wars and all of us bonded together as a kind of wall of protection, I guess, against the dealers and the junkies and the young violent gangs. Harlem was a wasteland; we had no services and there were a lot of vacant lots, abandoned buildings, filthy supermarkets, methadone clinics, junkies lined the streets, and only the bravest shopkeepers kept decent hours. Every shopkeeper hid behind bulletproof glass, and there was lots of crack on the streets and lots of storefronts that sold drug paraphernalia. Everyone did lots of cocaine in the '80s and Harlem was no exception. In those days we were newcomers to the neighborhood so we were regarded with a great deal of suspicion. The building underwent many dark days of no elevator service, no heat, no hot water. Lots of break-ins. At the same time, there was lots of camaraderie; we helped each other. We also had our own storage bins in the basement; we had a Laundromat in the basement. We had our share of hardships too.

I never knew what Julie's job was. I'll have to ply the fog from my memory. I was an activist in the tenant's association; I was the secretary. It was so difficult getting the older, more longtime tenants to work cooperatively. I'm not sure whether Julie died of the plague; it seems she may have had another ailment. Does it matter? It's still during the time of the plague.

April 8, 2020

Tenants are complaining about the theft of packages delivered by UPS and FedEx, which are left in the entry foyers of each building. So far I've not had a problem but residents in Houses 1 and 2 are really bitching about it. Our building has had scaffolding around it for at least two years now. It's mandated by the city and is supposed to be there so that buildings can be inspected for loose bricks but nothing has happened and it encourages people to hang out there. It feels less safe and I had an incident not too long ago where I felt menaced by a pair of young passersby as I was returning home loaded down with groceries and fumbling for my keys as I was trying to enter the gated entry to our courtyard. Luckily, I had the presence of mind to keep my fears suppressed while at the same time projecting an aggressive attitude like, "I'm not the one you want to be messing with." Fortunately, nothing happened but the incident left me a bit shaken when I thought about it afterwards. Made a mental note to stay alert and to not put myself into a vulnerable position like that again, i.e., to have my keys readily available by the time I reach the gate.

Sidetracked today by Anne Moody, the late civil rights activist and author from Gloster, Mississippi, my hometown. Learned so much about her and her work. Didn't know anything about her really and so sad that when I was told that her sister, Adeline Moody, wanted me to introduce her to Danny Glover in 2014, I didn't have enough curiosity to follow up. I did go by their spread though, but everything was gated and awfully unwelcoming. I listened to rumors, no gossip, instead, i.e., that Anne had dementia and the family was secretive and private. It was Dave at the Afro-American History Museum in Natchez who came to see me to tell me Adeline Moody wanted me to introduce her to Danny Glover because she wanted to approach him about doing a movie about Anne's life. If I recall correctly he said that Adeline wanted to be assured though that she'd maintain total artistic control . . .. That turned me off. I was also so focused on my own shit I didn't bother.

It was my first visit for the summer arts camp and I was absorbed trying to get all of that together. I have to revisit my notes to see if I can recall exactly what unfolded. We did go up to the museum though, but I now wonder what would've been the result of that had I taken the time. At the same time, I'd met Austin Straus, who'd spent a couple of days with us in Harlem, after he left Bob Holman's. Austin was such a pain in the ass. OMG. A fantastic artist, he was so self-absorbed and he filled my head with negative ideas about Anne, to whom he'd been married for 10 years and about her sister. Austin claimed he'd been the one to encourage Anne to write her book and that he was in a fight to get co-ownership of her papers, which in my reading today, I learned were sold to Emory University in 2013, which would've been around the time I met Austin. He also told me that his son Sasha was living in Gloster with Anne, and that Anne and her family had turned his son against him. He indicated that Sasha had some kind of mental health issue as did Anne, according to him, so perhaps those things influenced me in a way they shouldn't have. Now six years later I'm reading all this stuff about Anne's life and that E.L. Doctorow had been the editor of her first book, *Coming of Age in Mississippi.* I don't know whether I'd inquired whether Austin and Anne had lived in New York City. I don't think I did nor did I inquire about any of their history I don't think. Learned in my reading today that indeed they'd met in New York at NYU and that Austin was a poet (he may've also told me he was a poet, since he subsequently married Wanda Coleman). I think, too, Austin was so bedraggled and smelly as if he hadn't had a bath or shower in ages that it was hard for me to focus on what he was telling me for the funk emanating from his body. Quincy made him take a shower. Just came right out and said it, "Austin, you need to take a shower." Once he washed up, he turned out to be quite a good-looking man who I imagined must have been killer-looking in his youth. Certainly charming.

He was on a tour selling his art books and sold three to us at an astronomical rate which I ended up not paying for altogether as it turns out because I realized that they were not done on archival paper and were beginning to fade. He stopped bugging me about the payments after a while once I told him that he'd overcharged me. He donated one to my nonprofit and the others I paid for, about $1,000 I think. Must check my records.

I'm beginning to lose interest in the daily briefings from Andrew Cuomo and the nonstop coverage of the coronavirus. It was said that perhaps the number of deaths and the extent to which the plague will kill people may have been overblown. That would not be surprising given how the press is so quick to hype disasters for the ratings I'm sure. Yet, my confidence and everyone else's has been so undermined to the extent that I don't even feel comfortable venturing out. We're still being advised that the worst is yet to come, but we (I) don't really know what the worst is, as far as I'm concerned we are in the worst right now!

April 9, 2020

The first time I've been outside in about two weeks or so. I am wearing my army issue pilots jumpsuit, a lightweight raincoat, my Andrew Yang

MATH cap, a 3M mask that Lisa and Roddey sent me and a pair of purple rubber gloves they also sent. It's warm about 52 degrees, and the trees are blooming. There has been a light rain today and a more serious storm is forecast. I have to go to the pharmacy and decide to do a bit of grocery shopping. I also intend to run the engine of my car, a 2006 Pontiac Grand Prix. It's been sitting on 117th Street one car in from St Nicholas Avenue for two weeks. I think I need to run the engine for at least half an hour to avoid it losing any functionality.

Almost everyone I see on the street is wearing a facemask and/or gloves, except for what appears to be two couples, both apparently millennials, and both have young children. One couple is white the other couple is black. The white couple has a toddler and an infant, a newborn, in a stroller, neither husband nor wife is wearing any protective coverings, neither mask nor gloves; neither is the toddler nor the newborn. My mouth drops open but I hold my tongue. They are walking in front of my building. There's a light rain this morning, so perhaps they think the rain has cleaned the air of any potential virus threat. The toddler has a scooter.

I stopped in Fine Fare Supermarket on my way to the CVS Pharmacy between 115th & 117th Street on Malcolm X Boulevard (Lenox Avenue to us old timers). The last time I was at Fine Fare, they'd begun to control the number of shoppers they allowed entry and so we had to wait in a line outside in order to enter. Today they've a sign that explains why we're waiting outside and how far we need to stand apart in consideration of the social distancing directives. The line is short today, only three of us when I first get in line. The person ahead of me is a young Latino, perhaps, male wearing a DKNY black puff jacket and a surgeon's mask. He's talking on his cellphone. Ahead of him and at the front of the line is an elderly black man with a red shopping cart. He's fully decked with a mask that looks like the white N95 that I'm wearing but it's not the 3M brand I'm wearing. He's wearing a hat and also regular black faux leather gloves. The young man is telling the person, I think it's his woman, that he's talking on the phone with that he doesn't believe the dangers of the virus are real. And the black man interrupts him and says, "If you don't believe it's real, why are you wearing a mask?" The Latino guy mumbles something I can't quite hear. But the young guy doesn't take off the mask. The elderly black man says, "That don't make no sense. If you don't believe it's real, why would you wear a mask?" The Latino man ignores this and continues to talk on his cellphone, mostly about how annoyed he is that we're standing outside the store for what seems like an eternity while several shoppers exit the store, about six or so, and several deliverymen enter the store by manually opening the automatic sliding doors. I too am annoyed and so is the elderly black man at the head of the line but we keep quiet.

Then I see a single black young woman exit the store. She's wearing a gold-colored puff jacket, no hat, no gloves, no eye covering, and she walks down the street. She returns after about ten or fifteen minutes and re-enters the store through the exit door so I assume perhaps she works inside although by her clothing I can't imagine she does and also because she's not wearing any protective clothing. Five minutes or so later, she exits with a small child about three years old and a young man who may be her husband or partner; none of them are wearing any protective clothing.

Inside the store they've put up a transparent shield at all the cash registers and all the cashiers are wearing facemasks and gloves. Stock boys are wearing masks too; I don't pay attention whether they're wearing gloves. No more than about 20 shoppers are inside the store, which is fairly well stocked. I find everything I need without too much difficulty. The only items that seem to be scarce are the dishwashing liquids, hand soap, although I find three, and my brand of floor detergent (lavender Fabuloso) is sold out, so I buy a small bottle of concentrated Pine Sol. I don't know when I'll start cleaning the house. The very thought of it is depressing. The apartment is huge and at this point in my life, the very last chore I want is to clean it.

Two doors down from Fine Fare is a CVS Pharmacy. I go there to pick up prescriptions for Quincy and me. CVS has a self-checkout counter at the front and the pharmacy is in the rear of the store. In fact I visit CVS first before I go to Fine Fare because I know they're not going to have the prescriptions ready and I was right. When I enter, there are two greeters at the entry, they also have sanitation wipes at the entry and the greeters are wearing masks and gloves. I bypass them markers on the floor six feet apart and the counter has been marked off as well. It's ten o'clock in the morning or so and there are very few shoppers. Counting me there are no more than five shoppers inside. There's one person ahead of me. She's wearing the mask and gloves. They've hung clear shower curtains at all the counters and behind the counters the workers are wearing masks. The cashier is wearing gloves but no mask. He beckons the woman ahead of me to come forward and she stands behind the six-foot marker. He can hardly hear what she says so he beckons her to approach closer. I don't know why they have the six-foot marker at the counter since they have the transparent plastic shower curtain there hung from the ceiling with a cutout opening near the debit card reader and an opening to pass the items through. They are well protected. I'm impressed with the changes they've made and stunned that it's taken so long—at least a month or two—to get this done.

Perhaps it's because according to news reports more people of color and in particular African Americans have died of this plague. Perhaps it has taken the general public this long to figure out this novel coronavirus is really real. After picking up my prescriptions and completing my shopping, I walk back to Seventh Avenue to my apartment and decide I'll stop by the deli on the corner of my block to see if they have *The New York Times* and *Daily News*. I also want to buy a lottery ticket. At the deli, they've taken the door off the entryway altogether and they've put down the masking tape six-foot markers. The cashiers are not wearing masks but they are elevated behind a counter, perhaps standing two feet or so above the ground floor. They are wearing gloves and I notice they are constantly cleaning off the card readers. Most of the people in the store, about six or so including me, stand in line behind the six-foot markers and wait to play the numbers or buy our lottery tickets. I bought the last copy of *The New York Times* and *Daily News*. The rain has stopped. And I cross the street, which I can do even though the light is green because there's hardly any traffic. I feel lucky today and hope I win something. I also hope I haven't picked up the virus.

# POETRY

# "Cora or Soccer Serenade"

by Victor Hernández Cruz

Is a different
Same poetry writes,
The ball is kicked with the feet,
Goes off flight air,
The player surprise who it finds
Could be opposite team.
Sings to his hip knee,
Head ras

Is it not like the writing of poetry,
If the images take place the ball
Bouncing at random, surprise where
It falls,
The players kick it with authority
Dexterity, strength within rapid
Running thought improvisation, swift in
As if sometimes the ball moves itself
Determines its flight,
As in these metaphors that I find
Sometimes ambush me.

Spontaneity similar to basket ball
Split second movements
Which your play partners figure

Instant in tune
What is faster light.

The Tainos used to call it Batu,
Not sure if they had to pass the ball
Through a loop.
If the losers were sacrificed to
The Sun
Or was it the winners
The game was a ceremony
In the batey near statues of Cemis,
After game all broke into feast
173
Under Ceiba trees
Cotton blankets' thrown near
Guayaba bushels
Flesh open.

Alive in soccer is the element of chance
We could say this is luck
Some have it some escape,
It could depend upon cloud formations,
The trajectory of a fly,
A peep a bu of nada,
The ball navigation
Factors the wind, the sun,
If morning afternoon ether,
Terreno upon of which those who run
Earth or artificial green reality grass,
Chance improvisation, luck,
Cora is like life,
The possibilities as to where
We might all land
This Maria go around,
Random seems but look

In silence peace
Pattern shows
As all the befores become afters
Mold this

Something is kicking us around
Forward towards what net,
Or netting
Pink spider webs
An infinity of silence
Felted blue echoes
Our goals are spell bound.

The earth is the ball we bounce
Upon
The hold this Cora game has
Upon the populous
Living Morocco
I tell you when the national team
Has a game everything paralyzes
I mean halt
Grocery Stores close
80 percent population,
Packed into Café
Or home frozen teli,
Collective roars come out
Of Cafes when home team goals,
Beyond fever it is an addiction
So much narrative they get
Out of the foot shuffling
Point toe heel kicks
Backward, right through
Split second open legs,
They just eat the ball,
Observe close the dance,

Swift mambo, early tap-dance
In sideway mode,
Mohammed Ali shuffle
Pre-punch,
Imagine Hakimi stomping roaches
In a New York tenement,

In the antiquity of Latin Americas
Natives Cora football arose
As in China and Japan
All had approximations of the game,
What the British did
What they always do
Was set up a series of rules,
Centuries before they even knew
Of the game,
Natives naked were bouncing balls
Through loops to reach the other
Side of a wall
There was no goals
Play till exhaust.
Team that tired out lost,
On to the dance.
Food, chicha.

The Guarani were primordial
Upon novel soccer
And the origin of the maraca
As its shaking awoke
Dormant spirits in the atmosphere,
Combine with tobacco
A resin circle flies off boundaries
Into Guayaba bushels,
Into the marisco with yucca bowls,
The game must go on

Till the players faint,
There are no winners
There are no losers,
Moton triumph
And the frijoles were amazing.

The ancient world total
Saw something round rolling,
The Greeks, Romans, Scots,
Centro America
Go to Paraguay to see the game
Pure passion
Obsession
Appear surprise chance,
Improve, quick thinking shifts
Thought in flight
Cora is life itself
Destiny Changes
Feet dance flamenco mambo
All movement never rest
Some players have taken their
Last kick and the ball landed
In paradise as the player died.
Soccer is serious occasions
It is the occasion of the question,
Itself
Think air enclosed in rubber
In horse hide,
The Olmec were called the rubber
People by the Aztecs,
They traded in rubber
Full Mesoamerica balls which were bouncing
Near the pyramids,
Through jungle valleys, the tune
Of conch shells gathers the tribe,

Testicle played testicle
Seashell against seashell,
Sometimes men and women
Play in unison,
The swing of the hammock
Corn aroma, saltine hot moist,
Juicy air, a sweet secret fruit
In my hands,
Punta pie upon a spot
Of the circumference of the bola,
Trajectory projected,
Keep mental fixed
As the ball has its own mind,
Goes above net
Skyway the stands,
Hits beer cup in some hands,
Ruben Blades song
"la vida tiene sorpresas"
Melody on
This game is a balance of
Talent and luck, chance.

Military strategist let the generals
Come out
Eleven men spread, the center
Kicks out towards the troops,
As forward charge in zig zagging
Math, the swift agitation dizzy
Opponents till dunk ball
Flew net
Ball in rectangular shape net
Target
Circle dip engaged.

Players sometimes take it
Slam nose, on the mouth,
Center ball on eye ball upon,
The back, knee, buttock culo ass,
If not opposite team's elbows
Head bangs I mean smash
Add the constant motion the
Hundreds who died from the workout,
Soccer can kill you,
As life can kill you as well,
With all the addition, subtraction
Of possible outcomes.
If we were just antiquity
And played till exhaustion
Current must be a winner.
Someone over someone else
National countries come into shine,
As Honduras El Salvador
Who actually went to war circa 1969
Behind a disputed call some referee,
Which prevented El Salvador
From reaching the finals
What WHAT
Was that for, the presidents discussed
The matter
Boiled over, armies amassed at
The borders
Yes el Salvador invaded Honduras,
Armies went at each other,
Both sides had used World War ll
Bomber planes, explosions away
All told 3,000 people on both
Sides were killed,
Behind that round little ball.

Cora is Cora

# Holler / Grito

by Juan Felipe Herrera

In memory of Tyre Nichols & Alonzo Bagley,
Rest in Power & so many killed w/o a cause

Tyre
we become you we
pummeled kicked down asphalt kicked again
choked chased
tasered shot whipped sprayed again dragged
policias w/ kevlar w/badge w/stripes
w/Glock w/ thick jackets glance
— once sisters once brothers
[Daunte Wright]/RIP
once our brothers once our sisters
they come forth they step back
last dance on Castlegate Lane corner
Memphis Tennessee
[Breonna Taylor] RIP

houses on the block quiet
lawn grasses turn to you
sharpened by the mower
[Atatiana Jefferson] RIP

we hold you up
we are here with you
bluish folds of night darkens
[Aura Rosser]RIP67

## Tyre

we become you
tonight falling & slide down
cop car door
broken we lift you up
miles away we hold you
we are here here

[Stephon Clark]RIP

you fall to the right
we lean to the right
you lean to the left you fall to the left
Tyre gone now

[Philando Castile]RIP

we wipe away your blood
swollen forehead
chest busted
heart kicked
Tyre Tyre Tyre you will not perish
you will not
fall again

[Alton Sterling]RIP

we carry you through green mist
we bring you home we wash your splintered
swollen body burst
inside we take you to Mama
thousand miles out & millions
cry w/our voices
w/our lives
set upon you you

[Freddie Gray]RIP68

love is infinite
gardens blossom Tyre
w/your last breath-sounds
your voice is our voice

[Janisha Fonville]RIP

we offer our gathering
our skateboards
rough painted torn sky brave
colors of street fire

[Michelle Cusseaux]

RIP
we offer our gathering
our skateboards
rough painted torn sky brave
colors of street fire

[Michelle Cusseaux]

RIP

[Tamir Rice]RIP
[Michael Brown]RIP

this caldron of massacres
shootings & stabbings & bullets
the firing hand the choking hand
the kicking boot the taser ring fingers at hand
whipping stick whipping
carving your back as if in slave time
[this time] :: gun hands same hands
so many violent Americas

[Tanisha Anderson]

RIP69
we become you we carry you
we write you poems
hit the high G's in the night choir

[Andre Hill]RIP

we carry you home
wet streets flaming boulevards
we are calling all
trains of Freedom

[Manuel Ellis]RIP

here we stand now
brave & determined

Saturday morning breakfasts
like in ’68 & ’69
murals of unity — Peoples’ Parks
sufferings of history
we remember John Brown
we remember Frederick Douglass
we remember & sing their names
your name so many names

[Botham Jean]RIP

we continue Tyre
today we carry you
this is our truth now
cornerground & underground

each night flower a song
each song a night candle
each night candle a poem70
each poem a night circle
each circle a people
all people all America

we holler Coltrane
your vastness across this Earth
we will plant kindness we will plant compassion
take the seed of friendship & humanity
to every house a Love Supreme
a Giant Sequoia rises below the fenders & breaks
out of the asphalt impossible arms &
takes account with impossible eyes
there
will be

no traffic stops no batons
no kicking boots no frenzied tasers
no hungry Glocks no melancholy AR’S

no bear sprays to death no plantation sticks
we will light & heal all the broken bodies
we will be marching together

[Akai Gurley]RIP

**For Those with a Gun, a Taser, a Night stick,**
**& Coiled Vestments of Power When One Moonbeam**
**on the Broken Corner Was Enuf —**

Once we were brothers sisters
when did violence unfold its volcanic shafts
its tentacles its coils & take you?
Why did you slash the Circle of Oneness?
Now you leave us bleeding on the edges
of all things

[George Floyd]RIP
[Alonzo Bagley]RIP71

Tyre
lead us to our new home
our non-violent America our true Freedom
with you we will become the infinite circle
the New America your name in every sunrise
winds pass through trees
leaves turn Tyre
doves wait on limbs
earth shakes the earth
this is when we shall holler
TYRE NICHOLS ¡PRESENTE!
true America
America Verdadera

from *California Brown*, Mouthfeel Press, 2024
Juan Felipe Herrera

**Sean Hill's Poems**

from *Blood Ties & Brown Liquor*
Silas Wright

from *Dangerous Goods*
Photograph

from forthcoming collection, *The Negroes Send Their Love*
*Musica Universalis* in Fairbanks
The White-headed Woodpecker
Imagine We're Ancestors Dreaming

Acknowledgments:

The Academy of American Poets' *Poem-a-Day*, "The White-headed Woodpecker"
*Alaska Quarterly Review*, "*Musica Universalis* in Fairbanks"

"Imagine We're Ancestors Dreaming" was commissioned by the Natural Resources Defense Council (NRDC) and published on their website alongside poems by Rachel Eliza Griffiths and Jane Wong as part of a Spring 2023 special poetry feature, Poets Imagine a Different Climate Narrative: https://www.nrdc.org/stories/poets-imagine-different-climate-narrative.

**Silas Wright at Age Seven 1914**

Silas Wright follows a fish's wriggle
In the shallows between reeds. He scribes the
Line in his tablet—as much pride in that line
As a man in his son. He almost giggles—
Still he goes on. The next letters come easy.
With this he'll have more than a mark to bind.
Rambling across the page again and again
In messy rows on it flows until he

Goes a little off the page's edge. He smiles.
He's surprised to hear when his mouth opens—
*That's mine.*

### A Photograph Taken in Duluth

My grandmother says *Beg Pardon* when she hasn't heard
        what you've said or is certain
you can't have meant what she heard like *I think the moon must*
        *have squinted at the dim light*
*of that gas lamppost and the three men that hung from it.*
        What I mean is three men, black,
in town with the circus, accused of the usual
        lynch-law crime were chosen
from six and dragged from jail one by one by men who'd formed a
        mob, propped up by thousands
of bystanders who didn't join in with the hoisting
        of these black men up the lamppost
for allegedly violating a white woman—of course—
        but registered approval
with fists and feet while they made way for the black men
        or didn't stop the hand or foot
of the woman or man next to them, so three beaten
        bodies violently shook,
shuddered, sputtered blood on those close by and came to rest.

        My grandmother says *Hush* when
she's heard what you've said and doesn't want to believe it.
        But I have a photograph—
proof of what happened in Duluth. For that I must say
        *Thank you kindly* (that's how
my grandmother always says it) to a photographer
        from just across the bay in
Superior, Wisconsin, on hand with the thousands
        of other souls crowding downtown

Duluth that June evening. I know he didn't take it
    for me. My grandmother says
*Have mercy* when she's heard a burdensome truth
    such as the photograph was soon
made into a postcard that sold quite well in local retail
    outlets as a memento.

My grandmother didn't know these men; she wasn't born
    yet, but doesn't need to be shown
this photograph to know the crowd of white faces
    staring into the searchlight.
Some lean forward and stretch their necks to make certain they're
    in the picture, one smiles while
Elias Clayton's body lies face down at his feet
    (hung so high they had to cut
him down to be in the shot) and Isaac McGhie
    and Elmer Jackson hang with their
necks stretched, heads lolled to the side, faces turned as if they
    should be the ones bearing
the shame or regret. This photo isn't necessary
    for my grandmother to know
that this happened, and can still happen. And that's why
    my grandmother sighs and says *Hush*.

### ***Musica Universalis*: A Nocturne**

– October, Fairbanks, Alaska

Each night this 21st-century frontier town settles
enough for me to hear the thrum and hiss in my ears,
my tinnitus, which I choose to think of as the harmony
of my firmament—all so far away—like the whoosh
and hiss from Nana's gas heater that warmed the winter-
chilled bedroom in Georgia while she got the skillet sizzling
with country-cured ham in the kitchen. My refrigerator
occasionally wakes this hour to clear its throat and rumble

on over the sounds in my ears. And some nights I get out
of bed to go stand under the generosity of stars here—I've
decided that must be the collective noun for all the stars
in one's gaze as it must also be for any number of scars, the way
we refer to a flock of starlings as a murmuration. I stand
there and use my hand to shade my eyes from the streetlights
to better see the stars. Our new light competes with the old
the way the clamor of our fleets in this age after sails is said
to interfere with the songs of whales. Here I sometimes see
the aurora borealis, silent, which seems impossible like the end
of the world for what we know of light in the sky—lightning
and, its often not-far-off companion, thunder—seems to say
something will always follow. Some say the northern lights
sizzle—an impossibility, a synesthetic weaving of the senses
exalting this light, or a lark like the bird which we call
an exaltation when in numbers great or small—more than
a handful, the way a friend used to count lovers when we
were younger, told me he was on to the second hand.
Love, while a lark, still handled carefully in those days.
I should drive out of town to view these lights against
the sky—black as a raven. They often fly in pairs or groups
—a conspiracy, a storytelling, an unkindness of ravens.

first appeared in the *Alaska Quarterly Review*

The White-headed Woodpecker

Quiet. Given to prying more than pecking, an odd member
of the family, lives only in the high pine forests of western

mountains like the Cascades, where I spent an afternoon
almost a decade ago in Roslyn, Washington looking for what

I could find of Black people who'd migrated from the South
almost a century and a quarter prior. The white-headed

woodpecker doesn't migrate and so is found in its
home range year-round when it can be found. Roslyn,

founded as a coal mining town, drew miners from all over
Europe—as far away as Croatia—across the ocean, with

opportunities. With their hammering and drilling to extract
a living, woodpeckers could be considered arboreal miners.

A habitat, a home range, is where one can feed and house
oneself—meet the requirements of life—and propagate.

In 1888, those miners from many lands all in Roslyn came
together to go on strike against the mine management.

And so, from Southern states, a few hundred Black miners
were recruited with the promise of opportunities in Roslyn,

many with their families in tow, to break the strike. They
faced resentment and armed resistance, left in the dark

until their arrival, unwitting scabs—that healing that happens
after lacerations or abrasions. Things settled down as they do

sometimes, and eventually Blacks and whites entered a union
as equals. Black save for a white face and crown and a sliver

of white on its wings that flares to a crescent when they
spread for flight, the white-headed woodpecker is a study

in stark contrasts. Males have a patch of red feathers
on the back of their crowns, and I can't help but see blood.

first appeared in The Academy of American Poets' *Poem-a-Day*

## Imagine We're Ancestors Dreaming

And suppose the seas rose; what if megafires,
I mean, what if blossoms come too early, blooming
before the last frost, so starvation's looming for

the bees looking for petals to slide between.
Suppose a hundred-year drought for our loves
and bomb cyclones and hurricanes for what's

held in a palm and most all our conveniences
—our modern balms or what we take to be
necessities, things assuming roles as central

as the heart and our beloveds as we lean away
from our relations with human and nonhuman
beings, ones that if tended could blossom. Too

early blooming drives famished bears to scavenge
alleys for trash alms before they can retire to dens
under fur and fat blankets, warm. Imagine massacres

or holding folks as property, presuming a narrow
definition of worthy relations to screen others out
—the point of who is kin drawn keen. Suppose seas

of change rose once and can again, I mean, suppose
heart and imagination—hope in our time to remedy
questions or statements as dooming as *what if*

*blossoms come too early, blooming? Suppose*
*a hundred-year drought for our loves and balms.*

first appeared on the Natural Resources Defense Council (NRDC) website in their *Poets Imagine a Different Climate Narrative* feature

# Four poems

by Ishmael Angaluuk Hope

*Note: These poems are from Ishmael Angaluuk Hope's upcoming collection,* Story Lyric. *"Dance Practice" was first published on "Poem-a-Day" (online, 2020). "We Will Emerge" was written for PEN America, organized by Wajahat Ali and Dave Eggers. Ali and Eggers asked writers, leaders, and celebrities to write a response to the recent crises in America in recent times: the pandemic, the political instability. They were requested to start the writing with "We will emerge" and to end it with "We will emerge and find a better way," and to write as we wish in between. "Discourse Patterns" was originally written for a commission with Stuart Hyatt's audio project,* Remote Hymns, *at the Anchorage State Museum, 2020. "The Birth of Art" is in response to reading Tlingit writer Louis Shotridge's magnificent "The House of Sáanáxhéit in Dream Land," (University of Pennsylvania Museum of Anthropology, Louis Shotridge Digital Archives).*

### Dance practice

Fannie Akpik
leads her dance group
at the high school hallway in Utqiagvik.
Voice
clear as a loon's call,
tender

as the warm center of the lagoon where dreams come to surface.
Songs erupted from the Qargi,
flash in the dark,
piece of the moon bitten off,
landing at the tip of the drum stick.
Sealgut covering of prayers
whirring like wind slipping into tied-up hoods.
Whalers come home
to their Elders' voices,
their hands that shape sod and clear snowy pathways,
enunciating real people sounds that shiver
on the tunnel between the heart and throat.

**We will emerge...**

And watch opera,
host potlatches, complete
rites for the dead,
put on avant-garde exhibitions, stage
happenings.
We will give long hugs,
sing karaoke
after the night's reading, mingle
romance with art, make bold statements
and lots of babies.
We will figure a way out of this,
listen to Elders, learn languages,
reweave the symbiosis
that webs
the sliver of geology we briefly occupy.
We will hold
and hold, and
hold
the rings of the oldest tree,
the bear's den where the bear is sleeping

and hearing everything,
and the dreams that we came to be
from what the land told us.
We will emerge
and find a better way.

## Discourse patterns

The breath
organizes thought,
rearranges and makes strange,
bounds over its own mind, seeks glitches,
like Elders mapping the land
as if words have material body.
With each brushstroke,
I gesture to the abstract expressionists,
and the surrealists, too,
who were exposed to the old truths,
the totem carvers and mask makers,
burning from within,
like Rilke's vision of Apollo's torso,
like bioluminescent fur.
They ride the world's knife edge,
slip glimpses, make sculptures
so real they blink,
set off tiny love bombs in the heart,
tell more than what they know.
Nutrient-rich
watershed eddies,
nourishing the salmon
who settle in the cold.

## The birth of art

A young woman's dream became Northwest Coast art.
She told the people what she saw,
in the undersea house.
All these years later, her dream
is re-elicited,
multiplied,
spread out,
bloomed and wilted and replaced again,
from her dream.
It is an honor
to have loved,
mulled,
pondered,
over hundreds of hours,
the living drama of a young woman's beautiful dream.

# Three Poems

by Genny Lim

## Century of Rage

This country makes you weep
Half our forests, rivers and mountains ruined
This country makes you angry
Howling wolves, wild horses hunted down
This country dishonors life and praises
Death in battle hymns and flag-draped eulogies
Of twenty-five units gone to kill strangers
Twenty-two wiped out
Of the three returning, none revel in the
Glory of lost comrades and limbs

This country ransoms the flesh of migrants
And immigrants languishing in burning deserts
And prison camps after scaling a border wall
Where the sun and moon don't shine without
A crack of light to enter

These streets bury its shame and hoards
Its wealth in bank bailouts and stock buybacks
While the rest of us live paycheck-to-paycheck
In search of the American Dream

This country makes you forget its

History of betrayal with its
Counterfeit victories that rise
Like Twin Towers of illusion over
The specter of Sitting Bull's ghost

## From Here to Gaza

Death never saw itself coming
Only the eerie silence just before
heaven blew up and the
olive trees burst into flames
At that interminable moment
all the exits from Gaza were sealed
and the key to your home became
a souvenir in the mausoleum of your dreams
When the roof of darkness caved in
the Sea of Galilee turned red and
there was nowhere to go
Time was a thief your memory froze
Little did you know the terror in your heart
had been there all along from birth
like a little mouse trapped in a cage
Little did we Americans know that the
distance from here to Gaza was an illusion
and that the border between Palestine and
Israel did not truly exist, ever, except in fiction
History is occupied territory and
whoever lives to tell it is the victor
There are no more lions, only hunters
with power over life and death
What's left? Only stories of the Flower of Jericho?
Only the place where Jesus fasted for forty days and forty nights?
You've nothing but stones to fill the empty Temple Mount
Your hunger echoes in its desecrated ground and
through the tunnels of insurgent prayers

Never to be satisfied until the river returns
to the sea and the Right of Return is reality
You will know that moment, when life returns
with the infallibility of spring because
your spirit will soar on the chords of the wind
and life will know itself becoming!

## War

War is madness
You ask yourself
What lies beyond the power of a bomb?
Beyond the artillery of words?
Beyond the firing squad of the *'Liberator?'*
Who hands you a map in exchange for your land?
What is Empire but the slaughterhouse of dreams?
A hungry ghost that feeds on itself?
The President yells, 'Rise!'
Beating his chest in the display of chief gorilla
And everyone rises!
He raises the flag of victory over the wounded
And corpses of innocents, as if their blood were
The Biblical parting of the Red Sea
War doesn't forgive, nor does it accept
The law of cause and effect
Above the conquest of nature
As if killing were godly
And fighting, the endgame for peace
War is death
It's mangled limbs, smoldering roofs, iron walls
Turned to rubble and ash
It's a black cloud of meaningless suffering
Under which both, victor and loser
Cling, as parasite to host
Consuming humanity

# Six Poems

by Nancy Mercado

### New York at 42

Twenty-five years later New York
and I'm still in love with you
like the husband I've never had
who is patient and tends to me
and is beautiful

I see the friends I love in you New York
and smell our home cooked meals
taste our arroz con gandules
our sushi and chicken korma
our tortellini and crème caramels

and hear the many tongues
that describe what you are

New York City

Your pedestrian-ridden streets
of men on Washington Heights corners
whistling daily at women going by
of frenzied Herald Square shoppers

and SoHo's privileged class

and hear the many intricate songs
of birds flying in Central Park

New York City

The songs of those
migrating over your rivers

Grateful for all that you are
for years of lessons I learned
in Harlem and Morningside
for the memories you gave
a naïve young girl

New York City

of the massive beauty
of your stacked skyline

**Ushering in Armageddon**
on the eve of trump's election

We rapidly disappear all drinkable water
ramming engorged steel pipes
like a rapist's penis into the earth
injecting its insides of vile poisons
lacerating its core
leaving warm radiant grasslands
stippled of dark gray gaseous machines

Rusting oozing mucus onto the countryside
choking-vaporous clouds rising from rivers
waterways cloaked with upended salmon
beaver

birds
assorted insects we'd yet to encounter

Mass extinctions
of other life forms run amuck
before us
because of us

We indulge in gluttony
zealots for crude oil
nuclear fuel and intangible futures

We indulge in greed
crazed for imbecilic video games
prime time and commercial ads
making others rich
and our minds poor

We coddle our narcissism
the idea that we are invincible
all-knowing
masters of the universe
superior to all life forms
yet ignorant of countless creatures
inhabiting the black depths at the bottom
of our own planet's seas

We sentence ourselves to wrath
placing madmen at the helm of a nuclear empire

We fornicate
with money and palm oil lovers
torching vast swaths of earth's forests
decimating acres at whim

We sentence ourselves to deception
choosing fanciful illusions

We are leviathan stars
on a global stage
existing only inside
the flat screens of our cracked skulls

We sentence ourselves to sloth
lethargically sitting by
witnessing the implosion
of even our own families
never lifting a finger
never troubling our carcasses
out of cushy cheap sofas bought at Walmart
on Veteran's Day sales

We splatter everything over
with syrupy affirmations
that disguise our crimes
that masked our cataclysms
our inertia
our self-inflicted Armageddon

like a junkie shooting up
that last dose of bad endings
a rehashed nightmare

How utterly foolish we are.

## I Come to See for Myself: On the Anniversary of Hurricane Maria

I fly in to see for myself
below, blue tarps over the homes of my nation
like those silver blankets that cover the souls
of Mayan and Arawak children locked inside cages
on the US mainland I left behind.

Arriving home, I enter a mass of confusion
plantain crops walloped in their places of birth
five-foot-tall grass rebelliously advancing to heaven
my mother's lemon tree on her last leg
hunched over, barely breathing.

I witness it for myself
splintered wooden electrical poles
held up by a neighbor's twine
trees arrowed through one another
now growing sideways, surviving.

Not the palm trees though
the palm trees chose victory or death
no in-between half-hearted living
some growing new hair
others simply guillotined
by Maria's detonation.

I walk into the new growth of forest
detect the low lamenting sounds of the injured there
witness the anger etched into the undulating
mountains surrounding me in the distance.

I see the US cavalry arrived just in time
Cortez and Columbus repackaged
into a 21st century nightmare

armies in metallic flying machines
using talking devices, exchanging messages
in a foreign language through invisible airways.

I see the cavalry arrived to help
themselves to the casinos they built
to hurl paper towels at the local mortician
to seize their opportunity to maximize
on the extinction of the natives
keeping them in drawn-out darkness
with no power to run hospitals
no shelter, with no water.

I cross the land
from West to East, South to North
to see the revelers and the ruined for myself
to lend an ear to survivors and to the dead
see shuttered schools for miles along the route,
I run out of fingers
on which to count them all

*part of the plan to ruin us*
a small voice reminds me.

I walk along the turquoise shore
lined of amputated homes
crumbled fences
collapsed doorways into the sea
inside, bits and pieces of families remain
their vestiges now
across the Atlantic at the opposite end.

Back in Ponce, I sit in my mother's rocking chair
watch my neighbor's hummingbirds
who've arrived to visit her ruby coral bells
I think of my father's strength

in his humility, he walked in silence
built a house to withstand
a cyclonic catastrophe.

I've seen for myself
the natives are
the majesty of this world
together they've cleared the paths
sawing, hewing through mammoth
barriers of deceit and loathing
retrieved their own water
traversing the inundation
of Washington's elite
that vowed to drown them.

They went about their lives
by the light of a candle
or an old wooden light pole
they stitched back together
with all the love on Earth
maneuvering through a world of cadavers
inside Maria's eye
amid the tantrums of the privileged
a nation held its ground.

Now, raises its foundation
of ancestral eminence anew.

## Journey from the Plague

Hellish sirens bend with distance
through a day's gray mists
sounds of birds emerge
claiming my mind's eye

My childhood appears
my mother shields us from
freezing unbridled winds
using a butter knife
stuffing toilet paper into
our rattling cracked window frames

i follow her
mimic her at 7 or 8
i follow my mother from window frame
to porous window frame
 Then
sirens
dissolve my memory again
Returned to my cloistered quarantine

Do I hurl my self
into a shuttered city
emptied hollowed-out
save for ambulances transporting the dead
birds and pigeons insects and mice
the trees and the flowers of spring?

## My Black Family

The blue-black skin of my grandfather
is not to be sold or brought
or broken into pieces for your enjoyment

My Black and Brown family
with shimmering dark clouds for hair
enshrine humanity
they are not for slaughter or poisoning
or target practice for your pastime

They are the sovereign of this universe

They work for God

They birthed you and your family
invented food for your existence
prayed and sang-out for your absolution

Midnight-blue folk are the creators of things
from the moment you materialize into this world
they make your joy possible
ensure your progress in this existence

God's appointed guardians of this planet
They come from the third sphere of light

Hard as you try
you will not ever
do away with them.

## A Halo for Mahsa

*for Mahsa Amini*

My hair intimidates you?

The mane that tells the story of my family
what protects my beauty
my crown of glory?

My hair intimidates you?

These flowing threads sweeping the earth
what I fiddle with day and day
twisting combing brushing twirling releasing
what dresses me           my braided halo?

My hair intimidates you?

So much so that you ripped it from my skull
So much so that you left my body strewn across a filthy jail cell?
My hair? What now blankets my sinless grave?

# “Panoramic”

by Tracy K. Smith

I

If we’re lucky, it’ll go on, this
Poem we’re writing together,
Like a winding mountain pass,
A place to journey through on the way
to where we hope to get to.

That we’re writing it together
Doesn’t make it the same
For me as for you. My lines
Zag and ripple back: rain
On water in wind. Yours

Are cloudless, telegraphic:
Songbirds busy with morning’s
Matter. Can we trust us
To follow that future music
Past the edge of familiar

Woods? This tune for what
We’ve never yet thought
To sing or say to anyone?
Can we ferry hope?
Can we outpace fright?

That we write it together
Doesn't guarantee what it will
Mean to you, to me. Begun,
It hurries ahead. We scurry
To help it along to where

We say we hope to get to.

II

Do you—
Can you see it?

At the horizon seam
Of undifferentiated sea?

What we are just now
Fathoming into being?

hadows surge beneath
A roof of waves.

Sunlight tilts and pools
Above. The nothing

That isn't possible
Flares in the mind

Of a school
of squid, becoming
The everything
That is.

III

*If we're lucky, it'll go on, this poem*
*We're writing together—a place*

*To journey through on the way*
*to where we hope to get to—*

Strike lucky, insert: brave.
Strike hope, insert: need.
Strike together, insert:
There is no difference between

What waits for you and
What's coming for me. Strike
Place, insert: where I am
no longer afraid. Strike hope,

Insert: remember. Insert:
What has been frightened
Into hiding, scrolled up,
Buried deep. Strike

Where we say we hope to get to.

Insert whatever in your mouth
Means: Everyone, Every One,
Every ever-once-was-one,
Insert: Where everyone is free.

# TRIBUTES

## Tribute to the late Rudolfo Anaya

by Jimmy Santiago Baca

Rudy,

I can see you now, you had a little jaunt in your step, a scarcely visible skip and roll, the result of childhood polio. That thick black and graying hair could have made you in Hollywood, I envied the hell out of it. But there was nothing to compare to your smile when you welcomed people, always willing to give your time and consejos to young writers, including me. We come from the same area, el llano, and from where you grew up it's only a half day's ride by horse to Estancia, where I was living with my grandparents for a time before the authorities took me and my brother away to a boarding school and then a catholic orphanage where I stayed for 12 years. And believe it or not, when I got out 12 years later and went to live with my tia Charlotte y tio Tranquelino, I attended Harrison Jr. High for a week or so before deciding never to go back. This was the school where you taught and were a counselor, and I've often wondered what the hell happened in you to strike such a masterpiece as your novel, *Bless Mi Ultima*. I mean, you were an accountant, a teacher, a counselor, and then the muse came down. You're an MMA fighter on the top rope lunging down all six-hundred pounds raw savagery on you and boom! cabron, you wrote a masterpiece. How the hell does that happen? You shot into global fame and never forgot your roots or your gente.

You loved your trees and flowers and mother earth. When I first rolled into Burque on my 45 Pan Head Harley, pistol in my waistband, and not entirely clean but struggling with my addiction, you took me in into your trust no questions asked. You respected my work and showed it by offering me help signing up at UNM and hiring me to landscape your house and paint all 40 of your apartments that you owned by the zoo. They were a mess and I went down there every day to paint and scrape and renovate and you'd stop by almost every day to chat and share tacos. I felt so terrible when I borrowed your wife Pat's truck, handed to her by her father, and Bob and I went to gather rocks for a fireplace I was building at my place, and after loading up, we stopped at an Indian bar in San Felipe and Bob got drunk and we ended up in a brawl, in the midst of which we hightailed it out and got into the truck and I spun rubber out of there and flipped the truck over and screwed it up bad—the whole body bent and dented and scraped up. I felt horrible. I had to tell Pat what I did, and she forgave me and you shook your head and said it happens, and I promised to fix it up and I did, near to new as possible.

There were things happening in my life that saddened you. When my house burned down and I drove up that night to find red lights and fire trucks and firemen sloshing around the charred debris, there you were waiting in your car and you walked up and took my infant boy from my wife's arms and said you'd take care of him while we dealt with the fire. There were times you called to give me readings offered to you just so I could have a little extra money for a growing family with bills and debts. You invited me over to your pad so many times and fed me and we laughed and joked and took walks, you mentioning often what a gift I had, for poetry and never to abuse it.

But I did. I quit writing, I befriended gangsters and criminals and you helped pull me out, appointing me to scholarly committees, UNM panels, literary festivals and conferences, we joined forces as literary giants and spoke for our Raza, demanded equity in publishing, took on racist school policies, spoke out when we had public forums. It was a wonderful time, the academic and the Vato teaming up, in unbreakable carnalismo.

I regret not having gone to see you more in the later years. We grew apart. Distant. But my feelings toward you have never changed, you were a true warrior, a relentless defender of my cultura, someone who really made a difference for us Chicanos, you, through your brilliant work and visions, made the world respect us and accept us as equals—for which we continue to honor your memory.

# Bob Callahan—A tribute

by Pat Goggins

"I'll cross that Bridge," Bob Callahan said to me.

He was referring to a beau monde mind & soul set—We had met halfway in San Francisco's Irish community, Bob from Connecticut & Columbia and me from Montana & Notre Dame.

Bob had done what a princely black Beatnik in Mike's North Beach Pool Hall had once counseled me to do— "Get Hip to Yourself." Bob knew who he was—a multi-cultural phenomenon—and he looked like it—the hair of a Bohemian and the flair of a maestro. Bob and his bold poet wife Eileen had hooked up and down with diverse thinkers, doers and free academics to form Turtle Island Press, an American publisher of fiery alternative writers, including Jaime de Angulo, Edgar Anderson, Carl Sauer and Ishmael Reed.

During my tour of duty ranked as an officer of the Irish Literary & Historical Society I was frequently referred to establishmentarian publications such as "Eire-Ireland" of the Irish American Cultural Institute out of St. Paul, Minnesota, as the standard bearer of worthy Irish American writing or "The Recorder" of the American Irish Historical Society out of New York or even "Literature in Irish" published by the Department of Foreign Affairs in Dublin. All were excellent, of course, with their reps of accepted writers. I even recommended a couple original writers submit manuscripts to the lofty above—and I lick my lips with laughter when I remember them receiving instant denials—**because** they did not have PhDs. They were just creative. Turtle Island

Titles therefore provides the oxygen we need to breathe relief and sigh with gratitude. With Life.

Throughout 60s and 70s I was civil rights and anti-war involved with cousins of all color and particularly with Indians on the Montana/Dakota Reservations I grew up on and around. Thus I found sync with Bob Callahan and was always revivified.

In 1980 I was with an Irishman, who was nursing a phony Irish coffee, at the Star and Plough Irish Pub in San Francisco—name of Jarlath O'Connor of Harrington's Moving and Storage. The "Troubles" in Northern Ireland had us vexed and we decided to educate ourselves, and others, on the violent conflict by creating a fair platform to present authentic voices to speak for themselves rather than be demonized by de-tractors from across the whole damn spectrum! Boom! Demonstrations and bomb threats resulted within such bastions of San Francisco freedom as Grace Cathedral and the University of San Francisco. Because it was taboo and mortal sin to talk with any opposition.

Our first two Northern Ireland speakers were from the non-sectarian Alliance Party.

Bob Callahan joined Irish Forum and connected us with our first speaker from the Republic of Ireland, Tim Pat Coogan, author of *On the Blanket* about protesting Irish Republican prisoners in the "North." Coogan himself said the California Irish Forum members themselves comprised amazing diversity.

This event was a significant exemplar of Turtle Island extension as Bob Callahan brought black author Ishmael Reed to the San Francisco Irish Center way out on the avenues where the Irish live and thrive. Ishmael met noted Ireland author Tim Pat and also mingled with the San Francisco Irish daredevil journalist Warren Hinckle, all while getting a taste of the Irish social/politico craic. The ballroom attendees eyeballed Ishmael too as the quite well known African American writer sportingly acquitted himself in that Hiberno civil rights activity. The undersigned Pat Goggins who had worked with black politico leaders like John George who became the first black Chair of the Board of Supervisors in Alameda County was thrilled to welcome Ishmael, a champ of independent thought and social movement. This drop-in by Ish is in his signal scouring book *Airing Dirty Laundry* (1993).

Growing Forum guests included principal Anglo/Irish conflict protagonists and Forum membership grew to 1800 workers, attorneys, doctors, teachers, students, etc. in five California cities. Bob, a valued critic, wrote an even-handed report of our outreach activities. We all absorbed our sweet differences. For example, I discovered that the powerful Orange Order upholding "Protestant Northern Ireland for a Protestant People" had been having secret annual global meetings hidden in the Bay Area. So we recruited the Order's Grand Dragon leader Rev. Martin Smyth to speak at the SF World Affairs Council. Bob and another journalist embraced the Gonzo Journalism style of Hunter S. Thompson and cheerily re-arranged the WAC international flags to devilishly implant the Israeli flag immediately behind Rev. Smyth. Because of my strict non-partisan role as Forum Executive Director, I simply redressed the hi-jinks. Tension was already high. Dear Charlie Laverty, former Sinn Fein prison ship prisoner in Northern Ireland, was so distraught with the Orange Order that he chose to beat his own Irish forehead against the wall drawing blood. (Charlie himself was a Forum speaker.) During the post-talk press conference, a wee lad asked me if he could take an envelope in to Rev. Smyth and I obliged. Then when we walked the guest speaker and party to the Union Square parking lot, Rev. Smyth showed me the envelope—it was a death threat. In our Forum decade of promoting dialogue for Peace we had over 300 speakers here and in Ireland . . . with boundless surprises. Bob also gave us downhome humor. Celtic Twinkle.

The Forum tenaciously introduced Bob to community leaders and groups and helped him organize events for his brilliant *Callahan's Irish Quarterly* and his fantastic *Big Book of American Irish Culture*. The first ad, a full page, in *Callahan's Irish Quarterly* premier issue on the inside cover, was from the Irish Forum; a photo entitled "Shopping in Belfast" with a boy casually eating his ice cream cone while holding his mother's cone as she is being searched by armed British soldiers.

We share these legacies with Bob, Eileen, son David and all ye Turtle Islanders.

We know that Bob Callahan is still bridging—untamed, wild and beautifully loved.

With appreciation to Professor James Duran and popular historian Sean Prendiville for their inspiration.

# “As long as the Work Gets Done”: Remembering Andy Hope

by Peter Metcalfe

*Andrew “Andy” John Hope III died at the age of 58 on August 7, 2008, following a brief battle with cancer. At the time of his death, he was executive director of “Sharing Our Knowledge: Conference of Tlingit Tribes and Clans.” Hope previously served as regional coordinator of the Alaska Rural Systemic Initiative of the University of Alaska, as a tribal enrollment officer for the Bureau of Indian Affairs, and as administrator of the Sitka Tribe of Alaska. Andy became a board member in 1976, and during the early 1990s served as president of the Before Columbus Foundation.*

Andrew John Hope III was born to be a leader. His grandfather, Andrew Hope, was a founder of the Central Council of Tlingit and Haida Indian Tribes of Alaska, the regional organization his father, Andrew “John” Hope, later led as President/CEO. Among their many leadership positions, Andy’s grandfather and father both served as Grand Camp Presidents of the Alaska Native Brotherhood, an organization founded in 1912 that championed civil and Indigenous rights. Rather than feeling entitled by this legacy of leadership, Andy assumed the responsibility that came with it by doing the hard work of organizing, promoting, and advocating the interests of Alaska Natives.

The traditional ceremony held in Sitka two days after he passed away served to remind us of Andy’s many foundational contributions to the modern renaissance of Tlingit cultural traditions. It is now commonplace for people of Tlingit heritage to know their Tlingit names and matrilineal clans and clan houses, as well as their fathers' clan associations. More than most, Andy Hope deserves credit for younger generations reclaiming their names and clans.

Andy was my senior by a few years, both of us coming of age in the late 1960s, he in Sitka and me in Juneau. We came to know about each other through our fathers who broadcast basketball games together. Before that, my father Vern served with Andy's grandfather in the Alaska Territorial Legislature of the early 1950s.

When Andy and I became acquainted in our mid-20s we discovered a natural affinity through our family connections, although Andy was of Tlingit heritage, while I am not.

My awakening to Indigenous culture was gradual, but even in my early youth I noted the willful ignorance of White society to the Native culture that was all around us. Andy, naturally, was more aware than I of the gross failure of White people to understand or appreciate Alaska Native culture and history, and he could hardly have ignored the visceral loathing of many Whites for Native language, foods, and lifestyles.

Alaska did not have a tribal reservation system and as Andy and I came of age, segregation was a thing of the past, but racism in all its subtleties had yet to fade away. In those days, I can't remember any Alaska Native grocery baggers or bank clerks. Apparently, my White contemporaries did not want Natives touching their food or money. Those who did not know me well felt free to share their racist sentiments and jokes. It was then exceptional for any of my Native contemporaries to introduce themselves by their Native names and clan affiliations.

As young men, we rebelled against the "establishment," reeling as we were from the threats of being drafted into the Vietnam War, the shocking assassinations, and our awareness of the environmental sacrifices being made at the altar of progress. For me, most damning of all was learning about the atrocities that had been perpetrated against Indigenous populations. Both Andy and I had been raised on the Hollywood cowboy and Indian movies, only a bit more than comic book portrayals of how the "west was won." Not until the early 1970s did that begin to change.

The more I learned about the underlying conspiracy that had suppressed Alaska Native language, culture, history, and folkways, the more I was struck by how incredulous it all was: People I respected, people older and more learned than I—teachers, political leaders, historians—had little to no interest in Native culture.

In the spring of 1970, about the time Andy was attending college classes in Sitka, I graduated from Juneau-Douglas High School. That summer, I took a job as a campaign worker in a statewide U.S. Senate campaign for a Democrat, a "peace candidate ." Soon after my candidate's inevitable loss in the election of November 1970, I took a job in Juneau as a community organizer joining an otherwise all-Tlingit staff of a "War on Poverty" program.

In Sitka, Andy became involved in the serious study of Indigenous topics. With Richard and Nora (Marks) Dauenhauer, two seminal figures in Tlingit and Indigenous studies, he founded Tlingit Readers Inc. in 1972 and became the general editor. With no staff and hardly any funding, Andy managed—with encouragement and involvement of the other founders—the re-publishing of several out-of-print books, essays, and papers by Indigenous Alaska intellectuals (Louis Shotridge, Olaf Abraham, Robert Davis). The team also initiated the "Tlingit Readers Series" that included a "literacy sampler" of Indigenous history, oratory, poetry; a Tlingit/English dictionary; and a key to Tlingit orthography. In 1975, Andy authored "Founders of the Alaska Native Brotherhood," the first such published compilation documenting the lives of the twelve men and one woman who created the organization that was to win civil rights for Alaska Natives and forge the means of winning reparations realized in the 1971 Alaska Native Claims Settlement Act.

While Andy was engaged in this important work, I took a different path. Demoralized by my hometown's inability to shed its latent racism, I went commercial fishing,* briefly attended college, then dropped out

* One minor experience in an otherwise dramatic and life-changing two-years of fishing the Gulf of Alaska with Sam Demmert, a Tlingit from Yakutat, illustrates a cultural tipping point. In the summer of 1972, before heading out into the Gulf of Alaska we made a final fuel stop at Pelican, a tiny, mostly White fishing port. I was hoping for a much needed cleansing. Standing before a bunkhouse clerk, I handed

entirely. By 1976 I was back in Juneau fulfilling an ambition to create a new concept bar, which became the Crystal Saloon and Ballroom. The timing was right— the peak years for baby boomers, well-paid Alaska Pipeline workers rotating through town, and a booming state government, Juneau's mainstay employer. The Crystal became a highly successful business but ultimately a failed partnership. During my two-year tenure as a young bar owner, I sponsored many musical events— Merle Travis, Taj Mahal, Sonny Terry & Brownie McGhee, Mose Allison— but none more memorable than Jim Pepper and the San Francisco All-stars.

As I was to find out, Andy had sponsored a Pepper concert in Sitka a year before me. When he learned that I too was a fan, he sought me out. This is how Andy and I first became acquainted in 1977— through our mutual admiration of Jim Pepper (1941-1992), the great Native American jazz musician.

Google "Witchitai-To," a peyote chant that Jim Pepper put to jazz. The song became a cross-over hit and a staple on FM radio stations across the country. Listening to it, imagine Jim and his band on stage at the Crystal Saloon and Ballroom with a special appearance of his father Gil Pepper (Kaw-Muscogee Cree), both Peppers expert fancy-dancers, chanting the Witchitai-To lyrics, Gil's dewclaw rattle punctuating Jim's soaring tenor sax— an unforgettable performance— and you'll get a hint of the pride I felt in presenting such a brilliant musical event.

Andy and I sponsored other appearances of Pepper and his band in Juneau and Sitka. Much later, in 1993, a year after Pepper's untimely death of cancer, we co-produced a two-hour radio show tribute to Jim that featured his music and interviews with his parents, friends, and fellow musicians.

In the late 1970s, after my business partnership failed, I attempted a return to commercial fishing, but times and circumstances had changed. At loose ends, I was contracted by my former boss from my

---

him the sauna fee, but before he handed me the key, I had to answer the question: "Are you on a hippie or an Indian boat?" It seemed there was no good answer, so I told the truth: an Indian boat. That gained me admission.

community organizer days who was now executive director under John Hope of the regional Tlingit and Haida tribe. The project was to write and produce a history of the "Central Council of Tlingit and Haida Indian Tribes of Alaska," an assignment that launched my now nearly 45-year career in communications.

Again, Andy and I found common purpose: me as a writer/publisher and him as the executive director of the Sitka Community Association, a federally recognized tribe. Andy hired me to produce an annual report for the organization. Over the next 25 years, as close friends and associates, we were to collaborate on many publishing projects, media productions, and cultural events.

One of Andy's greatest contributions to those studying clan lineages lives on in the "Traditional Tlingit Country" map for which he engaged my services to publish. The map lists every Tlingit clan and clan house. To look at this poster, one could be forgiven for not appreciating the decades it took Andy to complete the research, find consensus among Native tradition bearers, achieve agreement on a spelling system (orthography), and then raise the money to pay for successive printings as minor typos and errors of omission were corrected.

Recognizing the obvious intrinsic worth in each of these undertakings, it never occurred to me to say no to Andy. In 2008, during his memorial services in Sitka, I listened as one person after another recalled how Andy had roped them into working with him. It all sounded familiar especially when someone referred to the simple question that began so many of Andy's phone calls: "Is it done yet?"

Andy's leadership was undramatic. He led by example and persistence. But as low key as he was, he never withheld his opinion about anything, including sports, politics, jazz, poetry, Tlingit history and culture, and Alaska Native education, of which he was especially passionate. His trenchant observations, almost always laced with profanities, were wickedly amusing. Upon hearing yet another lacerating opinion about a Native leader who had fallen short of his expectations, I'd throw back at him one of his favorite expressions: "Don't sugar coat it, Andy; tell me how you really feel!"

Time and again, however, Andy revealed his ability to change his mind and to generously acknowledge when someone he may have previously criticized had stepped up to do the right thing.

If Andy wasn't Alaska's first tribal leader of the post-1975 Indian Self-Determination era, he was the movement's guiding light. Under his leadership, the Sitka Community Association (now the *Sitka Tribe of Alaska*) became the model for other Alaska tribal organizations. There are now more than 200 federally recognized tribes in Alaska, but back in the early 1980s, only about a dozen tribes were active in the state, and few if any were as advanced as SCA. Andy was quick to seize on the mandates of new federal laws that empowered tribes. He led the way for other tribes by presiding over the creation of social service, economic development, employment, energy assistance, and housing programs, as well as the development of a tribal court, the adoption of tribal ordinances, and the funding of preschool and cultural education.

One of the things Andy did best was to get people working toward a common goal. In the late 1970s, he organized the first Conference of Southeast Alaska Tradition Bearers. In 1983, he co-founded the United Tribes of Alaska and, in the early 1990s, the Southeast Alaska Native Educators Association. And all along, from the early 1970s forward, he organized seminars on Native culture, arts and language, tribal courts, and Alaska Native education.

From correspondence I have found in Andy's archives, it was his love of poetry that led to a 30-year on-again/off-again involvement in the Before Columbus Foundation, an aspect of Andy's life of which I was at the periphery. Documents in several file folders track his participation with the organization led by Ishmael Reed that is dedicated to promoting "public awareness and appreciation for contemporary American multi-cultural literature and related or other art forms." Reed's Wikipedia entry describes him as "American poet, novelist, essayist, songwriter, composer, playwright, editor and publisher [as well as] jazz pianist and band leader." Little wonder Andy and he came together.

The earliest BCF documents in Andy's files are dated 1976, the last 2006. Following the thread, it appears Ishmael Reed and he discovered each other in the mid-1970s. As chief administrator of the Sitka tribe, Andy used his influence in the community to raise funds for Reed to visit Sitka in 1976 to join a poetry and Native arts workshop that featured readings by him and Andy.

Annual meeting minutes of the Before Columbus Foundation on December 13, 1976, list Ishmael Reed as chairman and Andy as executive secretary. In 1978, Andy organized another poetry reading in Sitka featuring Reed, Andy, and Andy's wife Elizabeth "Sister" Goodwin (an Iñupiat of Northwest Alaska), an event promoted as a celebration of the first publication released by Raven's Bones Foundation, Andy's creation, and the publication of an essay by Reed, "God Made Alaska for the Indians," in which he described his first interactions with Andy: "After dinner, I wanted to talk about Raven myths, but Andy Hope . . . wanted to talk about Cecil Taylor and Sonny Rollins. His interests were international and multicultural."

In the early 1990s, Andy accepted an assignment to edit an "Alaska issue" of the quarterly *Before Columbus Review of American Multicultural Literature*, but it appears he was foiled by his reluctance to placate the artists and academics in such an inherently fractured organization. In a May 1991 letter to a BCF board member who had criticized Andy's "lack of professionalism," he responded that he "had long since lost any enthusiasm for the issue . . .. (As) I stated to the board, if this operation continues to be a volunteer one, we'll get what we pay for."

Although an Alaska issue wasn't published, throughout his association with BCF Andy was a frequent contributor to the quarterly. In a 1992 edition, he reviewed "Vol. 6 Subarctic," of the Smithsonian Institution's series of handbooks on North American Indians. In his review, Andy reveals his disdain for the academic arrogance common at that time, which affected the studies of Native American peoples. He pointed out that there were few Native Americans among the hundreds of contributors to the handbooks. "There are a number of reasons for this, the main one being that the Handbook [series] was organized more than 20 years ago, and the Smithsonian's emphasis at that time was (and arguably still is) on 'established scholars.' The ivory tower approach resulted. There were few Native American 'established scholars' in 1970 and there are few in 1992. The rich sources embodied in tribal oral traditions were also disregarded by the editors of this volume."

Characteristic of Andy, he did not dismiss what he described as the "fine source material" available in the series, but it underlines the genesis of an idea he had nurtured for many years that would come to fruition in 1993: the "Sharing Our Knowledge" conferences of Tlingit, Haida, Tsimshian Tribes and Clans (and their Canadian kin).

The first "Clan Conference," as it was then known, was held in 1993 in Haines/Klukwan. Andy organized it with his frequent collaborators Richard and Nora Dauenhauer. My services were engaged to supervise and produce video coverage of the three-day conference. From the start, the Clan Conferences staked out a unique position in the study of Indigenous cultures. To my knowledge, this was the first such event that brought together on the basis of mutual respect and equal participation Indigenous tradition bearers and academics to share and absorb knowledge of Native cultures—the antithesis to an "ivory tower approach." Attendance in 1993 exceeded all our expectations as several hundred people crowded into Haines and Klukwan, ancestral territories of the Chilkoot and Chilkat peoples.

Andy single-handedly organized two more Clan Conferences in the mid-1990s, but ten years were to elapse before the March 2007 "Sharing Our Knowledge Conference"— when Andy changed the name— a well-funded event that attracted over 500 people to Sitka's convention center. Academics from institutions in Europe, Russia, and North America shared research with and learned from tradition bearers and others who study, promote, and live Southeast Alaska Native languages, traditions, and cultures.

Andy, the conference executive director, asked me to supervise the video documentation as I had in 1993. In the middle of this five-day event in Sitka I was racing between three camera crews covering concurrent workshops when he and I huddled to share a few words. I expressed my amazement at how many people were in attendance. "There's a hunger for this," he observed.

Since the early 1980s, Andy had championed the concept of a tribal college. I had my doubts, but with Andy I had learned to wait and see.

During the conference in Sitka, it finally made sense as I witnessed participants jam the lobby making their way to workshops, the topics of which included linguistics, archaeology, museum studies, cultural anthropology, education, ethnohistory, art and music, traditional ecological knowledge, Indigenous protocols, and fisheries. Seemed like college to me.

For the last evening of that 2007 conference, Andy had organized several poets and writers to give readings. The tribal theater on Katlian Street, modeled on a Tlingit longhouse, was packed until the wee hours. I recall the shocked appreciation he expressed to me the day after for what had happened: the crowd rising in repeated ovations. "For poetry?" he said. "Amazing!"

Early in 2008, Andy invited me to take photos of himself with his grandchild, the first child of his son Ishmael whom he had named after his friend Ishmael Reed. Months later, Andy asked me to take photos at an event he had organized to honor Indigenous authors. On my office computer I downloaded and titled the photos. A few days later I computer-searched for images of "Andy Hope." The two recent photos from January and May came up next to each other. I was alarmed. In five months he had aged years. It was then I realized my friend had something much worse than the extended flu he had complained about. I told my wife that Andy was obviously very sick. We both encouraged him to go to the emergency room. He put it off for a week. When I gave him a ride to the hospital, it was the last time I saw him alive. He was immediately transferred by medevac to the Native regional hospital in Anchorage, then to the Native hospital in Sitka where he died of cancer on August 7, 2008. At his son's call, I had flown to Sitka, arriving at Andy's bedside moments after he passed away.

A deathbed wish told to his daughter Tillie was to place his files in my care. I've taken seriously the task of being Andy's literary executor and have maintained an archive of over a dozen file boxes bulging with research, correspondence, and publications, as well as a carton of his book *Will the Time Ever Come: A Tlingit Source Book* (about the first Clan Conference). The Traditional Tlingit County poster is now in its seventh printing. With support from a tribally administered

U.S. Department of Education grant, I curated the "Andrew John Hope III Legacy Project," a collection of videos, publications, and other materials Andy produced for and about the Sharing Our Knowledge conferences. Several dozen newsletters and essays by Andy are now available on the Sharing Our Knowledge website, along with a catalog of over 650 individual video-recorded presentations from 1993 through 2024, all accessible on the SOK YouTube channel. Seems like an online tribal college to me.

Preparing his obituary, I talked with Andy's family. They quickly agreed that a comment we had all heard from him more than a few times best summed up his attitude toward so much of what he had accomplished: "You don't need to take the credit; let others take the credit, *as long as the work gets done*."

We, his friends and family, continue his work. His legacy lives on with the Sharing Our Knowledge conferences and his many publishing efforts, and with his son Ishmael Hope through his own work as a published poet and author, a professional storyteller, and as an increasingly fluent Tlingit speaker and transcriber.

The 2009 conference in Juneau was dedicated to his memory and the 2012 conference in Sitka included workshops and the presentation of papers recognizing contributions including Andy's on the centennial of the Alaska Native Brotherhood. These conferences continue to be held every two years and remain eagerly anticipated and well-attended events featuring academic presentations, cultural activities, and field trips. (See sharingourknowledge.org and the menu item "Founding Documents.")

In life, Andy did not take credit for much. In his memory, let us acknowledge all for which he deserves recognition. Whenever I hear a young person speaking Tlingit, or reciting her or his clan lineage, or talking about Northwest Coast culture, I think of Andy. He is not forgotten.

# AFTERWORDS

# Maxine Hong Kingston's 2023 Lifetime Achievement Award Acceptance Speech

Thank you, everybody. This award means a lot to me, especially that it was presented by Shawn Wong. This means that there is some rapprochement coming among writers who were arguing: who do those stories belong to, and who is authentic? In other words, who is true, who is Chinese and who is Chinese American. And for Shawn and me, we were on opposite sides of this argument. And so his words today mean that there is rapprochement, if not reconciliation.

A thousand years before Columbus, Chinese ships sailed here, and they came to Turtle Island. And in those days, the Chinese exploration ships carried artwork, they brought the culture of the Middle Kingdom as far as they could go. So those ships were loaded with sculptures and scrolls and paintings, musical instruments, drums, compasses. And when they got here to Turtle Island, the culture that they found here, that they received, was that this was the land where women were the most powerful. And actually they came here to Turtle Island, but they called it the Land of Women. And what impressed them was, there was no war and no taxes.

Maybe about thirty years ago, Earll and I were living at the Grand Canyon, and we went to visit the Hopis. And one of the Hopi women was showing us around and I thought, *Look, look up there. They have curved roofs, and in the curved roofs there are ceramic or clay sculptures of animals and people.* And I said, "Oh, we have those too." And then she said, "Well, what village do you come from? But what tribe are you from?" I said, "Oh, no, no, no, no, I'm talking about China." And she said, "Oh, we came from there 5,000 years ago. We came across five rocks." And then I said, "Wow, those rocks must be the islands of Hawaii." And they got here. And then years later, in China, I saw everywhere sculptures of bronze or iron. And they're turtles. And they actually look like Volkswagen bugs. They're about that same size. And on their backs is a stellae. And on these stellae, on the backs of the turtles, there's poems. And what they say is that turtles brought writing to China. And so I think, *Wow, I'm looking at these sculptures, at these roofs, both in China and at Hopi.* And I think, *Wow, we must have gotten together somewhere.*

And then a few years ago, maybe about thirty years ago, this was in the 1980s and the Cultural Revolution was just ending. I was traveling with Leslie Marmon Silko through China. Toni Morrison was there too. We were traveling together. And Leslie was wearing a poncho, and it had all kinds of Laguna Indian designs on it. And then we were looking at rugs in China. And she looks at the rug and she says, "Wow," and she holds up her poncho. She holds up the rug. It's the same designs, the same symbols. And so she bought one of those rugs and she's gonna bring it back. And then we were at a temple. And there's these columns. And the columns were a turquoise blue and Chinese red with white trims. And Leslie says, "Wow." And then she goes like this. [Indicates showing her earrings.] And you see her earrings dangling down, and they're the same as those columns. And so then we looked at each other and we're saying, "Wow." And then we're saying, "Yeah, there was a rainbow bridge. And the rainbow bridge is a two-way street." Or even as bell hooks and the Buddhists would say, we are one. And Shakespeare reminds us that kindness and kin come from the same roots.

# Anne Waldman Acceptance Speech for a Lifetime Achievement Award

## The American Book Awards, Oakland CA. Oct 25, 2015

Salutations. When I received news of this prestigious award, known for its panoramic awareness of the range of literary diversity—experimental, radical, avant-garde, community-minded—I was extremely moved. I wanted to dance around the block! I wanted to sing from the mountaintop! I actually bowed to the Continental Divide. I was in the middle of the third week of the Jack Kerouac School of Disembodied Poetics Summer Writing Program at Naropa University in Boulder with its theme of "Braided River: The Activist Rhizome," a creative writing program I co-founded with Allen Ginsberg and Diane di Prima in 1974 and have shepherded for over 40 years. The usual intensities of any conglomeration of creative people was in play; it is never static at Naropa, never fully "institutional," always generative and progressive in its pedagogy and writing practices and performance. It also holds a backdrop with a Buddhist view, of non-competitive education. The award confirms that I was on the right path to help nourish this poetry school after nearly a decade at The Poetry Project at St. Mark's Church in-the-Bowery in New York's Lower East Side. Thank you on behalf of Infrastructure Poetics, an important ingredient to sustain artistic community.

I have also had the good fortune to be involved recently in projects involving poetry and education in Morocco, India, and China. And recent performances at Montreal POP and the Henry Miller Library in Big Sur. And keynotes addresses in Belgium and France.

When I got the news of the Award I also thought of all the people—now passed on—involved in my long path of poetry and cultural activism. Allen Ginsberg, Frank O'Hara, Ted Berrigan, William Burroughs, Bob Creeley, Lorenzo Thomas, Leslie Scalapino, Akilah Oliver, Amiri Baraka, Adrienne Rich, Judith Malina. Many others, friends and colleagues in the mix. I think of all those active now who continue the work in poetic and artistic communities all over the world. And so many younger people. And also work for racial and gender justice, and for the priceless freedom of imagination.

Part of the poet's job is to look into the darkness of our time, and rather than be paralyzed, we can feel the generative power we still have as poets and artists to affect change of view. The activism flows specifically with projects related to climate change, anti-nuclear proliferation and social justice, working in performance with my family and many others.

The writing continues with recent publications from Penguin Poets and Coffee House Press. A new book-length poem is coming out this spring: *Voice's Daughter of a Heart Yet To Be Born*, a meditation on Blake's *The Book of Thel*. A new manuscript, *Future Feminism*, is scheduled for Penguin in 2017. *CROSS WORLDS: Transcultural Poetics* was published recently.

The Before Columbus Award gives me renewed energy and enthusiasm. I am extremely grateful to my editors as well. Lawrence Ferlinghetti who launched *Fast Speaking Woman*, Paul Slovak at Penguin, Chris Fischbach and Erika Stevens at Coffee House, and Simone Fattal at Post-Apollo Press. And I thank my son Ambrose Bye, a frequent collaborator, for being here in my stead. And bow to you, the Before Columbus Foundation, and want to thank Justin Desmangles and the staff. And a deep deep deep bow to Ishmael Reed, a great writer, thinker, artistic force, publisher, and cultural activist.

This means the world coming from you, Ishmael.

Thank you all, so very much.

# APPENDIX

# American Book Award Winners

## 1980-2024

### 1980s

*1980*

- Douglas Woolf for *Future Preconditional: A Collection*
- Edward Dorn for *Hello, La Jolla*
- Jayne Cortez for *Mouth on Paper*
- Leslie Marmon Silko for *Ceremony*
- Mei-mei Berssenbrugge for *Random Possession*
- Milton Murayama for *All I Asking for Is My Body*
- Quincy Troupe for *Snake Back Solos*
- Rudolfo Anaya for *Tortuga*, a novel

*1981*

- Alta for *Shameless Hussy*
- Alan Chong Lau for *Songs for Jadina*
- Bienvenido N. Santos for *Scent of Apples: A Collection of Stories*
- Helen Adam for *Turn Again to Me & Other Poems*
- Lionel Mitchell for *Traveling Light*
- Miguel Algarín for *On Call*
- Nicholasa Mohr for *Felita*
- Peter Blue Cloud for *Back Then Tomorrow*
- Robert Kelly for *The Time of Voice: Poems 1994–1996*
- Rose Drachler for *The Choice*
- Susan Howe for *The Liberties*
- Toni Cade Bambara for *The Salt Eaters*

*1982*

- Al Young for *Bodies and Soul*
- Duane Niatum for *Songs for the Harvester of Dreams: Poems*
- E. L. Mayo for *Collected Poems*
- Frank Chin for *The Chickencoop Chinaman* and *The Year of the Dragon*
- Hilton Obenzinger for *This Passover or the next, I will never be in Jerusalem*
- Him Mark Lai, Genny Lim, Judy Yung for *Island: Poetry and History of Chinese Immigrants on Angel Island, 1910–1940*
- Jerome Rothenberg for *Pre-Faces and Other Writings*
- Joyce Carol Thomas for *Marked by Fire*
- Leroy Quintana for *Paper Dance: 55 Latino Poets*
- Lorna Dee Cervantes for *Emplumada*
- Ronald Phillip Tanaka for *The Shino Suite: Japanese-American Poetry*
- Russell Banks for *Book of Jamaica*
- Tato Laviera for *Enclave*

*1983*

- Barbara Christian for *Black Women Novelists: The Development of a Tradition, 1892–1976*
- Cecilia Liang for *Chinese Folk Poetry*
- Evangelina Vigil-Piñón for *Thirty An' Seen a Lot*
- Harriet Rohmer for *Legend of Food Mountain: LA Montana Del Alimento*
- James D. Houston for *Californians: Searching for the Golden State*
- Jessica Tarahata Hagedorn for *Pet food & Tropical Apparitions*
- John A. Williams for *Click Song*, a novel
- Joy Kogawa for *Obasan*
- Judy Grahn for *The Queen of Wands: Poetry*
- Nash Candelaria for *Not by the Sword*
- Peter Guralnick for *Lost Highway: Journeys and Arrivals of American Musicians*
- Seán Ó Tuama for *An Duanaire: An Irish Anthology: 1600-1900, Poems of the Dispossessed*

*1984*

- Cecil Brown for *Days Without Weather*
- Gary Snyder for *Axe Handles: Poems*
- Howard Schwartz, Mark Podwal for *The Captive Soul of the Messiah: New Tales About Reb Nachman*
- Imamu Amiri Baraka for *Anthology of African American Women: Confirmation Men*

- Jesús Colón for *A Puerto Rican in New York, and Other Sketches*
- Joseph Bruchac for *Breaking Silence: An Anthology of Contemporary Asian-American Poets*
- Maurice Kenny for *The Mama Poems*
- Mei-mei Berssenbrugge for *The Heat Bird*
- Miné Okubo for *Citizen 13660*
- Paule Marshall for *Praisesong for the Widow*
- Ruthanne Lum McCunn, You-shan Tang, Ellen Lai-shan Yeung for *Pie-Biter*
- Thomas McGrath for *Echoes Inside the Labyrinth*
- Venkatesh Kulkarni for *Naked in Deccan*
- William J. Kennedy for *O Albany!*

*1985*

- Angela Jackson for *Solo in the Box Car Third Floor E*
- Arnold Genthe, John Kuo Wei Tchen for Genthe's *Photographs of San Francisco's Old Chinatown*
- Colleen J. McElroy for *Queen of the Ebony Isles*
- Gary Soto for *Living Up The Street*
- Peter Irons for *Justice at War*
- Keiho Soga, Taisanboku Mori, Sojin Takei, Muin Ozaki for *Poets Behind Barbed Wire*
- Louise Erdrich for *Love Medicine*, a novel
- Maureen Owen for *Amelia Earhart*
- May Sarton for *At Seventy: A Journal*
- Robert Edward Duncan for *Ground Work: Before the War*
- Ron Jones for *Say Ray*
- Sandra Cisneros for *The House on Mango Street*
- Sonia Sanchez for *Homegirls and Handgrenades*
- Julia Vinograd for *The Book of Jerusalem*
- William Oandasan for *Round Valley Songs*

*1986*

- Anna Lee Walters for *The Sun Is Not Merciful: Short Stories*
- Cherríe Moraga, Gloria Anzaldúa for *This Bridge Called My Back: Writings by Radical Women of Color*
- Helen Barolini for *The Dream Book: An Anthology of Writing by Italian American Women*
- Jeff Hannusch for *I Hear You Knockin : The Sound of New Orleans Rhythm and Blues*
- Linda Hogan for *Seeing Through the Sun*

- Miguel Algarín for *Time's Now/Ya Es Tiempo*
- Natasha Borovsky for *A Daughter of the Nobility*
- Raymond Federman for *Smiles on Washington Square: A Love Story of Sorts*
- Susan Howe for *My Emily Dickinson*
- Terence Winch for *Irish Musicians/American Friends*
- Toshio Mori for *Yokohama, California*

*1987*

- Ai for *SIN*
- Ana Castillo for *The Mixquiahuala Letters*
- Cyn Zarco for *Cir'cum.nav'i.ga'tion*[6]
- Daniel McGuire for *Portrait of Little Boy in darkness*
- Dorothy Bryant for *Confessions of Madame Psyche: Memoirs and Letters of Mei-Li Murrow*
- Etheridge Knight for *The Essential Etheridge Knight*
- Gary Giddins for *Celebrating Bird: The Triumph Of Charlie Parker*
- Harvey Pekar for *The New American Splendor Anthology: From Off the Streets of Cleveland*
- James Welch for *Fools Crow*
- John Wieners for *Selected Poems: 1958–1984*
- Juan Felipe Herrera for *Face Games*
- Lucia Chiavola Birnbaum for *liberazione della donna: feminism in Italy*
- Michael Mayo for *Practicing Angels: A Contemporary Anthology of San Francisco Bay Area Poetry*
- Septima Poinsette Clark, Cynthia Stokes Brown for *Ready from Within: A First Person Narrative*
- Terry McMillan for *Mama*

*1988*

- Allison Blakely for *Russia and the Negro: Blacks in Russian History and Thought*
- Charles Olson for *The Collected Poems of Charles Olson: Excluding the Maximus Poems*
- Daisy Bates for *The Long Shadow of Little Rock: A Memoir*
- David Halberstam for *The Reckoning*
- Edward Sanders for *Thirsting for Peace in a Raging Century: Poems 1961–1985*
- Gerald Vizenor for *Griever: An American Monkey King in China*
- Jimmy Santiago Baca for *Martin & Meditations on the South Valley*
- Kesho Y. Scott, Cherry Muhanji, Egyirba High for *Tight Spaces*
- Marlon K. Hom for *Songs of Gold Mountain: Cantonese Rhymes from San Francisco Chinatown*

- Benjamin Hoff for *The Singing Creek Where the Willows Grow: The Mystical Nature Diary of Opal Whiteley*[2]
- Ronald Sukenick for *Down and in: Life in the Underground*
- Salvatore La Puma for *The Boys of Bensonhurst*
- Toni Morrison for *Beloved*
- Tek Lum Lum for *Expounding the Doubtful Points*

*1989*

- Alma Luz Villanueva for *The Ultraviolet Sky*
- Askia M. Touré for *From the Pyramids to the Projects: Poems of Genocide and Resistance!*
- Audre Lorde for *A Burst of Light*
- Carolyn Lau for *Wode Shuofa: My Way of Speaking*
- Emory Elliott for *Columbia Literary History of the United States*
- Eduardo Galeano for *Genesis*
- Frank Chin for *The Chinaman Pacific and Frisco R.R. Co.*
- Henry Louis Gates for *The Signifying Monkey: A Theory of Afro-American Literary Criticism*
- Isabel Allende for *Eva Luna*
- J. California Cooper for *Homemade Love*
- Jennifer Stone for *Stone's Throw*
- Josephine Gattuso Hendin for *The Right Thing to Do*
- Leslie Scalapino for *way*
- Shuntaro Tanikawa for *Floating the River in Melancholy*
- Charles Fanning for *The Exiles of Erin: Nineteenth-Century Irish-American Fiction*
- William Minoru Hohri for *Repairing America: An Account of the Movement for Japanese American Redress*

## 1990s

*1990*

- Adrienne Kennedy for *People Who Led to My Plays*
- Barbara Grizzuti Harrison for *Italian Days*
- Daniela Gioseffi for *Women on War (Essential Voices for the Nuclear Age)*
- Elizabeth Woody for *Hand into Stone: Poems*
- Hualing Nieh for *Mulberry and Peach: Two Women of China*
- Itabari Njeri for *Every Good-Bye Ain't Gone*
- James M. Freeman for *Hearts of Sorrow: Vietnamese-American Lives*
- John C. Walter, J. Raymond Jones for *The Harlem Fox: J. Raymond Jones and Tammany, 1920–1970*

- John Norton for *Light at the End of the Bog*
- José Emilio González for *Vivar a Hostos*
- Sergei Kan for *Symbolic Immortality: The Tlingit Potlatch of the Nineteenth Century*
- Lloyd A. Thompson for *Romans and Blacks*
- Martin Bernal for *Black Athena: The Afroasiatic Roots of Classical Civilization*
- Michelle T. Clinton, Sesshu Foster for *Invocation L.A.: Urban Multicultural Poetry*
- Miles Davis for *Miles: The Autobiography*
- Paula Gunn Allen for *Spider Woman's Granddaughters: Traditional Tales and Contemporary Writing by Native American Women*
- Shirley Geok-lin Lim, Mayumi Tsutakawa, Margarita Donnelly for *The Forbidden Stitch: An Asian American Women's Anthology*

*1991*

- Alejandro Murguía for *Southern Front*
- bell hooks for *Yearning: Race, Gender, and Cultural Politics*
- Bruce Wright for *Black Robes, White Justice: Why Our Legal System Doesn't Work for Blacks*
- Charley Trujillo for *Soldados: Chicanos in Viet Nam*
- D. H. Melhem for *Heroism in the New Black Poetry: Introductions & Interviews*
- Deborah Keenan for *Looking for Home: Women Writing About Exile*
- Jessica Hagedorn for *Dogeaters*
- John Edgar Wideman for *Philadelphia Fire*, a novel
- Joy Harjo for *In Mad Love and War*
- Karen Tei Yamashita for *Through the Arc of the Rain Forest*
- Lucia Berlin for *Homesick: New and Selected Stories*
- Mary Crow Dog for *Lakota Woman*
- Meridel Le Sueur for *Harvest Song: Collected Essays and Stories*
- Mill Hunk Herald Collective for *Overtime: Punchin' Out With the Mill Hunk Herald Magazine*
- Nora Marks Dauenhauer, Richard Dauenhauer for *Haa Tuwunaagu Yis, for Healing Our Spirit: Tlingit Oratory*
- R. Baxter Miller for *The Art and Imagination of Langston Hughes*
- Thomas Centolella for *Terra Firma*

*1992*

- A'Lelia Perry Bundles for *Madam C.J. Walker*
- Art Spiegelman for *The Complete Maus: A Survivor's Tale*
- Benjamin Alire Sáenz for *Calendar of Dust*

- Donna J. Haraway for *Simians, Cyborgs, and Women: The Reinvention of Nature*
- Fritjof Capra for *Belonging to the Universe: Explorations on the Frontiers of Science and Spirituality*
- José Antonio Burciaga for *Undocumented Love/Amor Indocumentado: A Personal Anthology of Poetry*
- Keith Gilyard for *Voices of the Self: A Study of Language Competence*
- Lucy Thompson for *To the American Indian: Reminiscences of a Yurok Woman*
- Norma Field for *In the Realm of a Dying Emperor: Japan at Century's End*
- Peter Bacho for *Cebu*
- Peter Kalifornsky for *Dena'ina Legacy: K'tl'egh'i Sukdu: The Collected Writings of Peter Kalifornsky*
- Raymond Andrews for *Jessie and Jesus and Cousin Claire*
- Sandra Scofield for *Beyond Deserving*
- Sheila Hamanaka for *Journey*
- Stephen R. Fox for *The Unknown Internment: An Oral History of the Relocation of Italian Americans During World War II*
- Steven R. Carter for *Hansberry's Drama: Commitment Amid Complexity,*
- Verlyn Klinkenborg for *The Last Fine Time*
- William B. Branch, Amiri Baraka, August Wilson for *Black Thunder: An Anthology of African-American Drama*

*1993*

- Asake Bomani, Belvie Rooks for *Paris Connections: African American Artists in Paris*
- Christopher Mogil, Peter Woodrow for *We Gave Away a Fortune*
- Cornel West for *Prophetic Thought in Postmodern Times*
- Denise Giardina for *Unquiet Earth*
- Diane Glancy for *Claiming Breath*
- Eugene B. Redmond for *The Eye in the Ceiling*
- Francisco X. Alarcón for *Snake Poems*
- Gerald Graff for *Beyond the Culture Wars: How Teaching the Conflicts Can Revitalize American Education*
- Jack Beatty for *The Rascal King: The Life and Times of James Michael Curley*
- Leroy V. Quintana for *The History of Home*
- Katherine Peter for *Neets'aii Gwiindaii: Living in the Chandalar Country*
- Nelson George for *Elevating the Game: Black Men and Basketball*
- Ninotchka Rosca for *Twice Blessed*, a novel

*1994*

- Giose Rimanelli for *Benedetta in Guysterland*
- Eric Drooker for *Flood!: A Novel in Pictures*
- Graciela Limón for *In Search of Bernabe*
- Gregory J. Reed for *Economic Empowerment Through the Church*
- Janet Campbell Hale for *Bloodlines: Odyssey of a Native Daughter*
- Jill Nelson for *Volunteer Slavery: My Authentic Negro Experience*
- Lawson Fusao Inada for *Legends from Camp*
- Nicole Blackman for *Aloud: Voices from the Nuyorican Poets Cafe*
- Paul Gilroy for *The Black Atlantic: Modernity and Double-Consciousness*
- Ronald Takaki for *A Different Mirror: A History of Multicultural America*
- Rose L. Glickman for *Daughters of Feminists*
- Tino Villanueva for *Scene from the Movie GIANT*
- Virginia L. Kroll for *Wood-Hoopoe Willie*

*1995*

- Abraham Rodriguez for *Spidertown*, a novel
- Herb Boyd, Robert L. Allen for *Brotherman: The Odyssey of Black Men in America—An Anthology*
- Denise Chávez for *Face of an Angel*
- John Egerton for *Speak Now Against the Day: The Generation Before the Civil Rights Movement in the South*
- John Ross for *Rebellion from the Roots: Indian Uprising in Chiapas*
- Thomas Avena for *Life Sentences: Writers, Artists, and AIDS*
- Linda Raymond for *Rocking the Babies*, a novel
- Li-Young Lee for *The Winged Seed: A Remembrance*
- Marianna De Marco Torgovnick for *Crossing Ocean Parkway*
- Marnie Mueller for *Green Fires: Assault on Eden: A Novel of the Ecuadorian Rainforest*
- Peter Quinn for *Banished Children of Eve, A Novel of Civil War New York*
- Sandra Martz for *I Am Becoming the Woman I've Wanted*
- Gordon Henry Jr. for *The Light People*
- Tricia Rose for *Black Noise: Rap Music and Black Culture in Contemporary America*

*1996*

- Agate Nesaule for *A Woman in Amber: Healing the Trauma of War and Exile*
- Arthur Sze for *Archipelago*
- Chang-Rae Lee for *Native Speaker*
- Chitra Banerjee Divakaruni for *Arranged Marriage*
- E. J. Miller Laino for *Girl Hurt*

- Glenn C. Loury for *One by One from the Inside Out: Race and Responsibility in America*
- James W. Loewen for *Lies My Teacher Told Me: Everything Your American History Textbook Got Wrong*
- Joe Sacco, Edward Said for *Palestine*
- Kimiko Hahn for *The Unbearable Heart*
- Maria Espinosa for *Longing*
- Robert Viscusi for *Astoria*
- Sherman Alexie for *Reservation Blues*
- Ron Sakolsky, Fred Weihan Ho for *Sounding Off!: Music as Resistance / Rebellion / Revolution*
- Stephanie Cowell for *The Physician of London: The Second Part of the Seventeenth-Century Trilogy of Nicholas Cooke*
- William H. Gass for *The Tunnel*

*1997*

- Alurista for *Et Tu ... Raza*
- Derrick Bell for *Gospel Choirs: Psalms Of Survival In An Alien Land Called Home*
- Dorothy Barresi for *The Post-Rapture Diner*
- Guillermo Gómez-Peña for *The New World Border: Prophecies, Poems, and Loqueras for the End of the Century*
- Louis Owens for *Nightland*
- Martín Espada for *Imagine the Angels of Bread: Poems*
- Montserrat Fontes for *Dreams of the Centaur*, a novel
- Noel Ignatiev for *Race Traitor*
- Shirley Geok-lin Lim for *Among the White Moon Faces: An Asian-American Memoir of Homelands*
- Sunaina Maira for *Contours of the Heart: South Asians Map North America*
- Thulani Davis for *Maker of Saints*
- Tom De Haven for *Derby Dugan's Depression Funnies*, a novel
- William M. Banks for *Black Intellectuals: Race and Responsibility in American Life*
- Brenda Knight for *Women of the Beat Generation: The Writers, Artists and Muses at the Heart of a Revolution*

*1998*

- Allison Adelle Hedge Coke for *Dog Road Woman*
- Angela Y. Davis for *Blues Legacies and Black Feminism: Gertrude "Ma" Rainey, Bessie Smith, and Billie Holiday*
- Brenda Marie Osbey for *All Saints: New and Selected Poems*

- Don DeLillo for *Underworld*
- Jim Barnes for *On Native Ground: Memoirs and Impressions*
- John A. Williams for *Safari West: Poems*
- Nancy Rawles for *Love Like Gumbo*
- Nora Okja Keller for *Comfort Woman*
- Sandra Benitez for *Bitter Grounds*, a novel
- Scott DeVeaux for *The Birth of Bebop: A Social and Musical History*
- Thomas Lynch for *The Undertaking: Life Studies from the Dismal Trade*

*1999*

- Alice McDermott for *Charming Billy*
- Anna Linzer for *Ghost Dancing*
- Brian Ward for *Just My Soul Responding: Rhythm and Blues, Black Consciousness, and Race Relations*
- Chiori Santiago for *Home to Medicine Mountain*
- E. Donald Two-Rivers for *Survivor's Medicine: Short Stories*
- Edwidge Danticat for *The Farming of Bones*
- Judith Roche, Meg McHutchison for *First Fish, First People: Salmon Tales of the North Pacific Rim*
- Gioia Timpanelli for *Sometimes the Soul: Two Novellas of Sicily*
- Gloria Naylor for *The Men of Brewster Place*, a novel
- James D. Houston for *The Last Paradise*
- Jerry Lipka, Gerald V. Mohatt, Ciulistet Group for *Transforming the Culture of Schools: Yup¡k Eskimo Examples*
- Trey Ellis for *Right Here, Right Now*
- Josip Novakovich for *Salvation and Other Disasters*
- Lauro Flores for *The Floating Borderlands: Twenty-Five Years of U.S. Hispanic Literature*
- Luís Alberto Urrea for *Nobody's Son: Notes from an American Life*
- Nelson George for *Hip Hop America: Hip Hop and the Molding of Black Generation X*
- Speer Morgan for *The Freshour Cylinders*
- Gary Gach for *What Book!?: Buddha Poems from Beat to Hiphop*
- Chiori Santiago, author, Judith Lowry, illustrator, *Home to Medicine Mountain*

**2000S**

*2000*

- Esther G. Belin for *From the Belly of My Beauty*
- Allan J. Ryan for *The Trickster Shift: Humour and Irony in Contemporary Native Art*

- Andrés Montoya for *The Ice Worker Sings and Other Poems*
- Camille Peri, Kate Moses for *Mothers Who Think: Tales of Real-Life Parenthood*
- David A. J. Richards for *Italian American: The Racializing of an Ethnic Identity*
- David Toop for *Exotica*
- Elva Trevino Hart for *Barefoot Heart: Stories of a Migrant Child*
- Emil Guillermo for *Amok: Essays from an Asian American* Perspective; With an Introduction by Ishmael Reed
- Frank Chin for *The Chinaman Pacific & Frisco R.R. Co.*
- Helen Thomas for *Front Row at the White House : My Life and Times*
- Janisse Ray for *Ecology of a Cracker Childhood*
- John Russell Rickford, Russell John Rickford for *Spoken Soul: The Story of Black English*
- Leroy TeCube for *Year in Nam: A Native American Soldier's Story*
- Lois-Ann Yamanaka for *Heads By Harry*
- Michael Lally for *It's Not Nostalgia: Poetry & Prose*
- Michael Patrick MacDonald for *All Souls: A Family Story from Southie*
- Rahna Reiko Rizzuto for *Why She Left Us*, a novel
- Robert Creeley for *The Collected Poems of Robert Creeley, 1975–2005*
- Editor/Publisher: Ronald Sukenick
- Jack E. White, Journalism
- Frank Chin: Lifetime Achievement Award
- Robert Creeley: Lifetime Achievement Award

*2001*

- Amanda J. Cobb for *Listening to Our Grandmothers' Stories: The Bloomfield Academy for Chickasaw Females, 1852–1949*
- Andrea Dworkin for *Scapegoat: The Jews, Israel, and Women's Liberation*
- Carolyne Wright for *Seasons of Mangoes and Brainfire*
- Chalmers Johnson for *Blowback, Second Edition: The Costs and Consequences of American Empire*
- Cheri Register for *Packinghouse Daughter: A Memoir*
- Chris Ware for *Jimmy Corrigan: The Smartest Kid on Earth*
- Diana Garcia for *When Living Was a Labor Camp*
- Elizabeth Nunez for *Bruised Hibiscus*
- Janet McAdams for *Island of Lost Luggage*
- Philip Whalen for *Overtime: Selected Poems*
- Russell Leong for *Phoenix Eyes and Other Stories*
- Sandra M. Gilbert for *Kissing the Bread: New and Selected Poems, 1969–1999*

- Ted Joans for *Teducation*
- Tillie Olsen for *Silences*
- William S. Penn for *Killing Time With Strangers*
- Malcolm Margolin, Editor
- Ted Joans: Lifetime Achievement Award
- Tillie Olsen: Lifetime Achievement Award
- Philip Whalen: Lifetime Achievement Award

*2002*

- Aaron A. Abeyta for *Colcha*
- Susanne Antonetta for *The Body Toxic: An Environmental Memoir*
- Rilla Askew for *Fire in Beulah*
- Tananarive Due for *The Living Blood*
- Gloria Frym for *Homeless at Home*
- Dana Gioia for *Interrogations at Noon*
- LeAnne Howe for *Shell Shaker*
- Alex Kuo for *Lipstick and Other Stories*
- Michael N. Nagler for *Is There No Other Way? The Search for a Nonviolent Future*
- Donald Phelps for *Reading the Funnies: Looking at Great Cartoonists Throughout the First Half of the 20th Century*
- Al Young for *The Sound of Dreams Remembered: Poems, 1990–2000*
- Jessel Miller for *Angels in the Vineyards*
- Lerone Bennett: Lifetime Achievement Award
- Jack Hirschman: Lifetime Achievement Award

*2003*

- Kevin Baker for *Paradise Alley*
- Debra Magpie Earling for *Perma Red*
- Daniel Ellsberg for *Secrets: A Memoir of Vietnam and the Pentagon Papers*
- Rick Heide, ed. for *Under the Fifth Sun: Latino Literature from California*
- Igor Krupnik, Willis Walunga, Vera Metcalf, and Lars Krutak, editors for *Akuzilleput Igaqullghet = Our Words Put to Paper: Sourcebook in St. Lawrence Island Yupik Heritage and History*
- Alejandro Murguía for *This War Called Love: Nine Stories*
- Jack Newfield, for *The Full Rudy: The Man, the Myth, the Mania*
- Joseph Papaleo for *Italian Stories*
- Eric Porter for *What Is This Thing Called Jazz?: African American Musicians as Artists, Critics, and Activists*
- Jewell Parker Rhodes for *Douglass' Women*, a novel

- Rachel Simon for *Riding the Bus with My Sister: A True Life Journey*
- Velma Wallis for *Raising Ourselves: A Gwich'in Coming of Age Story from the Yukon River*
- Max Rodriguez for *QBR: The Black Book Review*

*2004*

- Diana Abu-Jaber for *Crescent*, a novel
- David Cole for *Enemy Aliens: Double Standards And Constitutional Freedoms In The War On Terrorism*
- Charisse Jones and Kumea Shorter-Gooden for *Shifting: The Double Lives of Black Women in America*
- Kristin Hunter Lattany for *Breaking Away*
- A. Robert Lee for *Multicultural American Literature: Comparative Black, Native, Latino/a and Asian American Fictions*
- Diane Sher Lutovich for *What I Stole*
- Ruth Ozeki for *All Over Creation*
- Renato Rosaldo for *Prayer to Spider Woman / Rezo a la Mujer Arana*
- Scott Saul for *Freedom Is, Freedom Ain't: Jazz and the Making of the Sixties*
- Michael Walsh for *And All the Saints*

*2005*

- Bernard W. Bell for *The Contemporary African American Novel: Its Folk Roots And Modern Literary Branches*
- Cecelie Berry for *Rise Up Singing: Black Women Writers on Motherhood*
- Jeff Chang for *Can't Stop Won't Stop: A History of the Hip-Hop Generation*
- Julie Chibbaro for *Redemption*
- Richard A. Clarke for *Against All Enemies: Inside America's War on Terror*
- Alisha S. Drabek and Karen R. Adams, for *The Red Cedar of Afognak, A Driftwood Journey*
- Ralph M. Flores for *The Horse in the Kitchen: Stories of a Mexican-American Family*
- Hiroshi Kashiwagi for *Swimming in the American: A Memoir And Selected Writings*
- Robert F. Kennedy, Jr. for *Crimes Against Nature: How George W. Bush and His Corporate Pals Are Plundering the Country and Hijacking Our Democracy*
- Don Lee for *Country of Origin*, a novel
- Lamont B. Steptoe for *A Long Movie of Shadows*
- Don West for *No Lonesome Road: Selected Prose and Poems*, eds Jeff Biggers and George Brosi
- Journalism Award: Bill Berkowitz

*2006*

- MacKenzie Bezos for *The Testing of Luther Albright*, a novel
- Matt Briggs for *Shoot the Buffalo*
- David P. Diaz for *The White Tortilla: Reflections of a Second-Generation Mexican-American*
- Darryl Dickson-Carr for *The Columbia Guide to Contemporary African American Fiction*
- Thomas Ferraro for *Feeling Italian: The Art of Ethnicity in America*
- Tim Z. Hernandez for *Skin Tax*
- Josh Kun for *Audiotopia: Music, Race, and America*
- P. Lewis for *Nate*
- Peter Metcalfe for *Gumboot Determination: The Story of the Southeast Alaska Regional Health Consortium*
- Kevin J. Mullen for *The Toughest Gang in Town: Police Stories from Old San Francisco*
- Doris Seale and Beverly Slapin, editors, for *A Broken Flute: The Native Experience in Books for Children*
- Matthew Shenoda for *Somewhere Else*
- Carlton T. Spiller for *Scalding Heart*
- Chris Hamilton-Emery: Editor Award
- Jay Wright: Lifetime Achievement Award

*2007*

- Daniel Cassidy for *How the Irish Invented Slang: The Secret Language of the Crossroads*
- Michael Eric Dyson for *Come Hell or High Water: Hurricane Katrina and the Color of Disaster*
- Rigoberto González for *Butterfly Boy: Memories of a Chicano Mariposa*
- Reyna Grande for *Across a Hundred Mountains*, a novel
- Ernestine Hayes for *Blonde Indian: An Alaska Native Memoir*
- Patricia Klindienst for *The Earth Knows My Name: Food, Culture, and Sustainability in the Gardens of Ethnic Americans*
- Gary Panter for *Jimbo's Inferno*
- Jeffrey F. L. Partridge for *Beyond Literary Chinatown*
- Judith Roche for *Wisdom of the Body*
- Kali VanBaale for *The Space Between*

*2008*

- Moustafa Bayoumi for *How Does It Feel to Be a Problem Being Young and Arab in America*

- Douglas A. Blackmon for *Slavery by Another Name: The Re-Enslavement of Black Americans from the Civil War to World War II*
- Jonathan Curiel for *Al' America: Travels Through America's Arab and Islamic Roots*
- Nora Marks Dauenhauer, Richard Dauenhauer, and Lydia T. Black for *Anóoshi Lingít Aaní Ká. Russians in Tlingit America: The Battles of Sitka, 1802 and 1804*
- Maria Mazziotti Gillan for *All That Lies Between Us*
- Nikki Giovanni for *The Collected Poetry of Nikki Giovanni: 1968–1998*
- C. S. Giscombe for *Prairie Style*
- Angela Jackson for *Where I Must Go*, a novel
- L. Luis Lopez for *Each Month I Sing*
- Tom Lutz for *Doing Nothing: A History of Loafers, Loungers, Slackers, and Bums in America*
- Fae Myenne Ng for *Steer Toward Rock*
- Yuko Taniguchi for *The Ocean in the Closet*
- Lorenzo Thomas for *Don't Deny My Name: Words and Music and the Black Intellectual Tradition*, ed. Aldon Lynn Nielsen
- Frank B. Wilderson III for *Incognegro: A Memoir of Exile and Apartheid*
- J. J. Phillips: Lifetime Achievement Award

*2009*

- Houston A. Baker, Jr. for *Betrayal: How Black Intellectuals Have Abandoned the Ideals of the Civil Right Era*
- Danit Brown for *Ask for a Convertible*
- Jericho Brown for *Please*
- José Antonio Burciaga for *The Last Supper of Chicano Heroes: Selected Works of José Antonio Burciaga*, editors for Mimi R. Gladstein and Daniel Chacón
- Claire Hope Cummings for *Uncertain Peril: Genetic Engineering and the Future of Seeds*
- Stella Pope Duarte for *If I Die in Juarez*
- Linda Gregg for *All of It Singing: New and Selected Poems*
- Suheir Hammad for *Breaking Poems*
- Richard Holmes for *The Age of Wonder*
- George E. Lewis for *A Power Stronger than Itself: The A.A.C.M. and American Experimental Music*
- Patricia Santana for *Ghosts of El Grullo*
- Jack Spicer for *My Vocabulary Did This to Me: The Collected Poetry of Jack Spicer*, ed. Peter Gizzi and Kevin Killian
- Miguel Algarín: Lifetime Achievement Award

**2010s**

*2010*

- Amiri Baraka for *Digging: The Afro-American Soul of American Classical Music*
- Sherwin Bitsui for *Flood Song*
- Nancy Carnevale for *A New Language, A New World: Italian Immigrants in the United States, 1890–1945*
- Dave Eggers for *Zeitoun*
- Sesshu Foster for *World Ball Notebook*
- Stephen D. Gutierrez for *Live from Fresno y Los*
- Victor LaValle for *The Big Machine*
- François Mandeville for *This Is What They Say*, translated by Ron Scollon from Chipewyan
- Bich Minh Nguyen for *Short Girls*
- Franklin Rosemont and Robin D. G. Kelley, editors, for *Black, Brown, & Beige: Surrealist Writings from Africa and the Diaspora*
- Jerome Rothenberg and Jeffrey C. Robinson, editors, for *Poems for the Millennium: Volume Three: The University of California Book of Romantic and Postromantic Poetry*
- Kathryn Waddell Takara for *Pacific Raven: Hawai`i Poems*
- Pamela Uschuk for *Crazy Love: New Poems*
- Katha Politt: Lifetime Achievement Award
- Quincy Troupe: Lifetime Achievement Award

*2011*

- Keith Gilyard for *John Oliver Killens*
- Akbar Ahmed for *Journey Into America: The Challenge of Islam*
- Camille Dungy for *Suck on the Marrow*
- Karen Tei Yamashita for *I Hotel*
- William W. Cook and James Tatum for *African American Writers and Classical Tradition*
- Gerald Vizenor for *Shrouds of White Earth*
- Eric Gansworth for *Extra Indians*
- Ivan Argüelles for *The Death of Stalin*
- Geoffrey Alan Argent, editor, for *The Complete Plays of Jean Racine: Volume 1: The Fratricides*, translated by Argent from French
- Neela Vaswani for *You Have Given Me a Country*
- Sasha Pimentel Chacón for *Insides She Swallowed*
- Miriam Jiménez Román and Juan Flores, editors, for *The Afro-Latin@ Reader: History of Culture in the United States*

- Carmen Giménez Smith for *Bring Down the Little Birds*
- Luis Valdez: Lifetime Achievement Award
- John A. Williams: Lifetime Achievement Award

*2012*

- Annia Ciezadlo for *Day of Honey: A Memoir of Food, Love, and War*
- Arlene Kim for *What Have You Done to Our Ears to Make Us Hear Echoes?*
- Ed Bok Lee for *Whorled*
- Adilifu Nama for *Super Black: American Pop Culture and Black Superheroes*
- Rob Nixon for *Slow Violence and the Environmentalism of the Poor*
- Shann Ray for *American Masculine*
- Alice Rearden, translator; Ann Fienup-Riordan, ed., for *Qaluyaarmiuni Nunamtenek Qanemciput: Our Nelson Island Stories*
- Touré for *Who's Afraid of Post-Blackness? What It Means to Be Black Now*
- Amy Waldman for *The Submission*
- Mary Winegarden for *The Translator's Sister*
- Kevin Young for *Ardency: A Chronicle of the Amistad Rebels*
- Eugene B. Redmond: Lifetime Achievement Award

*2013*

- Will Alexander for *Singing In Magnetic Hoofbeat: Essays, Prose, Texts, Interviews, and a Lecture*, Essay Press
- Jacob M. Appel for *The Man Who Wouldn't Stand Up*, Cargo
- Philip P. Choy for *San Francisco Chinatown: A Guide To Its History & Architecture*, City Lights
- Amanda Coplin for *The Orchardist*, Harper Collins
- Natalie Diaz for *When My Brother Was An Aztec*, Copper Canyon Press
- Louise Erdrich for *The Round House*, Harper Collins
- Alan Gilbert for *Black Patriots and Loyalists: Fighting for Emancipation in the War for Independence*, University of Chicago
- Judy Grahn for *A Simple Revolution: The Making of an Activist Poet*, Aunt Lute Books
- Joy Harjo for *Crazy Brave: A Memoir*, W.W. Norton & Co.
- Demetria Martinez for *The Block Captain's Daughter*, University of Oklahoma Press
- Daniel Abdal-Hayy Moore for *Blood Songs*, The Ecstatic Exchange
- dg nanouk okpik for *Corpse Whale*, University of Arizona Press
- Seth Rosenfeld for *Subversives: The FBI's War On Student Radical and Reagan's Rise to Power*, Farrar, Straus & Giroux
- Christopher B. Teuton for *Cherokee Stories of the Turtle Island Liar's Club*, University of North Carolina

- Lew Welch for *Ring of Bone: Collected Poems*, City Lights
- Ivan Argüelles: Lifetime Achievement Award
- Greil Marcus: Lifetime Achievement Award
- Floyd Salas: Lifetime Achievement Award

*2014*

- Andrew Bacevich for *Breach of Trust: How Americans Failed Their Soldiers and Their Country*, Metropolitan Books
- Joshua Bloom and Waldo E. Martin, Jr. for *Black Against Empire; The History and Politics of the Black Panther Party*, University of California Press
- Juan Delgado (poetry) and Thomas McGovern (photography) for *Vital Signs*, Heyday Books
- Alex Espinoza for *The Five Acts of Diego León*, Random House[12]
- Jonathan Scott Holloway for *Jim Crow Wisdom: Memory and Identity in Black America Since 1940*, University of North Carolina Press
- Joan Naviyuk Kane for *Hyperboreal* for University of Pittsburgh Press
- Jamaica Kincaid for *See Now Then* Farrar, Straus and Giroux
- Tanya Olson for *Boyishly* YesYes Books
- Sterling D. Plumpp for *Home/Bass* Third World Press
- Emily Raboteau for *Searching For Zion: The Quest for Home in the African Diaspora*, Atlantic Monthly Press
- Jerome Rothenberg with Heriberto Yepez for *Eye of Witness: A Jerome Rothenberg Reader*, Commonwealth Books
- Nick Turse for *Kill Anything That Moves: The Real American War in Vietnam*, Metropolitan Books
- Margaret Wrinkle for *Wash*, Atlantic Monthly Press
- Koon Woon for *Water Chasing Water*, Kaya Press
- Armond White: Anti-Censorship Award
- Michael Parenti: Lifetime Achievement Award

*2015*

- Hisham Aidi for *Rebel Music: Race, Empire, and the New Muslim Youth Culture* (Vintage)
- Arlene Biala for *her beckoning hands* (Word Poetry)
- Arthur Dong for *Forbidden City, USA: Chinese American Nightclubs, 1936-1970* (DeepFocus Productions)
- Roxanne Dunbar-Ortiz for *An Indigenous Peoples' History of the United States* (Beacon Press)
- Peter J. Harris for *The Black Man of Happiness* (Black Man of Happiness Project)
- Marlon James for *A Brief History of Seven Killings* (Riverhead Books)

- Naomi Klein for *This Changes Everything: Capitalism vs. The Climate* (Simon & Schuster)
- Laila Lalami for *The Moor's Account* (Pantheon)
- Manuel Luis Martinez for *Los Duros* (Floricanto Press)
- Craig Santos Perez for *from unincorporated territory [guma']* (Omnidawn)
- Carlos Santana with Ashley Kahn and Hal Miller for *The Universal Tone: Bringing My Story to Light* (Little, Brown and Company)
- Ira Sukrungruang for *Southside Buddhist* (University of Tampa Press)
- Astra Taylor for *The People's Platform: Taking Back Power and Culture in the Digital Age* (Henry Holt)
- Anne Waldman: Lifetime Achievement Award

*2016*

- Laura Da' for *Tributaries* (University of Arizona)
- Susan Muaddi Darraj for *Curious Land: Stories from Home* (University of Massachusetts)
- Deepa Iyer for *We Too Sing America: South Asian, Arab, Muslim, and Sikh Immigrants Shape Our Multicultural Future* (The New Press)
- Mat Johnson for *Loving Day* (Spiegel & Grau)
- John Keene for *Counternarratives* (New Directions)
- William J. Maxwell for *F.B. Eyes: How J. Edgar Hoover's Ghostreaders Framed African American Literature* (Princeton University)
- Lauret Savoy for *Trace: Memory, History, Race, and the American Landscape* (Counterpoint)
- Ned Sublette and Constance Sublette for *The American Slave Coast: A History of the Slave-Breeding Industry* (Lawrence Hill Books)
- Jesús Salvador Treviño for *Return to Arroyo Grande* (Arte Público)
- Nick Turse for *Tomorrow's Battlefield: U.S. Proxy Wars and Secret Ops in Africa* (Haymarket Books)
- Ray Young Bear for *Manifestation Wolverine: The Collected Poetry of Ray Young Bear* (Open Road Integrated Media)
- Louise Meriwether: Lifetime Achievement Award
- Lyra Monteiro and Nancy Isenberg: Walter & Lillian Lowenfels Criticism Award
- Chiitaanibah Johnson: Andrew Hope Award

*2017*

- Rabia Chaudry for *Adnan's Story: The Search for Truth and Justice After Serial* (St. Martin's Press)
- Flores A. Forbes for *Invisible Men: A Contemporary Slave Narrative in the Era of Mass Incarceration* (Skyhorse Publishing)

- Yaa Gyasi for *Homegoing* (Knopf)
- Holly Hughes for *Passings* (Expedition Press)
- Randa Jarrar for *Him, Me, Muhammad Ali* (Sarabande Books)
- Bernice L. McFadden for *The Book of Harlan* (Akashic Books)
- Brian D. McInnes for *Sounding Thunder: The Stories of Francis Pegahmagabow* (Michigan State University Press)
- Patrick Phillips for *Blood at the Root: A Racial Cleansing in America* (W. W. Norton & Company)
- Vaughn Rasberry for *Race and the Totalitarian Century: Geopolitics in the Black Literary Imagination* (Harvard University Press)
- Marc Anthony Richardson for *Year of the Rat* (Fiction Collective Two)
- Shawna Yang Ryan for *Green Island* (Knopf)
- Ruth Sergel for *See You in the Streets: Art, Action, and Remembering the Triangle Shirtwaist Factory Fire* (University of Iowa Press)
- Solmaz Sharif for *Look* (Graywolf Press)
- Adam Soldofsky for *Memory Foam* (Disorder Press)
- Alfredo Véa for *The Mexican Flyboy* (University of Oklahoma Press)
- Dean Wong for *Seeing the Light: Four Decades in Chinatown* (Chin Music Press)
- Nancy Mercado: Lifetime Achievement Award
- Ammiel Alcalay: Lost & Found: The CUNY Poetics Document Initiative: Editor/Publisher Award

*2018*

- Thi Bui for *The Best We Could Do: An Illustrated Memoir* (Harry N. Abrams)
- Rachelle Cruz for *God's Will for Monsters* (Inlandia Books)
- Tommy Curry for *The Man-Not: Race, Class, Genre, and the Dilemmas of Black Manhood* (Temple University Press)
- Tongo Eisen-Martin for *Heaven Is All Goodbyes* (City Lights)
- Dana Naone Hall for *Life of the Land: Articulations of a Native Writer* (University of Hawaii)
- Kelly Lytle Hernández for *City of Inmates: Conquest, Rebellion, and the Rise of Human Caging in Los Angeles, 1771-1965* (University of North Carolina)
- Victor LaValle for *The Changeling: A Novel* (Spiegel & Grau)
- Bojan Louis for *Currents* (BkMk Press)
- Valeria Luiselli for *Tell Me How It Ends: An Essay in Forty Questions* (Coffee House Press)
- Cathryn Josefina Merla-Watson and B. V. Olguín for *Altermundos Latin@ Speculative Literature, Film, and Popular Culture* (UCLA Chicano Studies Research Center Press)

- Tiya Miles for *The Dawn of Detroit: A Chronicle of Slavery and Freedom in the City of the Straits* (The New Press)
- Tommy Pico for *Nature Poem* (Tin House Books)
- Rena Priest for *Patriarchy Blues* (MoonPath Press)
- Joseph Rios for *Shadowboxing: poems & impersonations* (Omnidawn)
- Sunaura Taylor for *Beasts of Burden: Animal and Disability Liberation* (The New Press)
- Sequoyah Guess: Lifetime Achievement Award
- Kellie Jones, *South of Pico: African American Artists in Los Angeles in the 1960s and 1970s* (Duke University Press): Walter & Lillian Lowenfels Criticism Award
- Charles F. Harris: Editor/Publisher Award
- Rob Rogers: Anti-Censorship Award
- Heroes Are Gang Leaders: Oral Literature Award

*2019*

- Frank Abe, Greg Robinson, and Floyd Cheung for *John Okada: The Life & Rediscovered Work of the Author of No-No Boy* (University of Washington Press)
- May-lee Chai for *Useful Phrases for Immigrants: Stories* (Blair)
- Louise DeSalvo for *The House of Early Sorrows: A Memoir in Essays* (Fordham University Press)
- Heid E. Erdrich for *New Poets of Native Nations* (Graywolf Press)
- Ángel García for *Teeth Never Sleep: Poems* (University of Arkansas Press)
- Tommy Orange for *There There* (Knopf)
- Halifu Osumare for *Dancing in Blackness: A Memoir* (University Press of Florida)
- Christopher Patton for *Unlikeness Is Us: Fourteen from the Exeter Book* (Gaspereau Press)
- Mark Sarvas for *Memento Park: A Novel* (Farrar, Straus and Giroux)
- Jeffrey C. Stewart for *The New Negro: The Life of Alain Locke* (Oxford University Press)
- William T. Vollmann for *Carbon Ideologies: Volume I, No Immediate Danger, Volume II, No Good Alternative* (Viking Press|Viking)
- G. Willow Wilson and Nico Leon for *Ms. Marvel Vol. 9: Teenage Wasteland* (Marvel Comics)
- Nathan Hare: Lifetime Achievement Award
- UCLA Chicano Studies Research Center: Editor/Publisher Award
- Moor Mother: Oral Literature Award

## 2020s

*2020*

- Reginald Dwayne Betts for *Felon: Poems* (W.W. Norton)
- Sara Borjas for *Hearts Like a Widow, Mouth Like a Cliff* (Noemi Press)
- Neeli Cherkovski, Raymond Foye, Tate Swindell (editors) for *Collected Poems of Bob Kaufman* (City Lights)
- Staceyann Chinn for *Crossfire: A Litany for Survival* (Haymarket)
- Kali Fajardo-Anstine for *Sabrina & Corina: Stories* (One World)
- Tara Fickle for *The Race Card: From Gaming Technologies to Model Minorities* (New York University Press)
- Erika Lee for *America for Americans: A History of Xenophobia in the United States* (Basic Books)
- Yoko Ogawa for *The Memory Police* (Pantheon)
- Jake Skeets for *Eyes Bottle Dark with a Mouthful of Flowers* (Milkweed Editions)
- George Takei, Justin Eisinger, Steven Scott and Harmony Becker for *They Called Us Enemy* (Top Shelf Productions)
- Ocean Vuong for *On Earth We're Briefly* Gorgeous (Penguin)
- De'Shawn Charles Winslow for *In West Mills* (Bloomsbury Publishing)
- Albert Woodfox and Leslie George for *Solitary: My Story of Transformation and Hope* (Grove Press)
- Eleanor W. Traylor: Lifetime Achievement Award
- Kofi Natambu Editor Award: *The Panopticon Review*
- Jasper Bernes, Joshua Clover, and Juliana Spahr
- Publisher Award: Commune Editions
- Amalia Leticia Ortiz: Oral Literature Award
- Walter & Lillian Lowenfels Criticism Award: Anthony Harkins and Meredith McCarroll (editors) for *Appalachian Reckoning: A Region Responds to Hillbilly Elegy*

*2021*

- Ayad Akhtar for *Homeland Elegies* (Little, Brown & Co.)
- Maisy Card for *These Ghosts Are Family* (Simon & Schuster)
- Anthony Cordy for *Borderland Apocrypha* (Omnidawn Press)
- Ben Ehrenreich for *Desert Notebooks: A Road Map for the End of Time* (Counterpoint)
- Johanna Fernández for *The Young Lords: A Radical History* (University of North Carolina Press)
- Carolyn Forché for *In Lateness of the World: Poems* (Penguin Press)
- John Giorno for *Great Demon Kings: A Memoir of Poetry, Sex, Art, Death, and Enlightenment* (Farrar, Straus and Giroux)

- Cathy Park Hong for *Minor Feelings: An Asian American Reckoning* (One World)
- Randall Horton for *{#289-128}: Poems* (University of Kentucky)
- Gerald Horne for *The Dawning of Apocalypse: The Roots of Slavery, White Supremacy, Settler Colonialism, and the Capitalism in the Long Sixteenth Century* (Monthly Review Press)
- Robert P. Jones for *White Too Long: The Legacy of White Supremacy in American Christianity* (Simon & Schuster)
- Judy Juanita for *Manhattan my ass, you're in Oakland* (Equidistance Press)
- William Melvin Kelley (author), Aiki Kelley (illustrator) for *Dunfords Travel Everywhere* (Anchor Books)
- Maryemma Graham: Lifetime Achievement Award
- Shana Redmond: Walter and Lillian Lowenfels Criticism Award for
- *Everything Man: The Form and Function of Paul Robeson*
- Jacob Soboroff Anti-Censorship Award: *Separated: Inside an American Tragedy*

*2022*

- Spencer Ackerman for *Reign of Terror: How the 9/11 Era Destabilized America and the Produced Trump* (Viking)
- Esther G. Belin, Jeff Burgland, Connie A. Jacobs, Anthony K. Webster for *The Diné Reader: An Anthology of Navajo Literature* (University of Arizona Press)
- Anthony Cordy for *Borderland Apocrypha* (Omnidawn Press)
- Emma Brodie for *Songs in Ursa Major* (Knopf)
- Daphne Brooks for *Liner Notes for the Revolution: The Intellectual Life of Black Feminist Sound* (Harvard University Press)
- Myriam J.A. Chancy for *What Storm, What Thunder* (Tin House Books)
- Francisco Goldman for *Monkey Boy* (Grove Press)
- Zakiya Dalila Harris for *The Other Black Girl: A Novel* (Atria Books)
- Fatima Shaik for *Economy Hall: The Hidden History of a Free Black Brotherhood* (The Historic New Orleans Collection)
- Edwin Torres for *Quanundrum: [i will be your many angled thing]* (Roof Books)
- Truong Torres for *Book of the Other: Small in Comparison* (Kaya Press)
- Mai Der Vang for *Yellow Rain* (Graywolf Press)
- Phillip B. Williams for *Mutiny* (Penguin Books)
- Michelle Zauner for *Crying in H Mart: A Memoir* (Knopf)
- Gayle Jones: Lifetime Achievement Award
- Jessica E. Teague: Walter and Lillian Lowenfels Criticism Award for *Sound Recording Technology and American Literature*
- Jeffrey St. Clair: Anti-Censorship Award

- Wave Books: Charlie Wright (Publisher)/Joshua Beckman (Editor in Chief): Editor/Publisher Award

*2023*

- Ayanna Lloyd Banwo for *When We Were Birds* (Doubleday)
- Edgar Gomez for *High-Risk Homosexual* (Soft Skulls)
- Kelly Lytle Hernández for *Bad Mexicans: Race, Empire, and Revolution in the Borderlands* (W.W. Norton & Company)
- Everett Hoagland for *The Ways: Poems of Affirmation, Reflection and Wonder* (North Star Nova Press)
- Anne Hyde for *Born of Lakes and Plains: Mixed-Descent Peoples and the Making of the American West* (W.W. Norton & Company)
- Jamil Jan Kochai for *The Haunting of Haji Hotak and Other Stories* (Viking)
- Aidan Levy for *Saxophone Colossus: The Life and Music of Sonny Rollins* (Hachette Books)
- Bojan Louis for *Sinking Bells: Stories* (Gray Wolf Press)
- Leila Mottley for *Nightcrawling* (Knopf)
- Darryl Pinckney for *Come Back in September: A Literary Education on West Sixty-Seventh Street, Manhattan* (Farrar, Straus and Giroux)
- Sherry Shenoda for *Mummy Eaters* (University of Nebraska Press)
- Mosab Abu Toha for *Things You May Find Hidden in My Ear: Poems from Gaza* (City Lights Books)
- Javier Zamora for *Solito: A Memoir* (Hogarth)
- Maxine Hong Kingston: Lifetime Achievement Award
- Neta Crawford: Anti-Censorship Award
- bell hooks: Walter and Lillian Lowenfels Criticism Award

*2024*

- Chitra Banerjee Divakaruni: *Independence: A Novel* (William Morrow)
- Debra Magpie Earling: *The Last Journal of Sacajewea: A Novel* (Milkweed Edition)
- Paul S. Flores: *We Still Be: Poems and Performances* (El Martillo Press)
- Aisha Abdel Gaward: *Between Two Moons: A Novel* (Doubleday)
- Gregg Hecimovich: *The Life and Times of Hanna Crafts: The True Story of the Bondwoman's Narrative* (Ecco)
- Nic Watts and Sakina Karimjee, adaptation of *CLR James: Toussaint Louverture, The Story of the Only Successful Slave Revolt in History* (Verso)
- R.F. Kuang for *Yellowface* (William Morrow)
- Felipe Luciano for *Flesh & Spirit: Confessions of a Young Lord* (Empire State Edition)

- Fae Myenne Ng for *Orphan Bachelors* (Grove Press)
- Roger Reeves for *Dark Days: Fugitive Essays* (Graywolf)
- John N. Roberts for *Changing the Commons: Stories About Place Making* (ORO Editions)
- Barbara D. Savage for *Merze Tate: The Global Odyssey of a Black Woman Scholar* (Yale University Press)
- Rachel L. Swarns for *The 272: The Families Who Were Enslaved and Sold to Build the American Catholic Church* (Random House)
- Henry Threadgill and Brent Hayes Edwards for *Easily Slip into Another World: A Life in Music* (Knopf)
- Valerie Wilson Wesley for *A Shimmer of Red (An Odessa Jones Mystery)* (Kensington)
- Rosanna Xia for *California Against the Sea: Visions for Our Vanishing Coastline* (Heyday)
- John Yau for *Please Wait by the Coatroom: Reconsidering Race and Identity in American Art* (Black Sparrow Press)
- Monica Youn for *From From* (Graywolf)
- Jessica Hagedorn: Lifetime Achievement Award
- Jeff Deutsch, publisher and Parneshia Jones, editor for *Divine Days*, by Leon Forrest, Seminary Co-op Offsets: Publisher/Editor Award
- Rabbi Michael Lerner: Publisher/Editor Award
- Jeffrey D. Sachs, Director, Center for Sustainable Development, Earth Institute: Anti-Censorship Award
- Asna Tabassum, Valedictorian, Class of 2024, University of Southern California: Walter and Lillian Lowenfels Criticism Award
- Lynnée Denise for *Why Willie Mae Thorton Matters* (University of Texas Press): Walter and Lillian Lowenfels Criticism Award
- Brenda M. Greene "Book Review: *Erasure* by Percival Everett, The Basis for American Fiction" (Our Time Press): Walter and Lillian Lowenfels Criticism Award
- Mehdi Hasan, for *Zeteo*: Walter and Lillian Lowenfels Criticism Award
- Kate Wagner for *Behind F2's Velvet Curtain* (Escape Collective): Walter and Lillian Lowenfels Criticism Award

# Acknowledgements & Permissions

Cover photo: Ishmael Reed and Andrew Hope III, former presidents of the Before Columbus Foundation. Photo by Peter Metcalfe.

"Imagining America" by Wajahat Ali. Reprinted by permission of the author.

"Tribute to the late Rudy Anaya" by Jimmy Santiago Baca. Reprinted by permission of the author.

"The Poorest Boy in Chicago" by Mitch Berman. Reprinted by permission of the author.

"Members Only-A Year in Zimbabwe" by Karla Brundage. Reprinted by permission of the author.

"Cora or Soccer Serenade" by Victor Hernández Cruz. Reprinted by permission of the author.

"Justin Desmangles introduces the 2024 American Book Award Ceremony." Reprinted by permission of the author.

Excerpt from *The Savage City* by T.J. English. Reprinted by permission of the author.

"Sharing the Darkness: An Essay on Ukraine" by Carolyn Forché. Reprinted by permission of the author. Featured Artwork: *Rooms 22* by Ashley Ashford-Brown. First published: *Fusion*, Fall 2023.

Preface to *Colored People* by Henry Louis Gates, Jr. Reprinted by permission of the author.

"Tribute to the late Bob Callahan" by J. Patrick Goggins. Reprinted by permission of the *Roo* author.

Two excerpts from *Catching the Light* by Joy Harjo. Reprinted by permission of the author and Yale University Press, © October 24, 2023.

"Holler / Grito" by Juan Felipe Herrera. Reprinted by permission of the author.

Five Poems by Sean Hill. Reprinted by permission of the author.

Four Poems from *Story Lyric* by Ishmael Angaluuk Hope. Reprinted by permission of the author.

"Hare Diary" by Maxine Hong Kingston. Reprinted by permission of the author.

Chapter One of *The Moor's Account* by Laila Lalami. Reprinted by permission of the author.

"Century of Rage" by Genny Lim. Reprinted by permission of the author.

"From Here to Gaza" by Genny Lim. Reprinted by permission of the author.

"My True Name" by Genny Lim. Reprinted by permission of the author.

Six Poems by Nancy Mercado. Reprinted by permission of the author.

"Tribute to the late Andy Hope III" by Peter Metcalfe. Reprinted by permission of the author.

"The Displaced," Introduction to the anthology *The Displaced*, edited by Viet Thanh Nguyen. Reprinted by permission of the author.

"Panoramic" by Tracy K. Smith. Reprinted by permission of the author.

Chapter one of *Homebase,* a novel by Shawn Wong. Reprinted by permission of the author.

# About the Contributors

**Wajahat Ali** is a *Daily Beast* columnist, public speaker, recovering attorney, and tired dad of three cute kids. *The Domestic Crusaders*, his play about a Muslin Pakistani American family post 9/11, started with a 2005 restaurant reading in Newark, California, and appeared at the Kennedy Center in 2010. His essays, interviews, and reporting have appeared in *The New York Times*, *The Atlantic*, *The Washington Post*, *The Guardian*, and *New York Review of Books* and his most recent book is *Go Back To Where You Came From: And Other Helpful Recommendations on Becoming American* (Norton, 2022).

**Jimmy Santiago Baca**'s last two published books are *The Misfits* and *American Orphan*, from Arte Publico press. He is running his farm in Northern New Mexico, and as always working on his novel and poetry.

**Mitch Berman** is the author of the novel *Time Capsule*, hailed by Kurt Vonnegut and Ishmael Reed and nominated by Putnam for the Pulitzer Prize. His stories have appeared in eight anthologies and in literary magazines including *Conjunctions*, *Gettysburg Review*, *Agni*, *Antioch Review*, *Michigan Quarterly Review*, *Southwest Review*, *Witness* and *Boulevard*; they've been nominated for seven Pushcart Prizes and have received special mention in *Best American Short Stories* and (twice) in the Pushcart Prize anthologies. His MFA in writing is from Columbia and he has taught creative writing at many universities, including UT Austin.

**Karla Brundage**, founder of the West Oakland to West Africa Poetry Exchange (WO2WA), is a poet, essayist and high school English teacher. An accomplished editor, she has curated several groundbreaking anthologies including *Our Spirits Carry Our Voices*, *Sisters Across Oceans*, and *Black Rootedness: 54 Poets from Africa to America*, which showcase the vibrant dialogue between African and American poets. Her latest poetry collection, *Blood Lies: Race Trait(or)*, continues her exploration of cross-cultural identity and connection.

**Nancy Carnevale** is Associate Professor of history at Montclair State University specializing in the history of migration, race and ethnicity in the modern United States and women's/gender history. Author of *A New Language, A New World: Italian Immigrants in the United States, 1890-1945* (University of Illinois Press, 2009), her scholarship in recent years has focused on postwar African American and Italian American relations. She has served as historical consultant for a variety of artistic and public history projects and is an editor of the *Critical Studies in Italian Migrations*, a book series with Fordham University Press.

**Victor Hernández Cruz,** born in Puerto Rico and raised in New York, has lived on the east and west coast, and currently in exile in Morocco. Having written for over one half a century, while still in high school, his neighbors took up a collection to help him self-publish a mimeograph booklet. *Papo Got His Gun. Guayacán* (Ishmael Reed Publishing, 2024) is his latest poetry collection.

**Justin Desmangles** is chairman of the Before Columbus Foundation, administrator of the American Book Awards, and creator of the radio broadcast New Day Jazz. A member of the board of directors of the Oakland Book Festival, Mr. Desmangles is also a program producer at the African-American Center of the San Francisco Public Library. His poetry and journalism has appeared in *Amerarcana*, *Black Renaissance Noire*, *Drumvoices Revue*, *Konch*, and *Musiqology*.

**T.J. English**, a former New York City taxi driver, has published ten non-fiction books. Four of his books have been *New York Times* bestsellers, and five have been nominated for an Edgar Award in the category of Best Fact Crime. In 2023, he received a PEN Oakland/Josephine Miles Literary Award for his book *Dangerous Rhythms: Jazz and the Underworld*.

**Carolyn Forché,** is a poet, memoirist, translator, and anthologist. Her most recent works include *In the Lateness of the World*, a finalist for the Pulitzer Prize in poetry and winner of the American Book Award, and the memoir *What You Have Heard is True: A Memoir of Witness and Resistance*, which won the Juan E. Mendez Book Award for Human Rights in Latin America and was a finalist for the 2019 National Book Award in Nonfiction.

**Henry Louis Gates, Jr.** is an American literary critic, professor, historian, and filmmaker who serves as the Alphonse Fletcher University Professor and the director of the Hutchins Center for African and African American Research at Harvard University. He is a trustee of the Gilder Lehrman Institute of American History. He rediscovered the earliest known African-American novels and has published extensively on the recognition of African-American literature as part of the Western canon.

**J. Patrick Goggins** was born in 1936 Montana to an Irish Railroad family and raised on the roads in Montana, New Mexico, Texas and the Dakotas, graduating from Notre Dame in 1958 and on to the US Army in Germany. He was and is anti-War. He sold lawbooks to lawyers for 34 years while prioritizing outreach to communities: including African Americans in Oakland, Mexican Americans in the Valley, Irish in San Francisco, Belfast, Dublin, London, DC, and Indians on Standing Rock, Rocky Boy's, Blackfeet reservations and currently Chinese in San Francisco and China. His home base is Mill Valley, California.

**Joy Harjo**, a member of the Mvskoke Nation, is a poet, musician, playwright, and performer. She has garnered many awards including the National Book Critics Circle Lifetime Achievement Award and a National Humanities Medal. She served three terms as 23rd Poet Laureate of the United States, from 2019-2022. She is at work on a new album of music and a musical that will restore southeastern natives to the origin story of blues and jazz.

**Juan Felipe Herrera** is an American poet, performer, writer, cartoonist, teacher, and activist. Elected a chancellor of the Academy of American Poets in 2011, he served as poet laureate of California from 2012 to 2015, and poet laureate of the United States from 2015 to 2017. He has written more than 30 books in various genres. His recent books of poems include *Every Day We Get More Illegal* (2020) and *Akrílica* (2022), a book in translation, and *The Cosmic Flow: Mandalas, Meditations and Kindness* (2024).

**Sean Hill** is the author of *Dangerous Goods* and *Blood Ties & Brown Liquor*, and the forthcoming collection, *The Negroes Send Their Love*. His poems have appeared in numerous journals including *Callaloo, Harvard Review, The Oxford American, Poetry, Tin House*, and in several anthologies including *Black Nature* and *Villanelles*. Hill lives in southwestern Montana with his family and is an Associate Professor of Creative Writing at the University of Montana.

**Ishmael Angaluuk Hope** is a Tlingit and Inupiaq poet, games writer, and Indigenous scholar of oral literature and visual art. He is named after Ishmael Reed, who was a close literary colleague and friend to his parents, Tlingit writer Andy Hope III (Xhaastánch), and Inupiaq poet Sister Goodwin (Elizabeth Freda Goodwin Hope, Taliiraq), and he published her collection, *A Lagoon Is In My Backyard* (1984). Ishmael Angaluuk Hope is currently writing curriculum resources on Tlingit intellectual history for the Douglas Indian Association and writing articles on Northwest Coast art and oral literature.

**Maxine Hong Kingston** writes fiction, non-fiction, essays, and poetry. She has taught every level of school. Some of her most thrilling moments are: receiving the National Humanities Medal from President Clinton, the National Medal of Arts from President Obama, and the Lifetime Achievement Award from the Before Columbus Foundation.

**Laila Lalami** is the author of six books, including the Pulitzer Prize finalist *The Moor's Account* and the National Book Award finalist *The Other Americans.* Her most recent novel is *The Dream Hotel.*

**Genny Lim** is the ninth San Francisco Poet Laureate and a former San Francisco Jazz Poet Laureate. The recipient of lifetime achievement awards from the city of Berkeley and PEN Oakland, she is a native-born San Franciscan. Her translations of poems written by Chinese immigrants on the barrack walls of Angel Island with the late Him Mark Lai in *Island: Poetry and History of Chinese Immigrants on Angel Island*, won the American Book Award.

**Nancy Mercado**'s work has been highlighted by the Academy of American Poets in their Poem-A-Day series. She is a distinguished recipient of the American Book Award for Lifetime Achievement and has been recognized as one of 200 living individuals who embody the spirit of Frederick Douglass. More information, @ nancy-mercado.com.

**Andrew Hope III**, the scion of a Tlingit family with deep involvement in the Alaska Native rights movement of the 20th century, was a longtime member of the Before Columbus Foundation. In the memoir included in this anthology, his life friend and literary executor, **Peter Metcalfe** of Juneau, Alaska, recalls Andy's many contributions and reminds us of Ishmael Reed's words that described Andy's broad range of interests as truly international and multicultural.

**Viet Thanh Nguyen**'s novel *The Sympathizer*, won the Pulitzer Prize for Fiction and was turned into an HBO limited series. The recipient of fellowships from the Guggenheim and MacArthur Foundations, his most recent publication is *A Man of Two Faces: A Memoir, A History, A Memorial.* His next book is *To Save and to Destroy: Writing as an Other*, forthcoming from Harvard University Press in 2025. He teaches at the University of Southern California, where he is the Aerol Arnold Chair of English.

**Ishmael Reed** has authored fifty works of fiction, poetry, non-fiction, plays, and librettos, and edited numerous anthologies. He has received prizes in every category. The fourth novel in his "Terribles" series, *The Terrible Fives*, is forthcoming from Baraka Books. Other recent works include *Why the Black Hole Sings the Blues* (2022), and *The Shine Challenge 2025*, premiered at NYC's Theater for the New City on January 30, 2025. Reed is also a cartoonist, songwriter, musician and composer, public media commentator and publisher.

**Tracy K. Smith** was Poet Laureate of the United States from 2017-2019. Her most recent and forthcoming books are *To Free the Captives: A Plea for the American Soul* and *Fear Less: Poetry in Perilous Times.*

**Gundars Strads** is currently a Senior Editor of California Management Review, based at University of California at Berkeley's Haas School of Business. He has been the Executive Director of the Before Columbus Foundation for over forty years and was a co-editor of *The Before Columbus Foundation Poetry Anthology: Selections from the American Book Awards, 1980-1990* (W.W. Norton, 1992) and *The Before Columbus Foundation Fiction Anthology, Selections from the American Book Awards, 1980-1990* (W.W. Norton,1992). He is a Latvian-America and the son of refugees. His parents were educators, and his father was also a writer and editor.

**Margaret Porter Troupe** creates projects that promote the arts, especially art created by people of African descent and other people of color, including New Bones, Porter Troupe Gallery, Harlem Arts Salon, and the Gloster Arts Project, a free summer arts camp for children in rural Southwest Mississippi. Her poetry and other writing have been published occasionally in journals and anthologies.

**Ann Waldman** is the author of more than 60 books, including the mini-classic *Fast Speaking Woman* (City Lights Books); a new collection of essays, interviews, letters, and poems entitled *Bard, Kinetic* (Coffee House Press, 2023); as well as her classic, *Vow to Poetry.* One of the founders and directors of The Poetry Project at St. Marks's Church in-the-Bowery, she also co-founded with—Allen Ginsberg and Diane di Prima—the Jack Kerouac School of Disembodied Poetics at Naropa University, the first Buddhist inspired University in the western hemisphere, which celebrated its 50th anniversary in 2024.

**Shawn Wong** is the author of two prize-winning novels, *Homebase* and *American Knees*, of which the latter was made into a feature film. He is the co-editor of the landmark anthology, *Aiiieeeee! An Anthology of Asian American Writers*, and is the Byron and Alice Lockwood Professor in the Humanities at the University of Washington.

Albuquerque, 1976 celebration for the Pueblo Revolt of 1680, a successful uprising by Native Americans against Spanish colonizers in New Mexico. Left to Right: Gundars Strads, Simon Ortiz, the late David Meltzer, Ishmael Reed, the late Rudy Anaya, Victor Hernández Cruz, the late Bob Callahan and Shawn Wong.

American Book Awards 2024. Left to right: Fae Myenne Ng, Rosanna Xia, Roger Reeves, John N. Roberts, Chitra Banerjee Divakaruni, Brenda Greene, Paul Flores, Felipe Luciano, Gregg Hechimovich, Brent Hates Edwards, Justin Desmangles, Debra Magpie Earling. (Photo by Tennessee Reed)

MIX
Paper
FSC® C100212

Printed by Imprimerie Gauvin
Gatineau, Québec